The Great Allegheny Passage Companion

Guide to History & Heritage along the Trail

by Bill Metzger

To Pittsburgh, PA

McKeesport

Boston

Buena Vista

West Newton

Cedar Creek Park

Whitsett

Layton/Perryopolis

Dawson

Connellsville

Bowest

Indian Creek

Bruner Run

Rockwood

Casselman

Garrett

Ohiopyle

Pinkerton

Laurel Ridge

Meyersdale

Ramcat

Fort Hill

Confluence

To Cumberland, MD

The Local History Company

publishers of history and heritage

Pittsburgh, Pennsylvania, USA

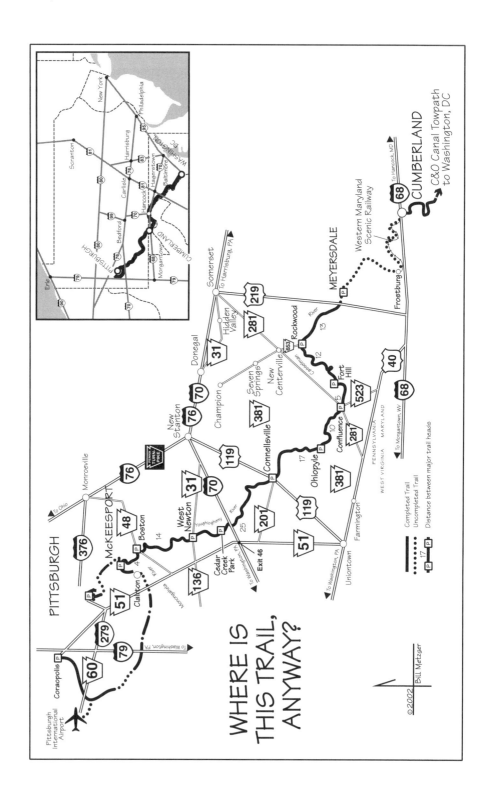

WHERE IS
THIS TRAIL,
ANYWAY?

©2002

Bill Metzger

The
Great Allegheny Passage
Companion

Guide to History & Heritage along the Trail

by Bill Metzger

To steve —
Enjoy the rest of the
ride & stay dry!
Bill Metzger
May 23 '05

The Local History Company
publishers of history and heritage

Pittsburgh, Pennsylvania, USA

The Great Allegheny Passage Companion
Guide To History & Heritage along the Trail
Copyright © 2003 by Bill Metzger

Published by
The Local History Company
112 North Woodland Road
Pittsburgh, PA 15232
www.TheLocalHistoryCompany.com
info@TheLocalHistoryCompany.com

The name "The Local History Company", "Publishers of History and Heritage", and its logo are trademarks of The Local History Company.

Unless otherwise credited, all photos, maps and images were courtesy of the author.

Back cover photo credits left to right: Bill Metzger; William Henry Jackson, courtesy Library of Congress, Detroit Publishing Company collection; R. A. Baker, Van Sickel collection.

Library of Congress Cataloging-in-Publication Data

Metzger, William
    The Great Allegheny Passage Companion: Guide To History & Heritage along the Trail / by William Metzger.
        p.   cm.
    Includes bibliographical references (p.) and index.
    ISBN 0-9711835-2-X (pbk.: alk paper)
    1. Pennsylvania—History, Local. 2. Pennsylvania—Description and travel. 3. Trails—Pennsylvania. 4. Historic sites—Pennsylvania. 5. Allegheny Mountains Region—History, Local. 6. Allegheny Mountains Region—Description and travel. 7. Allegheny County (Pa.)—History, Local. 8. Allegheny County (Pa.)—Description and travel. 9. Pittsburgh Region (Pa.)—Description and travel. 10. Pittsburgh Region (Pa.)—History. I. Title.

F150.M48 2003
974.8'7—dc21

                    2002012166

Printed in USA

FOR PAM

WHO MAKES EVERYTHING POSSIBLE

Table of Contents

ACKNOWLEDGMENTS

A book like this doesn't just happen without a lot of help from generous and knowledgeable people. Know that their efforts at guiding me were faultless; any error in passing on that information to you is mine alone. It is to them that I extend my sincere thanks for their enthusiasm for this project.

To the great friends and traveling companions who took the time to go out and experience the trail with me: first and foremost among them Jim Shaulis, without whom I would know nothing about the geology of the trail; Bob McKinley, whose knowledge of the trail continually amazes me; Tom Helm and Bill Finley, who fearlessly accompanied me on road trips; and Judy Marshall, who guided me through the wilds of Elizabeth Township.

To all the people who shared information: Tim Banfield; Cynthia Mason of the Meyersdale Library, a wellspring of local information and photos; Dave Dudjak for the Western Maryland track charts; Brett Hollern of the Somerset Planning Department for letting me hound him mercilessly; Bob Brendel, Roy Weil and Mary Shaw for their insights on publishing and allowing me to plagiarize their milepost numbers; Malcolm Sias for his information on Cedar Creek Park; Chris Davis and Bernard Means for their insights on the Native Americans; Judy Marshall, who ran down needed documents; Bob Holliday from Harnedsville; Director Dawn Davis at the Mary S. Biesecker Library in Somerset; the Ohiopyle State Park people: Environmental Information Technician Barb Drbal Wallace, Assistant Superintendent Dan Bickel and Superintendent Doug Hoehn; Dave Hamilton for his mining experiences; Hizzoner Joe Bendel who shared stories of McKeesport; Brad Clemenson for his erudite thoughts on the Grand Canyon of Pennsylvania; John Smith from the Pennsylvania State Game Commission and Gary Smith from the Pennsylvania Fish and Boat Commission; Dennis Millin from the U.S. Army Corps of Engineers; Kathy Ober from the Mt. Lebanon Library; Jim Steeley and the staff of the Westmoreland Historical Society; Rod Sturtz from the West Overton Museum; Bob Cupp for his encyclopedic knowledge of the Yough Valley history; Maynard Sembower, Ruben Knopsnyder and Jim Peters for their knowledge of the Markleton/Rockwood area; Pam Seighman from the Coal & Coke Heritage Center; Clarence "Clu" Johnson from Whitsett; and the Podluckys from Stoney's Brewery.

To all the people who shared photos: Carol Anthony; Linda Holliday; Miriam Meislik of the University of Pittsburgh Archives; Ron Baraff of the Steel Industry Heritage Corporation; Kurt Bell of the Railroad Museum of Pennsylvania; Pat Trimble, Mayor of Dawson; postcard collectors Eric Martin and Paul Dudjak; Kevin N. Tomasic; Dave Wright of the Allegheny County Engineers; the folks at the Western Maryland Historical Society; Jack Polaritz for the P&LE photos; Linc Van Sickel; Ed Lybarger of the Pennsylvania Transportation Museum Association;

John Carnprobst; Bill Colbert for all the great photos in his collection; Rod Sturtz of the West Overton Museum; Betty Albert of the Rockwood Historical Society; Nancy Velez of the Library of Congress; and Ron Morgenstern of the Elizabeth Township Historical Society.

Also many thanks to Russ Nirella for making the laptop work, Chuck and Sally Martin for the use of the cabin which made research infinitely easier, Deb and Lynn Sanner for the free ice cream and local information, and Kathy Dougherty for the lawn ball.

Special thanks to my wife Pam who is my sounding board, proofreader, shelter from the world, and great traveling companion who always hangs in there for "just one more picture."

And finally, to all the people of the Allegheny Trail Alliance, both volunteer and professional, who have not only built the first hundred miles but will be there until the job is complete and will be maintaining it long into the future: you are the finest bunch of folks I've ever met in my life. I'm proud to know each and every one of you. Keep up the good work.

Since this guidebook, like the trail, is a work in progress, the author welcomes any additional photos or information you may have. Feel free to contact the author via the publisher.

Unless otherwise credited, all photos, maps, and images are by the author.

Disclaimer
It should be noted here that the author has worked long and hard at becoming an opinionated old fart and that any opinions expressed herein are his and his alone and do not reflect those of the Allegheny Trail Alliance or The Local History Company.

INTRODUCTION

It was the last Saturday in October. My wife Pam and I had taken advantage of an experimental shuttle ride from Connellsville to Ohiopyle. The morning didn't hold much promise; it was cold and drizzly and when we crossed Chestnut Ridge, visibility went down to near zero in the fog. Delaying the inevitable, we had lunch at the Falls Market in Ohiopyle. But, joy of joys, we walked outside about the same time the sun came out. Maybe this wouldn't be so bad after all. Rain jackets were shed and we were on our way across the beautiful new bridge and down the trail.

The leaves were off the trees and we rode through a silver gray gothic arch of tulip poplar trees that had grown up since the railroad was abandoned—a miles-long cathedral through the heart of the mountains. There was no one else on the trail and we started screaming at the top of our lungs from the sheer joy of it all, reminding every small furry animal within earshot that the end of tourist season couldn't come soon enough.

The joy of it all. This is what the trail movement is all about. We can and do talk about the history of the corridor, preservation of the right of way and the natural environment, and the economic revitalization that the trail has brought. That's all true. But mostly, it's just fun.

It wasn't always that way. At the beginning of the twentieth century, the lower Yough valley was one of the most industrialized places on earth. Mines, mills, furnaces and ovens along the river belched smoke and fire that blotted out the sun in the daytime and lit the sky with a hellish red glow at night. A constant industrial roar punctuated by screaming whistles sang the song of prosperity. The river ran yellow.

The rhythms of life in the valley were the 4/4 time of the steam locomotive, the punctuation of passenger train and trolley schedules, and the relentless change of shifts relieved by Saturday night in town and Sunday morning in church. "Fun" would have been about the last word used to describe the Yough valley.

It's almost impossible to imagine that as you propel yourself by your own muscles through a quiet leafy canopy along a clean river under a blue sky. The occasional concrete foundation, overgrown grade, "gob pile", and red waterfall emerging from the side of the hill are all that's left of the great mines and mills that once employed thousands.

The industrial age in the Yough valley lasted just over a century. Nobody mines coal any more along the trail from McKeesport to Meyersdale or makes steel or burns coke or runs a steam locomotive. The last train on the track that's now the trail ran more than a decade ago. The industrial way of the life in the valley is gone forever, but it can't be forgotten. We're going to show you pictures and tell you stories about the way the trail used to be. We'll tell you about the heroes and the villains, about men who died suddenly in the mines and on the rails, and those who died slowly and painfully from industrially-induced illnesses. We'll tell you about the land and the water and the towns, ghost towns, and the people who lived there. You're going to learn a lot of stuff about the trail that you never knew.

And, we promise you, it'll be fun.

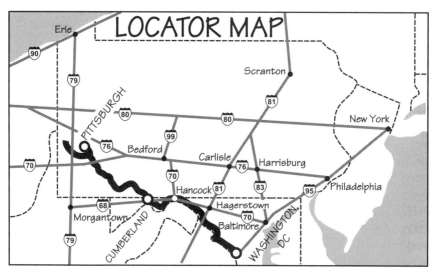

The locator map shows what eventually will be a continuous trail from Pittsburgh PA, to Washington, D.C. This guide covers the completed portion running from McKeesport, PA near Pittsburgh to Meyersdale, PA near the Maryland border. Directions to the Trail from Pittsburgh are included, as are directions from the Trail to Cumberland.

NUTS AND BOLTS

Things you need to know before you start your trip or begin reading this book.

Great Allegheny Passage

The Great Allegheny Passage is the longest multi-purpose rail-trail in the eastern United States, with 100 continuous miles of trail open from McKeesport to near Meyersdale, plus several smaller segments open in the Pittsburgh area. When finished in 2004 or thereabouts, the Passage will offer a total of 150 miles of non-motorized, nearly level trail between Cumberland, MD and Pittsburgh, with a 52-mile spur to Pittsburgh International Airport. At Cumberland, it joins the C&O Canal Towpath to expand the off-road linkage to Washington, DC. The Great Allegheny Passage is a project of the Allegheny Trail Alliance, a group of seven trail organizations united to build the trail from Cumberland to Pittsburgh (see Resources at the end of the book for more information on the individual trail organizations, museums, historical societies, and libraries mentioned throughout).

Pittsburgh to McKeesport and Back

Some day, you'll be able to ride your bike from downtown Pittsburgh to McKeesport on beautiful trails that will run much of the way on both sides of the river. That day is still several years away, and right now, the ride between the two cities is somewhat problematic.

Best bet is to hire a cab to take you out to McKeesport or Boston. But if you're determined to ride all the way from Downtown Pittsburgh to McKeesport, here's how we suggest you do it.

Eastbound

Leave the Amtrak or bus station and turn on to Grant Street. It's a 4-lane brick street, well marked, and begins at a 5-way intersection. You might want to walk your bike here. Take Grant all the way to Second Avenue and turn left. Again, be careful making this turn. Once on Second, follow the signs to the Eliza Furnace Trail. This is a fine trail that runs between the eastbound and westbound lanes of Interstate 376. When you get to the end of the trail, loop down to Second Avenue and turn left. Second Avenue will take you through the neighborhood of Hazelwood. Keep going east and cross the Glenwood Bridge. It's been undergoing construction for several years, so be careful crossing it.

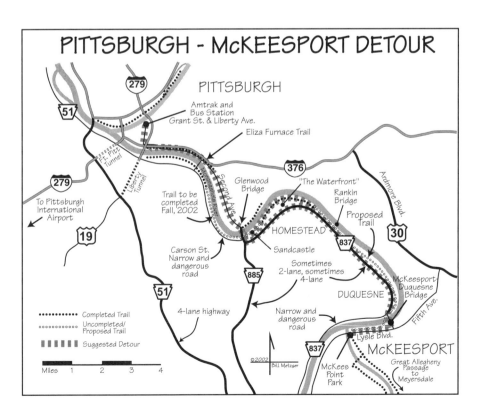

At the end of the bridge, there are two alternatives:

EASTBOUND ALTERNATIVE ONE:

If you're riding between Memorial Day and Labor Day, follow the signs to Sandcastle. It's a water park. When you get to the entrance of Sandcastle, take the two lane blacktop road along the railroad tracks. When you see the giant Lowe's Theater, turn left. You'll see a trail along the river. You can ride it or stay on the road through the Waterfront Commercial Development. When you see a big BLUE building, climb up the ramp and turn left on Route 837.

EASTBOUND ALTERNATIVE TWO:

If you're riding before Memorial Day and after Labor Day, follow the signs at the end of the Glenwood Bridge for Homestead and Route 837 East.

Follow 837 East through Homestead. After Homestead, this is a four lane divided highway with minimal shoulders, but there are "Share the Road with Bicycles" signs posted.

FROM BOTH EASTBOUND ALTERNATIVES

Stay on Route 837 East until you come to the McKeesport-Duquesne Bridge. Either ride the sidewalk or the road across the bridge, whichever you feel comfortable with.

Immediately at the end of the bridge, make a right on the first (currently unmarked) ramp. Take that down to Lysle Boulevard. Stay right on Lysle Boulevard, a 4 lane undivided street, past the *McKeesport Daily News* and City Hall. Make an easy right down the ramp at the War Memorial. The trail starts at the marina to the left under the bridge.

WESTBOUND

Turn right at the large brick building known as the Palisades and ride up the ramp to Lysle Boulevard. Lysle Boulevard is a 4 lane undivided street. Take it through town keeping the railroad tracks on your left until you get to a ramp to the right. Follow the signs to Duquesne and Route 837 West. Either take the sidewalk across the bridge or the roadway, whichever you feel comfortable with. At the end of the bridge, carefully merge on to 837 West.

This is a four lane divided highway with a narrow, dirty shoulder, but it is posted with "Share the Road with Bicycles" signs. There are two alternatives:

WESTBOUND ALTERNATIVE ONE:

If you're riding between Memorial Day and Labor Day, turn right at the ramp leading to the Waterfront. As you curve around the BLUE building, you'll see a trail on the right. Either take it or stay on the road. You're in the Waterfront commercial development. Stay on the main road keeping the river on your right. At the "T" intersection past Lowes Theater, turn right and stay on the blacktop highway past Sandcastle. Follow the signs to the Glenwood Bridge and Hazelwood, Second Avenue.

WESTBOUND ALTERNATIVE TWO:

If you're riding after Labor Day and before Memorial Day, stay on Route 837 through the town of Homestead on 8th Avenue. When you get to a series of ramps, follow the signs to Glenwood Bridge, Hazelwood and Second Avenue.

FROM BOTH WESTBOUND ALTERNATIVES:

After you cross the Glenwood Bridge, stay on Second Avenue until you see signs for the Eliza Furnace Trail. Take this trail into downtown. It's a great ride. At the end of the trail, turn left onto Second Avenue and right on Grant Street. The bus station and Amtrak station are at the end of Grant.

BIKING TO OR FROM PITTSBURGH INTERNATIONAL AIRPORT

 Don't even think of biking to or from Pittsburgh International Airport until we get some kind of trail built out there to connect to the Montour.

MILEPOSTS

The section of the Great Allegheny Passage from McKeesport to Meyersdale is made up of three individual trails, each with different ownership and a different set of mileposts. From McKeesport to Connellsville you're on the Yough River Trail North, which uses the old P&LE mileposts. Mile 0 is across the river from downtown Pittsburgh at Station Square. The first milepost you'll see on the trail is 18 at Dead Man's Hollow. There's no mistaking them—they're big white concrete triangle-shaped posts with the numbers painted on. They're almost always on the river side of the trail. These will take you to Connellsville, Mile 58. Once through Connellsville, through Riverfront Park and along Third Street, you'll be on the Youghiogheny River Trail South, which uses the old Route 281 bridge in Confluence as Mile 0. First milepost of theirs you'll see is 26. These are brown wooden 4x4s with the numbers routed into them. After Confluence, you're on the Allegheny Highlands Trail (PA). They also use painted 4x4s. Their mile 0 is at the Mason Dixon Line, but this is due to change. The official policy of the Allegheny Trail Alliance is that Mile 0 is at the Visitors Center in Cumberland, right where the C&O Towpath ends. That means everything is going to get renumbered. But for this edition of the guidebook, we're sticking with the mileposts as they are now since this is what you'll be seeing out on the trail. If you want a preview of the various mileposts, visit the web site: www.atatrail.org.

Milepost 52 on the Yough River Trail North is 52 miles from Station Square across the river from downtown Pittsburgh.

BIKES

The vast majority of this trail is paved with crushed limestone, and once it's set, it acts almost like concrete. Everyone assumes that because it's crushed stone, you need a mountain bike to ride it. You don't. Any road bike will do nicely.

HOWEVER, having said that, if you're really through-biking, a mountain bike or a hybrid is a good idea on the C&O Towpath, unless you're an experienced careful rider.

COMMERCIAL ESTABLISHMENTS AND THE WEBSITE

Businesses come and go and it's a daunting job keeping track of all the commercial activity that's happening along 100+ miles of trail. Fortunately, the folks of the Allegheny Trail Alliance who maintain the website www.atatrail.org are up to the task. Everything you need to know about where to eat, stay, and do your laundry is listed there and kept reasonably current. It's also a good idea to pick up a copy of *Linking Up* by Roy Weil and Mary Shaw. You can get it either through bookstores or through www.atatrail.org.

DIRECTIONS

The Yough and Casselman Rivers and the accompanying trail run toward every point of the compass. Compass directions are meaningless as is describing things on the right or left side of the trail. So, for the purposes of this guidebook, and to make things simple, we'll refer to things as either on the river side or the hill side of the trail. Since the trail follows the river and the river is cut through a gorge its whole length, there's always a hill.

Another thing you need to know about direction: that delightful tail wind that's been helping you along will become a vicious head wind just around the next bend in the river.

ACCESSIBILITY

The entire trail from McKeesport to Meyersdale is accessible to persons with disabilities. Where ramps are necessary to bypass bridges, they have been built to a maximum 5% grade. Benches are provided near major trail heads at least every half mile and often closer. Unless you are completely and totally bedridden, you can enjoy this trail.

Bicyclist's Responsibility Code

This is from Larry Walsh, who writes the monthly "Cycling" column for the *Pittsburgh Post-Gazette*. It is reprinted with his permission.

- *Wear a helmet. Always.*
- *Stay to the right of the trail.*
- *Pull well off the trail when you stop so others may pass safely.*
- *Ride single file.*
- *Enjoy the music of nature. Leave your headphones at home.*
- *Slow down and announce your presence when you are about to pass someone. A clear "On your left"—or "On your right" for the lane challenged—should suffice.*
- *Let your children set the pace so you can keep an eye on them. Make sure they don't pedal too far ahead or get in the way of others.*
- *Yield to nonbikers.*
- *Keep the trail clean. Pick up litter even if it isn't yours.*
- *Respect private property.*
- *When all else fails, use common sense.*

Pennsylvania Liquor Laws

If you like have a beer or a glass of wine after long day on the bicycle, you're going to have to work at it in Pennsylvania. You can only buy a single bottle or can of beer in a bar or restaurant with a liquor license and consume it on the premises. Same goes for a glass of wine. You can buy as much as a six pack of beer in a bar, but you can only buy a bottle of wine at a state liquor store or a winery. If you want more than a six pack of beer, you have to go to a beer distributor. You want to buy a bottle of beer or wine in a grocery store, keep on the trail 'til you get to Maryland and drink to your heart's content.

Security

This is a very safe trail. You are riding on a private right of way 99% of the time. That said, there are some common sense things you should do: If you're going to park your bike out of your sight, lock it. If you park your car at one of the trail heads, lock all your valuables in the trunk.

STARTING UP THE TRAIL

Western Pennsylvania is a relatively compact place that writers who don't know us try to put in the Midwest or Appalachia. We're not the Midwest. That begins at the Ohio border. We're not Appalachia or the South. They start where West Virginia begins—down at the Mason-Dixon Line. We're not part of the Great Lakes and their snow belt: that begins north of Interstate 80. What we are is western Pennsylvania—some would call us Westsylvania. This is a place that for 100 or so years was the industrial center of the world and supplied the country with steel, coal, aluminum, glass, and rye whiskey.

We're Slovenian, Slovakian, Serbian, Rusyn, Russian, Polish, Italian, African-American, Hungarian, Scotch-Irish and Asians of every persuasion. We brought our culture and our religion and our language with us and we haven't forgotten the old ways.

We're part of Pennsylvania because we got stuck with it a long time ago but we have little in common with our neighbors in Philadelphia and that includes language. A native Pittsburgh speaker and a born Philadelphian can barely understand each other. Spend any time with us and it becomes quite obvious.

You're traveling on a rail-trail. We pronounce that "rell trell." Steel mills are "still mills." Connellsville, Pennsylvania is "Connasville, Pennsavania." The plural of you is "yunz" or "yinz." When you start hearing "y'all," chances are you're in Maryland or West Virginia. We have a way with grammar, too. Our most famous is that we drop the infinitive. Things that "need to be cleaned" or "need cleaning" anywhere else in the English-speaking world "need cleaned" here. If Shakespeare would have written Hamlet's soliloquy about a Pittsburgher, Hamlet would have said, "Or not. That is the question." Oh, and most importantly to you, the happy trail user constantly in search of liquids, we don't drink soda here. We drink pop.

You're starting at McKees Point Park, where the Youghiogheny and Monongahela Rivers meet. This is your introduction to the Youghiogheny River. It's pronounced Yock-a-GAIN-ee, or Yock for short. We'll mostly refer to it as the Yough—it looks nicer in print. Since this is being written in English (thanks in no small part to events that took place along this trail corridor), Yough could also be pronounced "Yoff" as in cough, "Yow" as in bough, "Yew" as in slough (the ones along the river),

"Yo" as in dough, "Yaw" as in ought, or "Yuff" as in rough and tough. But it's not. There is a precedent. The Irish *lough* is the same as and is pronounced like the Scottish *loch* which is pronounced "lock". Like Yough.

The name Youghiogheny means, according to historians who know these things, "a stream flowing in a contrary direction" in some Native American language or another. Another source defines Youghiogheny as "four streams."

Both the Mon and the Yough flow northward. In Pennsylvania especially, we're used to our rivers flowing southward and this creates some confusion because southward is upstream and we think of south as down. So you have to get used to the idea that down is up. There's also some controversy about how Youghiogheny was spelled. As Tim Palmer observes in *Youghiogheny, Appalachian River* (1984; reprinted by permission of the University of Pittsburgh Press*)*:

> *"It may be only chance that has given us the spelling of Youghiogheny. The earliest reference to the river is a caption on a map drawn in 1737 by William Mayo: "Spring heads of Yok-yo-gane river a south branch of the Monongahela." In 1751, a map of Virginia and Maryland called the river the Yawyawganey. One year later a trader's map listed Ohio Gani. Captain Robert Orme of the Braddock expedition in 1755 called the river both Joxhio Geni and Yoxhio Geni. Nicholas Cresswell, an Englishman who traveled west to acquire land for a group of Virginians, wrote in 1775 that he "crossed the Yaughagany River at the Steward's Crossing." Local petitioners for a road from Uniontown to the river spelled it Youghiogheni in 1784, and in the same year, George Washington spelled it Yehiogany. In 1798, Robert Proud's The History of Pennsylvania referred to the "Yoxhiogany River." Early land grants spelled Yohogania, and other variations were Yochi Geni, Youghanne, and Yuh-wiac-hanne. For some reason, none of these spellings stuck."*

Also, while we're at it, it's pronounced Mon-on-ga-HAY-la. We call it the Mon, mostly. Native Americans called it "the river of sliding banks." These rivers, the Mon and the Yough, are part of the great Mississippi system. The waters you see here will flow over 2,000 miles to the Gulf of Mexico, part of a watershed that drains two-fifths (41%) of the continental United States. By the time it gets to New Orleans, water from the Yough will mix with water from the Milk River in Canada and the Canadian River in Texas. It'll join glacial meltwater from the Rockies in Montana and snow runoff from the Great Smokies in North Carolina. Down at the Big Easy, Old Faithful Geyser flows together with the Yough and the Yellowstone, the Red, the White, and the Little Blue and Big Blue Rivers.

Fourteen ten-thousandths (0.0014 percent) of the Mississippi's watershed is drained by the Yough and its tributaries. You're standing at McKeesport looking upriver; the great watershed is mostly to your back.

If you're heading west to east, you'll follow the Yough about 70 miles up to Confluence and then 30 more miles of its biggest tributary, the Casselman, to Meyersdale. Right now, you're about 752 feet (give or take a foot or so) above sea level. So the Ohio and Mississippi will only fall 752 feet in their 2,000 mile journey. (It works out to an average grade of .000068 percent.) Meyersdale is at 2,106 feet, so you'll climb 1,387 feet in 100 miles. The steepest railroad grade you'll encounter going east is .8 percent, but a whole lot of the time your trip will be flat.

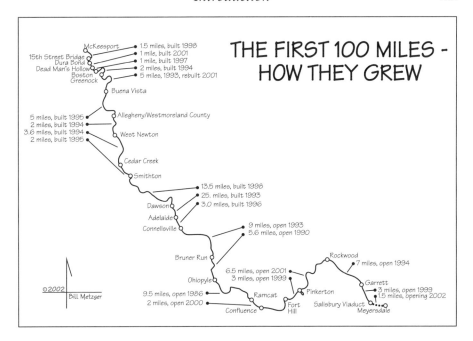

The Yough rises in western Maryland, hard by the West Virginia border, and drains a small sliver of the Mountain State. At its widest, the watershed is no more than 30 miles wide. Straight line, it's about 85 miles from the source to McKeesport. By the meandering river, it's 132. On its way, it manages to cut some fine gorges through the mountains and surrounding countryside.

You're following rivers because railroad builders followed rivers wherever they could and you're riding on a trail that was built on old railroad grades. Specifically, you're going to travel on the abandoned Pittsburgh and Lake Erie Railroad (P&LE) Youghiogheny Branch to Connellsville, and the Western Maryland (WM) Railway Connellsville Extension from Connellsville to Meyersdale.

Understand that this trail didn't just fall into place whole and ready to use. It was built over a period of 15 years in sections of anywhere from one to fifteen miles. This is no mere footpath through the forest. Because this is a rail-trail, it's built to railroad scale using massive structures that are hundreds, sometime thousands, of feet long, often weighing thousands of tons.

This trail is nothing short of a miracle. Consider that there were two abandoned railroads that were not only available but joined, and not only joined but ran through a series of beautiful river valleys. And not only did they run through super scenery, but they connected with the C&O Canal Towpath to join Pittsburgh and Washington, DC by trail. And not only was all this possible, but there was the leadership, both professional and volunteer, that rose to the occasion to visualize the trail and nurture it and to inspire the thousands of volunteers who actually made it happen.

It's not often you get to witness a miracle, let alone ride on one for a hundred miles, but that's exactly what you're doing when you take the trail from McKeesport to Meyersdale.

Map & Text Legend

TRAIL AMENITIES

P Trail Head, Parking Area

Rest Rooms

Chemical Toilet (In Season)

Picnic Pavilion

Picnic Area

Public Camping

X Snack Bar (Park Concessions only)

INDUSTRIAL SITES

Coal Mine

Coke Ovens

Industry

TEXT ITEMS OF NOTE

 Danger

Indicates Break For
Background Information

TRAILS

23 Milepost

Great Allegheny Passage

Trail in street, dirt road

Uncompleted Rail Trail

Hiking Trail

RAILROADS

Active Double Track RR

Active Single Track RR

+ + + + + + + + Abandoned Railroad

Abandoned Trolley Line

CHAPTER 1: McKEESPORT

The First Ward of McKeesport in the early 1920s. Aside from the Palisades, the long building along the river, most of the other buildings in this picture are gone. The bridge is the old 5th Street Bridge, which was replaced in the early 1930s. The smokestacks in the background belong to the U.S. Steel National Works. Courtesy Elizabeth Township Historical Society.

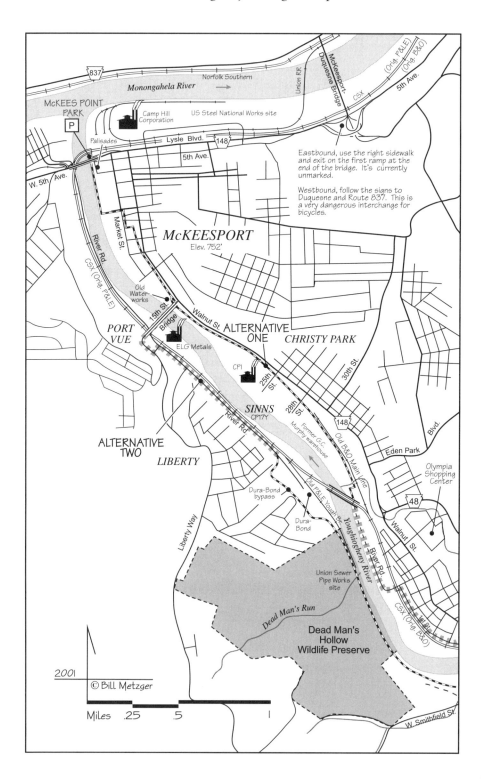

Mck Keesport was named for the McKees, father and son, who emigrated here from Scotland by way of Ireland and Philadelphia in 1755. Father David farmed here and established a ferry across both the Yough and the Mon Rivers. David died in 1795 at the age of 85 and passed the farm and ferry on to his son John, who established the town the same year his father passed away. It was originally known as McKees Ferry, then McKees Port.

The town prospered because of its excellent location for transportation and the ready availability of coal in the area. In 1833, there were 10 mines within a mile of town. Several steel mills located here, most notably the National Tube Works. National Tube, later U.S. Steel's National Works, made pipe and prospered with the growth of the oil industry. McKeesport became known as the Tube City. One of the offshoots of this was the unfortunately-named Tube City Beer, now mercifully defunct.

U.S. Steel closed the National Works in 1987 after a long decline. The Camp Hill Corporation, which makes pipe, is the only manufacturing remnant of the old mill, which covered two miles of Mon riverbank from the Yough River to below the McKeesport-Duquesne Bridge. Camp Hill purchased the most modern section in 1987 and made it a going concern.

The Baltimore and Ohio Railroad used to run right through town, which was both a blessing—residents of the town enjoyed excellent transportation before the advent of the automobile—and a curse. There were 24 grade crossings in McKeesport; the frequent trains (and there were dozens a day) tied the place in knots. But the town thrived in spite of it. McKeesport's downtown rivaled that of Pittsburgh.

Local politicians wanted the railroad out of town and finally, in 1971, the B&O relocated over to the P&LE side, a new railroad bridge was built across the Yough at Sinns (see map) and the tracks through town were abandoned. The only remnant of the old line in downtown is the tower where the operator who controlled the crossing signals worked.

Commuter trains ran from McKeesport to downtown Pittsburgh until 1989, when Allegheny County withdrew its subsidy. By the late 1980s, a combination of the closing of the steel mills, the loss of the G. C. Murphy corporate headquarters, some unfortunate urban renewal projects, the subsequent loss of downtown business to nearby malls, and the lack of rapid transportation to Pittsburgh caused a steep decline in McKeesport's fortunes. The flood of 1972 didn't help, either.

McKeesport's population was 55,000 in 1940; it was 24,000 in the 2000 census.

There are signs the place is coming back, but right now the trail runs through mostly open fields where thousands of people once lived and worked.

McKees Point Park has gone a long way toward cleaning up the Yough riverfront and will, in the future, be an important trail junction. The Steel Valley Trail will pass through here and join the Montour Trail to the south and the Three Rivers Heritage Trail into downtown Pittsburgh.

Before we leave McKeesport and the Mon River, we should say a word about river navigation. You may notice some very big boats pushing barges out on the Mon (they are called towboats even though they push their barges). The Mon is part of the inland waterway system and is navigable its entire length from the confluence of the Tygart and West Fork Rivers near Fairmont, West Virginia where it begins, down to where it joins the Allegheny (Al-a-GAIN-ee) River to form the Ohio River at the Point in Pittsburgh.

The Mon was a deep, slow-flowing river that didn't fall very far over its length, so it was easy to make navigable. "Canalize" was the term the engineers used, and they started work on making it navigable in 1836.

The mouth of the Yough is in the pool of Dam Number 2, located near Braddock about 6 miles downstream from here. The Army Corps of Engineers, which is in charge of construction and maintenance of the inland river network, is currently rebuilding the dam which will raise the river level five feet.

There are no mileposts to go by from here until you cross the river, either at the 15th Street Bridge or the Boston Bridge.

The Palisades

The big brick building at the trail head is the Palisades, a McKeesport institution. It was built before the turn of the century and has been a cigar factory and an auto dealership among other things, but the second floor has always been a community gathering place. It's been a dance hall and a roller skating rink, also a venue for boxing and wrestling. It's now owned by the City of McKeesport and has rest rooms in the ground floor that are open to happy trail users in season.

You'll begin at the Palisades and pass the John J. Kane Hospital, one of four skilled nursing hospitals run by Allegheny County. The vacant high rise next to it was once public housing. It's slated to be demolished. You'll also pass some occupied public housing.

After the trail leaves the park and the hospital, it runs through the area of the city known as the Second and Third Wards, also known as the Bottoms. This is a flood plain area that was particularly hard hit in the Hurricane Agnes Flood of 1972. Much of the land was bought up for redevelopment which has yet to happen.

Back in the unspecified old days, one of the attractions of the area was the famed Brick Alley which, according to an unnamed former mayor of the city, was "an attraction for late evening activities." This was where, if you had enough cash, you were guaranteed to get lucky. This being a family trail guide, that's as much as we'll say about it.

At 13th Street, the trail starts using the old Baltimore and Ohio main line, and was built by the City of McKeesport in 1998 under the leadership of then-mayor Joe Bendel.

The building with the conical roof down along the river by the 15th Street Bridge was the original McKeesport Water Works. When it was built at the turn of the last century, it was a model of its kind. Waterborne disease was rampant and the water works was built at the behest of the medical community. It eliminated the use of wells, rain barrels (people used to collect rain water that ran off their roofs) and river water delivery in wagons.

Today the building has a new roof and is being used for storage. The present water works is on the other side of the bridge.

You have two choices here: You can either cross the bridge and take the trail up to Boston on the south side of the river or stay on the trail on this side of the river up to Versailles. It's pronounced ver-SALES, just like in France.

ALTERNATIVE ONE

If you stay on this side of the river, you'll ride on the B&O main line on an asphalt trail paved by the City of McKeesport.

The plant you pass, CPI Industries, is the old U.S. Steel Christy Park Works. The long, yellow warehouses used to belong to the G. C. Murphy Company. When the trail ends at the McKeesport line, you'll continue up Douglas Street, cross the railroad tracks and turn right on First Street. Just before you get to the Boston Bridge, turn left on Kennedy Street and right when you get to the bridge. It's okay to ride on the sidewalk.

When you get to the other end of the bridge, keep bearing right until you get down to the trail head.

ALTERNATIVE TWO

Cross the 15th Street Bridge

When you cross the bridge, stop and take a look at the river. This is the first time you'll cross it on your trip up the trail. Look at the relatively clean water below you and know that well within living memory, the Yough down here was considered little more than a sewer; it ran in a foul rainbow of colors from all sorts of noxious industrial waste, mine drainage, raw human waste and anything else solid or liquid that anyone wanted to dispose of.

It's a pretty nice river now and getting nicer.

Except for the jet skis.

Mile 16 ELG Haniel

The industry directly under the 15th Street Bridge is ELG Haniel, a metal recycler, specializing in stainless steel.

River Road

Make a left just after you come off the bridge and turn right at the bottom of the ramp on to River Road. Trucks from Dura-Bond use this road during the week, so be careful. The good news is they don't use the road on weekends.

You'll be following the railroad tracks that are to your left all the way to Meyersdale. They belong to CSX, which stands for, uh, CSX. The tracks were originally part of the P&LE Youghiogheny Branch, but also were used by the B&O when it abandoned its line through downtown McKeesport in 1971 (see page 16).

Mile 17 Centralized Traffic Control

You can see the railroad up close and personal here, so this is a good place to talk about a bit of it. Those signals you're passing here are to tell the railroad crews what's happening. The lights are pretty simple: red means stop, green means go and yellow means proceed with caution. There are all sorts of combinations: green over red, red over green, etc., but unless you're studying to be a railroad engineer, you don't have to know them.

The signs on the silver box along the tracks say "Sinns" and "CP17Y." Sinns is the name the railroad gave the spot where the new line that bypassed downtown McKeesport cut over. On the other sign, the numbers mean, in this case, that we're roughly 17 miles from the old P&LE headquarters in what is now Station Square across the river from downtown Pittsburgh. P&LE's Milepost 0 was there. The kicker was P&LE mileposts went in both directions from Milepost 0 and that's why there's a Y at the end on this sign. The Y means this is the Youghiogheny Branch, or what's left of it. CP means this is a "controlled point," that is, a dispatcher in a remote location controls the switches which move the train from one track to another.

The system is called CTC, or Centralized Traffic Control. Before CTC, each station had a telegraph operator who relayed messages from the dispatcher to the train crews, threw the switches that moved trains from track to track and reported trains' locations to the dispatcher as each one passed. Advances in electronics made it possible for the dispatcher to control the trains from a remote (central) location and know their location at all times.

When this signal was installed, the central location was at Station Square. Now, since CSX bought the P&LE, the dispatcher is in Jacksonville, Florida. Yes, kids, those great big trains you see barreling by, and will see and hear all the way to Meyersdale, are being directed by a guy sitting at a console in a big dark room a thousand miles away. Ain't engineering wonderful?

Right before Dura-Bond, the main line of the railroad crosses back over to the other side of the river from the trail where it will stay all the way to Meyersdale. This marks end of the B&O's detour around McKeesport. The bridge across the Yough was built in 1968.

Mile 17.25 Dura-Bond

This was originally the location of the P&LE's 20-track Port Vue East Yard, where rail cars that came off the Yough Branch were sorted.

The Dura-Bond plant coats pipe for the petroleum and chemical industries. It's private property. Don't even think about trespassing through here.

The track leading into the plant is what remains of the P&LE Yough Branch.

Mile 17.25

Soon as you turn off River Avenue, you're on the Youghiogheny River Trail North and the Dura-Bond Bypass. This is the newest, last and most expensive section of the Yough River Trail North to be built. It was completed in the fall of 2001.

This is no ordinary rail trail. As befits its name, the Bypass was built to run around a tight spot created by the industry and a section of still-active railroad. It had to go up the hill, across a gully and back down the hillside.

The gully was filled with the earthly remains of McKeesport Public Housing's Building No. 16 which was imploded about three years ago.

Construction difficulties included land slipping and application problems with the erosion-resistant material due to the handicapped-accessible 5% grades.

A couple of things to note along this section: the wire baskets are called "gabions," which is French for "wire baskets full of rocks," and you can get a really good view of the Dura-Bond pipe yard from here.

Once you're up on the higher level, you can see the old clay diggings from the Union Sewer Works. They're kind of overgrown with scrub trees, but you can see the different grades along the way.

Harmony Society

The 19th Century in America was fraught with utopian schemes and the Harmony Society was no exception. They were a Christian communal industrial society founded by a German named Joseph Rapp, who came to this country in 1804. After trying two other locations, they founded the settlement of Old Economy, now Ambridge, in 1824. The group prospered on the 3,000 acres they owned.

The community generated bundles of cash—all profits went to the Society—and invested in local manufacturing industries. Their biggest investment was the Pittsburgh and Lake Erie Railroad, of which their leader at the time, Father Henrici, was the president for four years.

Alas, for all their financial success, the Society ultimately dissolved due to the quite simple fact that they were celibate. With nobody making any new Harmonites, the membership died out and finally quit in 1905. The property was sold off, most notably to the American Bridge Company who renamed the town.

Old Economy is now a state museum and can be toured daily except Mondays.

Mile 18 Dead Man's Hollow

Welcome to Dead Man's Hollow. It's a 400-acre wildlife preserve that's owned and operated by the Allegheny Land Trust. The site was destined to be a landfill until the Land Trust rescued it. The Hollow includes about 2.5 miles of hiking trails and is open to the public. Feel free to walk around, but lock your bike in the rack they provide for this purpose. They REALLY don't allow mountain biking on the trails.

It's been called Dead Man's Hollow for well over a hundred years. Let trail historian Bob Cupp tell you how it got its name: "there were at least four deaths as well as several questionable accidents, which resulted in serious injury.

"In 1874 a group of boys found a man hanging from a tree limb. The body was never identified and the killer(s) were never determined.

"In 1881 Robert (George) McClure was shot to death while in pursuit of the men who robbed his McKeesport store." One of the robbers was hung and one received 17 years for the crime.

In 1887, "Edward Woods, a 74-year-old Elizabeth Township resident was drowned in the Yough after crossing the river on the McClure Ferry." His body floated to the surface at Dead Man's Hollow.

In 1905, "at the Bowman Brick Works, an employee named Mike Sacco was crushed between an elevator and the third floor of the factory."

There were others. Two bank robbers met in the Hollow to split the loot. One killed the other and made off with the whole take.

The hollow has, according to Cupp, also been the site of an earthquake, a dynamite explosion, a mudslide, a lightning strike, a serious fire, and an explosion at the Youghiogheny Brick Company.

The Union Sewer Pipe Works was one of many industries that were once located in Dead Man's Hollow. The tracks in the foreground led from the banks where the clay was mined, then into the main building where it was molded into pipes. The round buildings to the right are the kilns where the pipe shapes were baked (the kilns' foundations are visible from the trail). Some of the product can be seen waiting to be loaded.
Pat Trimble collection.

Given all the industry that was located in there, it's surprising there were that few accidents. Industries in the hollow included the Union Sewer Pipe Works, the Bowman Brick Works, the Soles Brick Works, oil and gas wells, a coal mine and a stone quarry.

When you poke around the Hollow you can see the remains of some of these industries. But be careful, especially if you happen to find yourself in the Hollow around midnight on the full moon.

Understanding Railroad History

 If you're ready for a break, this is the time to learn a little history. If you're continuing along the Trail, you may want to skip ahead to the next chapter (look for the hiker & bike symbols).

RAILROAD 101

The Great Allegheny Passage is a rail trail. Rail trails are made from old railroads. But what's a railroad?

Julius Caesar and George Washington traveled at pretty much the same speed. True, in Washington's time, sailing ships had been much improved over Julius', and galley slaves had pretty much gone out of fashion, but the three forms of propulsion were still wind, water, and muscle. Wind powered sailing ships and the occasional windmill. Water powered most mills, and muscle power, be it human or animal, was what propelled you over land.

Around the turn of the 18th and 19th centuries, things started to change. First, the steam engine was invented. It was a big, slow, clunky stationary thing in its infancy, used for pumps and to power rudimentary machinery. But mechanics tinkered with it and made it smaller and portable. The first successful portable application was the steamboat, the first form of mechanized transportation the world had ever seen. There had been some attempts at steam-powered land carriages, but they came to naught, if for no other reason than because they scared the horses.

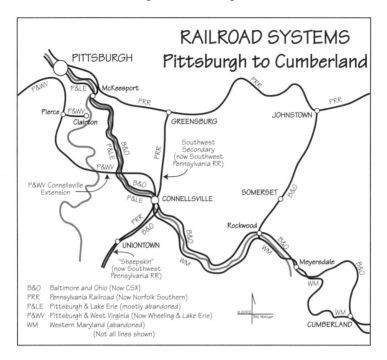

RAILROAD SYSTEMS
Pittsburgh to Cumberland

B&O   Baltimore and Ohio (Now CSX)
PRR   Pennsylvania Railroad (Now Norfolk Southern)
P&LE   Pittsburgh & Lake Erie (mostly abandoned)
P&WV   Pittsburgh & West Virginia (Now Wheeling & Lake Erie)
WM   Western Maryland (abandoned)
       (Not all lines shown)

Mine owners in England were experimenting with hauling coal out of their mines with carts on rails. This had the advantage of rolling easier because the wheels weren't bumping over rocks or bogging down in mud, the carts didn't have to be steered—the rails took care of that—and you could haul a lot more. So the first railroads were to haul coal from mine to market. They were originally short affairs and were powered by horses. Those same English mechanics started fooling around with putting steam engines on rails and things really got rolling. So to speak.

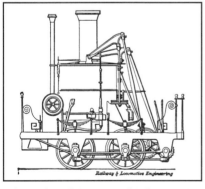

This early Baltimore & Ohio locomotive was called a "grasshopper" because of the way its rods thrashed up and down. Development of the Locomotive Engine, Sinclair, 1907, reprint.

Here's how a railroad works: a series of rails are laid end to end at a specified distance apart. This distance is called the gauge. Standard gauge in North America and Europe is 4' 8.5", or 56.5". The story goes that this was the distance that Roman chariot wheels were apart, but that's probably hokum.

The best story we've heard is that mine owners in England laid their rails 5 feet (a nice round figure) apart on the outside. They originally had the flanges (the things that hold the wheels on the rails) on the outside, but that proved to be impractical, so they put the flanges on the inside instead. The rails were 1.75" wide. So when you add two rails 1.75" wide you come up with 3.5". Subtract that from 5', or measure from the inside and you come up with standard gauge.

We adapted standard gauge in America because our first locomotives came from England. It's one of those things we're stuck with because we've always done it that way. It's sort of like sprocket holes in 35mm film.

Canals and waterways made it possible to overcome friction and travel freely where they exist, but railroads overcame friction quite nicely, too, and they can do it everywhere, day and night, summer and winter, without much worry about floods, drought or freezing. When people figured railroad technology out, there was no contest. Railroads handily won the day.

The first real attempt at a long distance railroad was the Baltimore and Ohio in 1828. Its founders invented the railroad as they went along and adapted it to use in the United States, where there was less population, more land and less money than in England. And they soon found themselves outdistanced by newer railroads that built on their mistakes. For example, the B&O and the Pennsylvania Railroads got to the Ohio River within a month of each other in 1852, but the Pennsylvania started 14 years later.

By the 1850s, railroads were being built all over the country, especially the northern states. Going to work for a railroad in, say 1855, was like going to work for Microsoft in 1985. This is where the action was. Andrew Carnegie got his start in business working for the Pennsylvania Railroad and became rich supplying steel to the railroads. The wonderful irony in Carnegie's case was that after he became successful, he fought the Pennsylvania Railroad every chance he got. You will read about some of these fights later.

A railroad does more than just overcome friction—it's also capable of carrying enormous weight. How? The track does all the work. If you took a locomotive or a loaded railroad car and tried to run it on the average highway, it would sink right through the asphalt. The new locomotives go 200 tons or better and a typical loaded railroad car today weighs well in excess of a hundred tons. The track not only spreads out the weight of these monsters, but it acts as a smooth running surface and a guideway. You don't have to steer a train. The track does that, too.

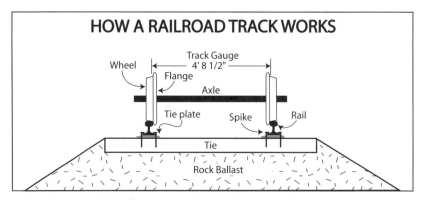

The rails, spaced 4'8.5" apart, are fastened to the tie by spikes and sit on tie plates which protect the tie from wear. Rock ballast holds the track in place and drains water away. Flanges on each wheel hold it on the track.

All a locomotive has to do is pull the weight of the train and because steel wheels on steel rails don't create much friction, a locomotive can pull a lot of weight. Next train you see going by, count the number of cars and multiply by 100. That's roughly how many tons the locomotives are pulling.

The railroad changed everything

It changed our notion of time. Journeys that once took weeks now took days; trips that took days now took hours. A riverboat or a stagecoach that left some-time in the afternoon or when it had a full load became a train that departed at 3:15, whether you were on it or not. No one even knew if the human body could survive traveling at speeds of 50 or 60 miles an hour. For a time 60 miles an hour was looked at as something akin to breaking the sound barrier or achieving earth orbit—a very hazardous goal to be achieved at great peril.

When a haphazard system of local time became inadequate, the railroads carved the country into four time zones in 1883. Railroad time became everyone's time. Congress finally agreed that this was a good idea and made the time zones manda-tory in 1919.

Business changed. Before the railroad, a company had offices or factories at one or two locations. The railroad had offices and facilities at each end and everywhere in between. Costs had to be accounted for like never before. Precise schedules had to be made and strictly adhered to. Huge numbers of people had to be recruited and trained to operate the railroad. Iron works and then steel mills had to be built and operated to supply raw material for the rails, cars, locomotives and bridges. Railroads not only hauled the raw materials in and the finished goods out of steel mills, they were also the mills' best customers.

Turning brake wheels on the top of a moving train in the snow was anything but romantic. Contrary to what you see in the movies, NOBODY is permitted atop a moving train today. The Railroad Up To Date (reprint from 1890).

A town that didn't have a railroad was doomed to obscurity. Everybody wanted one. There were literally hundreds of failed "sure fire" railroad schemes in Pennsylvania alone. Of the ones that did get built, some were fabulously success-ful. Others were less so. But you had to have a railroad then just like you need an Internet connection today. The railroad station became the center of the com-munity. Journeys great and small began and ended here; news in the form of telegrams, mail, out of town newspapers, and just plain gossip emanated from here; and this is where you picked up your mail-order chickens, plow or sewing machine.

And every boy—and a lot of their fathers—wanted to be a railroad engineer. In 19th century rural America, looking at the wrong end of a horse or cow didn't even come close to the promise offered by a glamorous life on the high iron, a life that beckoned every time a train blew its whistle for the local grade crossing.

The romance of the rails was the stuff of pulp fiction in the late 19th century, but the reality was often anything but romantic. Amputees were common due to the Civil War and the railroads. Until the invention of the air brake and the automatic coupler, railroaders were killed and maimed at an alarming rate. Before the air brake, brakemen were literally that. They walked along the tops of cars on moving trains and set hand brakes to stop the train. In the dark. In the snow. In the rain. Oh, and there were no handrails on the tops of the cars. Pittsburgh's George Westinghouse invented the air brake and made railroading infinitely safer.

Before automatic couplers, trains were held together with link and pin couplers. To couple two cars together, the same hapless brakeman had to stand between two cars and hold up a link in one hand and a pin in the other while the train backed up (on hand signals) to make the coupling. A veteran brakeman who had all his fingers was a rarity indeed.

Before efficient signaling and communications, trains proved the principal that no two objects could occupy the same track at the same time with regularity. And once a wreck occurred, the coal stoves in wooden passenger cars had a habit of catching the car on fire and burning trapped passengers to death. Steam heat and steel passenger cars solved that problem.

With safety problems solved and a nationwide railroad network in place, the railroads entered a golden age in the first two decades of the 20th century only to go into slow decline with the advent of the automobile and paved highways, government regulation, inbred management, and the decline of traditional "smokestack industries." World War II temporarily halted the decline only to see it return with a vengeance in the 1950s and '60s with interstate highways and jet airliners and relentless truck competition.

Fortunately, things changed for the better. Amtrak took away the burden of money-losing passenger trains, and freight deregulation in the early 1980s brought a rebirth of sorts with railroads being free to set rates for the first time in 70 years.

Today, the railroads are relatively strong and stable but a railroader of the 19th century would barely recognize the industry in the 21st.

You can still ride a train through the Yough valley any day of the week, (see discussion of Capitol Limited in the Resource chapter) but there's only one round trip a day where there used to be a dozen. Back then, every town of any size would have had a station that was manned, more often than not 24 hours a day. There were men who fueled, watered and repaired the steam locomotives, a crew every few miles who repaired the tracks, and each short train—and there were many of them

a day—had a five man crew. In the Yough valley alone, there were well over a thousand men who worked for the railroad. Now, long trains are the norm, pulled by diesel locomotives that

1881 Baltimore & Ohio "Ten Wheeler".
1881 Poor's Manual.

each have the power of a half dozen of the old steam engines. (Those diesel loco-motives cost in excess of 2.5 million bucks each, more than entire railroads used to cost.) Freight trains have two-man crews and there are no manned passenger stations on the old B&O between Martinsburg, West Virginia and Pittsburgh. The caboose is gone, replaced by a radio telemetry device on the end of the train. In almost every case on the railroad, technology has replaced manpower. Railroading has gone from a retail "all things to all people" business to a wholesale business dealing with big customers. Attempts have been made for years to declare the railroads dead. But they're not—not by a long shot. Just take notice of how many trains that you hear passing through the valley.

Baltimore and Ohio Railroad

As you've probably seen and heard if you're along the trail as you're reading this, or have read in these pages already, there's a railroad that parallels the trail all the way from McKeesport to Meyersdale and beyond. It's now the Keystone Subdivi-sion of CSX, but it was originally the Pittsburgh and Connellsville Railroad.

It was here first, which is a good reason why you're not riding a bike on its mortal remains.

In the early 1820s, the four Eastern Seaboard cities of Boston, New York, Phila-delphia, and Baltimore were about equal in population and income. The opening of the wildly successful Erie Canal in New York in 1824 threw the equation way out of balance. Now, New York became the port of choice for commerce to and from the west. New York was eating everybody's lunch.

The other cities howled. Boston couldn't build a canal because of the Berkshire Mountains to the west. (They ultimately built a network of railroads including a 4 3/4 mile tunnel that took 25 years to build.) Philadelphia started the Pennsylvania Main Line of Public Works, an ill-conceived railroad/canal combination that was

B&O system map.

cumbersome at best. Baltimore had a waterway of sorts up the Chesapeake Bay to the Susquehanna River, but it went north. There was precious little water to the west; the Patapsco River was short and steep, a poor candidate for a canal.

True, Baltimore had the National Road, but it was slow and expensive. Something else was needed. The merchants of Baltimore decided a railroad was just the ticket. Not only a railroad, but a railroad to the Ohio River, some three hundred miles to the west. If ever there was a bold undertaking, this was it.

On July 4, 1828, the first stone was laid for the railroad in the fine Masonic tradition. After the stone was declared four square, there was a great parade for which almost all the citizens of Baltimore turned out.

In truth, there were less than a dozen men in the whole city who could say with absolute certainty what a railroad was, which made the undertaking all the more audacious.

It so happened that on that very same day, about 35 miles to the south in Georgetown, in the District of Columbia, they turned over a spade full of earth for the Chesapeake and Ohio Canal. Chesapeake and Ohio, Baltimore and Ohio. Both were heading for the same Ohio. Up the same Potomac River valley. The same narrow Potomac River valley. This being America, even before the first stones were laid, the canal sued the railroad to cease and desist from buying land in said Potomac River valley.

There were more problems with the B&O. At first they built their structures to English standards—massive stone bridges of almost monumental proportions that still stand and carry trains to this very day. Fine for England where there were lots of people, money and short distances. For the B&O there was lots of land, most of it unpopulated, and precious little money.

What the Baltimore and Ohio was attempting to do was build a railroad that equaled the length of Great Britain at a time when there were exactly three other railroads in the United States, none more than a dozen or so miles long. The B&O found itself in the position of inventing the American railroad as it went along. It struggled with the type of power it should use, horses vs. locomotives. There's an excellent chance the legendary race between the steam locomotive Tom Thumb and a horse that you read about in history class didn't happen, but it was a while until locomotives became the preferred method of propulsion. The iron and wooden rail it started out with didn't stand up to constant wear—it took years to correct that problem. The original curves were often too sharp—they had to come back later and rebuild them. A relatively small hill became a formidable obstacle until more powerful steam locomotives were built to cross it.

Then there were political problems. The B&O not only had to deal with its own Maryland state legislature, but also those of Virginia and Pennsylvania. Pennsylvania granted it a charter to build to Pittsburgh in 1828, provided it did so in 15 years. That charter expired in 1843 when the B&O had just barely made it to Cumberland. They asked the Pennsylvania legislature for a new charter in 1846, coincidentally the same year the Pennsylvania Railroad was chartered. This time the Philadelphia interests who were backing the PRR stacked the deck against the B&O and wrote a charter that was impossible for the B&O to fulfill. To no one's surprise, it expired.

The Shenandoah, the Baltimore and Ohio's Pittsburgh to Washington train, rounds a curve just west of Casselman, PA in 1946. The locomotives are among the nation's first successful passenger diesels.   R.A. Baker photo, Van Sickel collection.

The B&O headed for Wheeling instead. It, too, was on the Ohio. And farther downstream. As a consolation prize, Wheeling wasn't bad. It was a thriving river port doing a bustling trade with the west.

But the Pennsylvania got Pittsburgh—which would prove to be the biggest of big enchiladas. By now, most of the bugs had been worked out of railroad building and the PRR had a relatively easy time of it building west from Harrisburg. Pittsburgh businessmen and the traveling public were less than enthused about the monopoly the "Pennsy" had on their town. A charter had been floating around for the Pittsburgh and Connellsville Railroad since 1837. Nothing had come of it. Through some legislative skullduggery, and those Pittsburgh boys could be as skullduggerous as the Philly guys, the Pittsburgh and Connellsville rose from the dead and started construction in 1854 from, of all places, West Newton.

Locomotives and rails came over the mountain from the east on the PRR, then were loaded into river barges and floated up the river. This was before the locks and dams on the Yough were washed away. They started this section because it was not only at the head of navigation, but it was the easiest to build. They opened it in 1855. The first locomotive to run over the section was named the "George Washington." Not much else was done to build eastward for quite a while.

Seems that the citizens of Turkey Foot (now Confluence) wanted no part of the railroad. They didn't want it to interfere with the business they were doing with the roads of the day.

The Pittsburgh & Connellsville did build toward Pittsburgh though, and the line was finished between its namesake towns in 1860, just in time for the coke boom to start. It took 11 more years and a new charter or two before the line was completed to Cumberland, but most of the traffic was coal and coke from the Connellsville District to the mills of Pittsburgh.

The Baltimore and Ohio formally took over the Pittsburgh and Connellsville in 1875—the B&O had backed the extension into Cumberland—and by the end of the 19th century it had become an important main line, which it remains to this day. After some difficulty, including a time when it was controlled by the Pennsylvania RR, the Baltimore and Ohio did well as a company; its lines ran to Cincinnati, St. Louis, and Chicago and it enjoyed its status as the first railroad in America. Its premier passenger trains, the National Limited and the Capitol Limited, enjoyed an excellent reputation with the traveling public. Residents of the Yough valley could count on seven passenger trains each way a day on the B&O.

In 1962, the B&O merged with the Chesapeake and Ohio Railroad (no relation to the canal). C&O-B&O became the Chessie System in 1973 (named for Chessie, the C&O's mascot cat) and merged into CSX in 1980.

Today, the line sees a passenger train each way a day and about 20 freight trains a day, but between Connellsville and McKeesport neither the passenger or freight trains stop. To the residents of the Yough valley where the railroad was once their only connection to the outside world, the old B&O is nothing more than something you have to stop for at a grade crossing.

And when the railroad quit stopping, the glory days of each town along the Yough valley were gone, too.

Pittsburgh, McKeesport & Youghiogheny Railroad

The trail you are now using, and will continue to use from here to Connellsville, began in no small part because Andrew Carnegie (we pronounce it Car-NEG-ee as opposed to outlanders who say CAR-neg-ee) was mad at the Pennsylvania Railroad (PRR). In 1880, the "Pennsy" had a virtual monopoly on the Pittsburgh steel market and could—and did—charge Carnegie what it jolly well pleased to haul his steel east. Carnegie, with all his money and power, could do little but fume and pay up. Never mind that Carnegie got his start in big business with the PRR—all's fair in love and railroads.

Enter William H. Vanderbilt of the New York Central Railroad Vanderbilts, arch-competitors of the PRR, who never passed up an opportunity to take a shot at their Philadelphia rivals. Carnegie wanted to hit the Pennsylvania Railroad where they lived, so he proposed building a railroad across the state of Pennsylvania from Pittsburgh to Harrisburg. He and Vanderbilt put up $5 million each and enlisted John D. Rockefeller, Henry W. Oliver, and other big industrialists of the day who were also stewed at the PRR. They cobbled together some long-dormant railroad charters and called the new railroad the South Pennsylvania Railroad. At the same time, the Pittsburgh and Lake Erie Railroad (P&LE) had just built a line from Pittsburgh west up to Youngstown, Ohio, and was doing a booming business in competition with the PRR. It was sponsored by local Pittsburgh folks, including the Harmonites whom we talked about earlier (see page 7).

The South Penn had a natural terminal at Port Perry, where Carnegie's big Edgar Thomson Works was located. But they needed to get west into Pittsburgh. Was the P&LE interested in building a line from Pittsburgh to Port Perry? You betcha

Number 97, a fine high-stepping passenger engine called an American type, poses on the Dickerson Run roundhouse turntable with its proud crew. Judging from its shiny appearance, this picture was taken not too long after the engine was built in 1893. Pat Trimble collection.

they were! And, come to think of it, the PL&E had a charter to build a railroad to Connellsville. But they were a bit strapped for cash at the moment and the Connellsville line had been put on hold.

"Strapped for cash, you say?" said Vanderbilt. "We have plenty. Let's talk." The deal emerged that Vanderbilt would build the new railroad, to be called the Pittsburgh, McKeesport & Youghiogheny (hereinafter known as the "P-Mickey") all the way to Connellsville, just coincidentally going by Port Perry and the Edgar Thomson Works. Vanderbilt would pay for the whole deal and lease it back to the P&LE. Through some smooth maneuvering, Vanderbilt wound up with the controlling interest in the P&LE. And the Harmonites walked away with a cool million of Vanderbilt's money.

Vanderbilt had his western outlet for the South Penn and access to the rich Pittsburgh market for his New York Central Lines. Not a bad deal.

Pittsburgh steelmakers, including Carnegie, were thrilled. The P-Mickey was finished into Connellsville in 1883 and construction was going great guns on the South Penn. It was expected to be open by 1886.

However, J. P. Morgan had a lot of money invested with both the Pennsylvania and the Vanderbilt interests. He was getting worried that the ruinous competition between the two would cost him a big chunk of change. In the legendary story, Morgan took both parties out in New York Harbor on his yacht *Corsair* and made them work out a deal. Nobody got off the boat until everybody agreed. When they disembarked from the *Corsair* on September 12, 1885, work stopped immediately on the three-quarters-completed South Penn and the line was sold to the Pennsylvania Railroad.

The P&LE got its railroad into Connellsville and tapped the rich coal and coke market, the Vanderbilts got their access to Pittsburgh, the Pennsylvania Railroad held onto its monopoly east for the time being, and Andrew Carnegie continued to fume.

And the South Penn? After some alteration, it became the Pennsylvania Turnpike in 1940.

The Pittsburgh and Lake Erie

After the P&LE was completed, it was said that it had a factory, mill or mine along every mile. This was a bit of an exaggeration, but it did run through the most industrialized area in the world. The P&LE became a money machine for its owners. The P&LE directly served U.S. Steel's National Works, Duquesne Works, Edgar Thom-

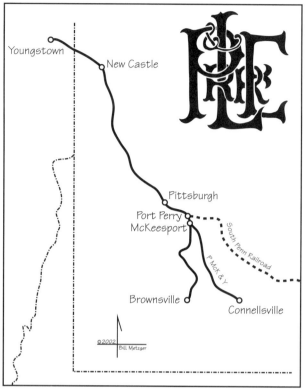

P&LE system map.

son Works, and Homestead Works; it also served Jones and Laughlin's (later LTV's) Pittsburgh Works and Aliquippa Works, and turned the traffic generated from these great steel mills and hundreds of other customers into piles and piles of cash. The New York Central, to its credit, was smart enough to mostly leave the P&LE alone. With some of the piles of cash, the P&LE built a beautiful terminal in Pittsburgh (now Station Square) and at the beginning of the twentieth century had a superb physical plant with a four-track main line and state of the art cars and locomotives. For a hundred years after its completion, the Pittsburgh and Lake Erie prospered. It was still controlled 93% by the New York Central, but along with the once-rival Pennsylvania Railroad, it purchased the Montour Railroad in the late 1940s and bought out the PRR's interest in 1975. (This purchase turned out to be extremely important to the rail-trail movement in Western Pennsylvania as we'll see.) The P&LE managed to avoid being included in the disastrous Penn Central merger of 1968, but was still controlled by PC, who stuck it for $12 million in a bad loan when the PC went bankrupt two years later. Penn Central, along with several other bankrupt railroads in the Northeast, became Conrail in 1976. Again, the P&LE dodged the bullet and wound up independent and prospering, but the bubble was soon to burst. In the early 1980s, steel mill after steel mill shut down and the newly-independent railroad found itself with a rapidly eroding traffic base. The mines played out on the Montour and it was abandoned in 1984. The once double-tracked Yough Branch was abandoned in 1990 and the rest of the P&LE was sold to CSX in 1992.

REGIONAL TRAIL CORPORATION

The abandonment of the Montour and the P&LE Yough Branch was bad news for the railroad and excellent news for the trail movement in Western Pennsylvania. Two years after the Montour called it quits, Peters Township in Washington County bought all six miles of the railroad inside its boundaries. It built the 4-mile Arrowhead Trail, which became an immediate hit with local residents. Spurred by the success of this project, the Montour Trail Council (MTC) was formed in 1989. Larry Ridenour, one of the original incorporators of the MTC, was aware of the imminent abandonment of the P&LE's Yough Branch and of its trail potential. At that time he worked for the Allegheny County Planning Department. At the same time, Dave Tremba, a retired hotel executive from Connellsville, was also aware of the P&LE and started talking it up as a possible connection to the Ohiopyle State Park trail. A series of public meetings about the trail took place in the Yough valley and the response was overwhelmingly positive.

Larry contacted Gordon Neuenschwander, president of the P&LE and the Montour, and asked for a year to line up political support and money. The president agreed. Both corridors were appraised and Neuenschwander took the word of the appraiser. What was intended to be a feasibility study evolved into a concept plan. The Regional Trail Corporation (RTC) was formed to buy the P&LE Yough Branch and the MTC raised the money to buy the Montour. Dick Wilson, an attorney who had worked for the P&LE and was a trail enthusiast, set up the corporation which was made up of representatives from Allegheny, Westmoreland and Fayette Counties. The counties kicked in for the property, the RTC raised "tons of money" to build the trail and the first trail went on the ground in 1993. RTC is still very much a going concern, with headquarters in West Newton (see Resources at the end of the book for contact information).

 Trail guide continues on page 21.

Chapter 2: Boston

A postcard of Boston, PA around the beginning of the 20th century. The first large building to the right of the tracks is the P&LE passenger station and the building across from it was the freight station. The railroad cars in the right foreground were loaded at Pittsburgh Coal Company's Yough No. 2 mine, which was located up the hollow where Route 48 runs today. None of the buildings between the stations and the original bridge still stand. Baseball fields occupy the wooded area in the left foreground today. Courtesy Elizabeth Township Historical Society.

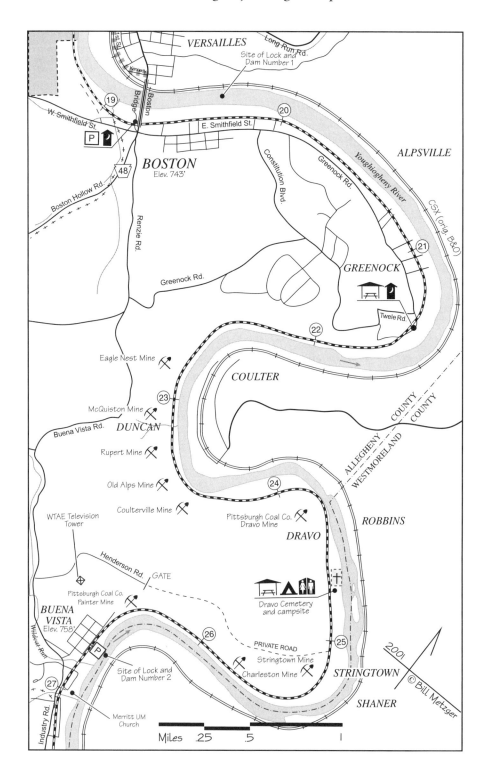

Mile 19 Boston

Boston was named for Boston, Massachusetts, but "there is little in the appearance of Boston to indicate the most remote resemblance to 'The Hub' of New England civilization." So said Thomas Cushing in *The History of Allegheny County* in 1889. Things haven't changed much in that regard; Paul Revere would have little to recognize here.

The field where the ball fields and trail head are located was known as "the fort field" during the French and Indian War. There was a small fort here where locals from the McKeesport area fled in times of trouble. In the 19th century, it was the head of navigation for the Yough River (it still is) and the site of a couple of coal mines. There was a ferry here, then a bridge, which was built in 1892. Donner Street, which runs down to the trail head, was the ferry landing and the bridge was just downstream from here. The bridge carried the trolley line from McKeesport to Scott Haven and was torn down in 1932 when the current bridge was built.

The current Boston Bridge is a cantilever structure with a clear span of 420 feet across the river. It was built by Allegheny County in the early 1930s when it was on a bridge-building binge and employed several hundred bridge engineers. This is a good place to brag about the fact that Allegheny County has, according to one count, 2,000 bridges longer than 8 feet long, one of the highest—if not the highest—concentrations in the world.

Allegheny County doesn't have any drawbridges or wooden covered bridges and that's just about the only type of bridge that it doesn't have. People come here just to tour the bridges.

Boston is the home of the Elizabeth Township Historical Society's headquarters on East Smithfield Street, which houses an excellent library and some interesting artifacts. Unfortunately, hours for the Society are sporadic.

In another historical note of local interest, the oil company just across the trail from the parking lot was where Hartley King, owner of the King's restaurant chain, got his start.

The Boston grade crossings are:

Mile 19.15   Donner Street
Mile 19.3   Drake Street—this is where the trolley crossed overhead
Mile 19.35   Walter Street—access to Elizabeth Township Historical Society
Mile 19.5   Harper Street—access to Boston Fire Hall
Mile 19.81   St. Davis Drive
Mile 20.75   Stoner Street

West Penn Railways' Scott Haven Line

West Penn Railways' Scott Haven trolley line began life as the Youghiogheny Valley Street Railway Company. It ran from McKeesport to Frank (Industry), which was across the river from Scott Haven, and was built in 1900. It served the mines and towns in that portion of the valley and at one time 13 trips a day made the 55-minute run in each direction. If you wanted to get to Scott Haven you had to take the sky ferry (see Sky Ferries on the next page).

Plans originally called for the trolley to be built to Sutersville and ultimately Connellsville, but Pittsburgh Coal Company wouldn't let them build through the narrow stretch of land between Industry and Blythedale, and the Suter family was

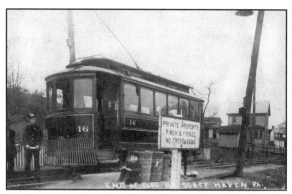

West Penn Railways Car Number 16 sits at the end of the line at Scott Haven ready for its run back to McKeesport. You can see by the sign how close the trolley tracks were to the railroad. Courtesy Pennsylvania Trolley Museum, Nathan Zapler Collection.

equally adamant about letting them build through Sutersville.

You could, if you really wanted to, take the West Penn trolley from McKeesport to Connellsville, but you had to work at it. It was much easier to take the train (see West Penn Railway discussion at the end of Chapter 9 on page 102).

The trolley line crossed the river on the original Boston Bridge, ran over the hill from Boston to Buena Vista, shortcutting the river on a line that included spindly wooden trestles and hairpin curves. It crossed the P&LE tracks on a wooden trestle at Drake Street, then zigzagged up the hill from there.

Among the more notable events in its history was a 1908 robbery in which two miscreants held up the motorman, the conductor, and the riders of a nighttime car. Later, after a gunfight, one of the desperadoes was killed and the other brought to justice. A 1912 accident killed five people and injured 25 when a car jumped the track and rolled down an embankment.

As was the case with most trolley lines of the era, the West Penn operated Olympia Park, an amusement park that was on the site of what's now the Olympia Shopping Center.

The trolley line was abandoned in 1932 when the county built the new Boston Bridge.

Sky Ferries

When railroads were the principal form of transportation in the Yough valley, residents played the schedules. For instance, you might go into McKeesport on the B&O on the east side of the river and come home on the P&LE on the west side. But at some point you had to cross the river. Or if you lived in Sutersville and worked in Smithdale before there were automobiles, you also had to cross the river.

Hence, the sky ferries. A typical sky ferry consisted of a car that ran on pulleys suspended from a cable attached to a tower on each side of the river. Sometimes they were hand powered, sometimes by steam, some electric. Some were free, some charged a nickel toll.

The story goes that while there was the brewery in Sutersville, the toll on the sky ferry over to Smithdale was free if you bought beer. Presumably, having a bit of a snootfull improved your chances of enjoying the ride. By all accounts, sky ferries were not for the faint of heart.

The Greenock sky ferry that ran across the river to the village of Alpsville, now a ghost town. The operator of the contraption is hand cranking the ferry across the river. The well-dressed riders are standing on a platform suspended above the river by what looks like one very thin cable. Courtesy Elizabeth Township Historical Society.

In Allegheny County, there were sky ferries from Greenock to Osceola, String-town to Shaner, Smithdale to Sutersville, Industry to Scott Haven and Dravo to Robbins. The last one to operate was from Smithdale to Sutersville. It quit in 1962.

Mile 21 Greenock

Greenock (pronounced "Greenoak") was named for Greenoch, Scotland by William Black, a Scot who settled there in 1840 and named his new home for the last place he saw when he left his native land. The town was inhabited by Germans who called it Greenock. Both the pronunciation and spelling stuck.

It was a coal mining and brick making town that has become a Pittsburgh area bedroom community.

Mile 21.08 Locust Grove Drive

Excel Tool & Die is the maintenance headquarters for the Mon Yough Trail Council.

Mile 21.28 Sandy Drive

This is the site of Greenock railroad station

Greenock station was a simple affair with a passenger waiting room at the right and a freight shed to the left. Note the flag hanging at the corner of the building. This station was literally a "flag stop" for some trains, meaning they only stopped if there was someone waiting to get on or off. Courtesy Elizabeth Township Historical Society.

Mile 21.32 Twele Road Park

The picnic pavilion here was built by the Mon-Yough Trail Council. Feel free to stop and take a break. The Council is a group of about 350 volunteers that maintains the trail from Dead Man's Hollow to the Westmoreland County line.

This is a fun outfit. They sponsor such events as the Yough and Roll, a 15- or 40-mile bike ride on the first Sunday in June, and Youghtoberfest, the first weekend in October. Both are held at the Boston trail head.

These are the folks who cut the grass, empty the trash cans and remove the downed trees. Support them by joining them. You get a nifty quarterly newsletter and the satisfaction of being a part of a great trail organization (see Resources at the end of the book for contact information).

Mile 21.6

When you pass the Tudor-style house after the little park, you immediately plunge into what's now a near-wilderness. Looks can be deceiving. Beginning in about 1850, when the locks were finished on the river, this was the scene of intense mining activity. The coal seam outcropped about 50 feet above the trail here and tipples were built with inclined tramways that led down to the river. All these mines were drift mines, that is they merely started digging into the side of the hill and followed the "drift" of the coal.

> The locations of all of the mines along the trail are for historic reference only. Under the best of circumstances, a coal mine is a dangerous place. An abandoned mine is a death trap. Although most of the mines are sealed, don't even think about entering one.

These are the mines on the trail side of the river. Their locations on the map are approximate.

- *Eagle Nest Mine owned by David Allen and opened in 1850. Sold to various operators and closed about 1900.*
- *McQuiston Mine owned by Robert McQuiston. Opened in 1860 and closed in 1862, about the end of river navigation. This was a big mine for its time; it built 15 houses for its workers, employed 50, and loaded 20 pairs of boats a year with coal for Louisville and New Orleans.*
- *Rupert Mine opened by Riley Rupert in 1860 and closed in 1863 at the end of river navigation.*
- *Old Alps Mine owned by the Alps Coal Co. Opened in 1860 and suspended in 1863.*
- *Coulterville Mine opened in 1851 by the Duncan, Cornell and Co. In 1859, the mine employed 50 to 60 men and shipped its coal to New Orleans.*

The best time for viewing the old mine works is in the late fall or early spring when the leaves are off the trees and there's no snow.

Mile 22.5

The cleared area along the river is the site of a train wreck that occurred here before the railroad was abandoned. It involved 15 cars loaded with bauxite—aluminum ore—and wasn't cleaned up until the railroad was sold and the trail was being built.

When you look at the small passenger shelter at Duncan (Duncan Hollow), consider that the same company that owned this humble edifice, the New York Central Railroad, also owned and operated Grand Central Station in New York, and, with a change of a train or two, you could ride there from here. The railroad put the world at your feet.
Courtesy Elizabeth Township Historical Society.

Mile 23.4 Duncan

The railroad named it for the Duncan & Cornell Co. All of these old names once were the site of railroad stations, even if they were only mere shelters. There were about a dozen houses here in the 1870s.

Mile 24

An archaeological dig took place near here in 1976. The Native American artifacts that were found were donated to the Carnegie Museum of Natural History in Pittsburgh.

Mile 24.9 Dravo Cemetery

The town was named for William Dravo, (pronounced Druh-VO) who opened a mine here in 1856. There were maybe a dozen houses here and the Newlin Methodist Episcopal Church, also known as the Dravo Church. The church was built in 1824, burned in 1863, rebuilt and burned again in 1909. It wasn't replaced.

Ten veterans, one from the war of 1812 and nine from the Civil War are buried in the cemetery, which is now owned by the Elizabeth Township Historical Society. In all there are 86 graves.

Volunteers from both the Society and the Mon-Yough Trail Council cleaned the cemetery up. Masons' Lodge 583 built the picnic pavilion which stands about on the site of the church. It's also oriented in the same direction.

There's a free campground here with water and a path down to the river where there's a nice sandy beach.

William Dravo's mine worked at least as late as 1919. It was still called the Dravo mine but was owned by the Lake Shore Gas Coal Co. It worked the Pittsburgh Seam and had 34 employees.

The Dravo name is well known in western Pennsylvania. The Dravo Corporation was, for about a century, a heavy construction and engineering firm that

SST Toilet. The quaint, seemingly wooden rest rooms with the big black stacks coming out the roof are SST toilets made of solid concrete. SST stands for "Sweet Smelling Toilet," a design developed by the U.S. Forest Service. The black stacks create a draft that carries objectionable odors away.

built dams, power plants and factories. It was particularly noted in World War II for building hundreds of LSTs (Landing Ship Tank) at its shipyards on Neville Island near Pittsburgh. After the war, the yards built towboats and barges for the inland waterways. Today Dravo manufactures lime for cleaning up the exhaust of coal-burning power plants. It's owned by the Carmeuse Group of Belgium.

Mile 25.0

The field on the river side was last known as the Philobaum pig farm before it was purchased by the Regional Trail Corporation. Queen Aliquippa's summer village, Cyrie, was located near here. The area has been replanted in native grasses.

 Stringtown is not a good place to go poking around because there are several old wells in the area with rotted coverings.

Mile 25.5 Stringtown

The woods past the field on the river side of the trail mark what's left of Stringtown, a ghost town that existed from about 1800 to the late 1930s. It was originally a farming community that became a mining town about 1857 when the Stringtown mine opened. This was a small operation that only lasted until 1861. An 1876 atlas of Allegheny County shows 20 houses in the Stringtown area.

As mining declined into the 20th century, the town did too. Elimination of the last Pittsburgh and Lake Erie passenger train in 1939 is said to have so isolated the community that the last few residents moved away. The last houses were torn down in the early 1950s.

Mile 26

The tower you can see from here belongs to WTAE, Channel 4, the local ABC affiliate. According to their chief engineer, it's 1,061 feet, 4 inches high from the base to the beacon. That's taller than several buildings in New York, Chicago and other major cities.

Mile 26.3 Painter Mine

The cattails here mark the site of Pittsburgh Coal Company's Painter Mine. It was a drift mine that worked the Pittsburgh Coal Seam and employed 173 miners in 1908.

WHAT IS THAT?

The poles on the river side of the trail are the remains of the railroad's telephone, telegraph, and signal lines. The steel boxes held relays for the railroad's signals that controlled both the movement of trains and grade crossings.

Chapter 3: Buena Vista/ Sutersville

When this picture was taken about 1919, three trains a way each day stopped at Buena Vista's trim little station from each direction. The number 173 on the side of the building is only temporary. It means that this was one of a series of photos taken for the U.S. Government by the railroad to determine its value. The government had taken over the railroads in World War I and these photos and other records were used to determine the amount of payment. Together, the valuation photos, records and maps make an incredibly useful resource for the historian. Courtesy Elizabeth Township Historical Society.

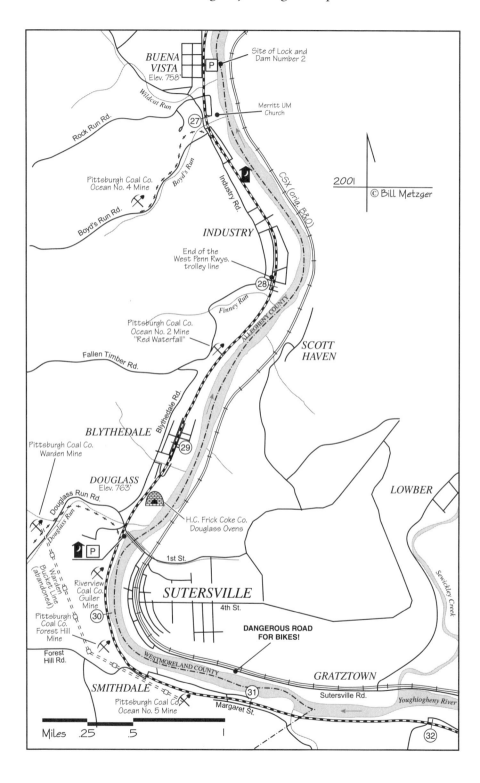

BUENA VISTA
Elev. 758'

Site of Lock and
Dam Number 2

Wildcat Run

Rock Run Rd.

Merritt UM
Church

27

Boyd's Run

Pittsburgh Coal Co.
Ocean No. 4 Mine

Industry Rd.

CSX (orig. B&O)

2001
© Bill Metzger

Boyd's Run Rd.

INDUSTRY

End of the
West Penn Rwys.
trolley line

28

Finney Run

ALLEGHENY COUNTY

SCOTT
HAVEN

Pittsburgh Coal Co.
Ocean No. 2 Mine
"Red Waterfall"

Fallen Timber Rd.

Blythedale Rd.

BLYTHEDALE

Pittsburgh Coal Co.
Warden Mine

29

LOWBER

DOUGLASS
Elev. 763'

Douglass Run Rd.

Douglass Run

H.C. Frick Coke Co.
Douglass Ovens

Warden
Bucket Line
(abandoned)

P

Sewickley Creek

1st St.

Riverview
Coal Co.
Guiler
Mine

SUTERSVILLE

Pittsburgh
Coal Co.
Forest Hill
Mine

30

4th St.

DANGEROUS ROAD
FOR BIKES!

Forest
Hill Rd.

WESTMORELAND COUNTY

GRATZTOWN

SMITHDALE

Sutersville Rd.

Youghiogheny River

Pittsburgh Coal Co.
Ocean No. 5 Mine

31

Margaret St.

Miles   .25   .5   1

32

Mile 26.5 Buena Vista

It's pronounced BEW-na VIS-ta, just like it is throughout the entire Span-ish-speaking world. Locals also refer to it as "BEWnie." The town was laid out in 1849 and named for the battle of Buena Vista in the Mexican War.

There was another battle of Buena Vista here in 1875 when striking coal miners battled with Italian "scabs" (the pejorative term for non-union workers brought in by the mine and mill owners to replace striking workers) from New York to break the strike. The miners won the fight when one of their leaders killed one of the scabs' leaders, labor negotiations being on something of a more personal level back then. (Note: Job functions were typically assigned along ethnic lines by the owners as a "divide and conquer" tactic.)

The P&LE railroad had a station here and a water facility for steam locomotives. Before the P&LE was built, there was a ferry across the river to the B&O.

This is an unincorporated village that has a public swimming pool about two blocks from the trail. It's open from Memorial Day to Labor Day.

Mile 26.6 Buena Vista Trail Head

Yough River Navigation

> *"The schemes of Youghiogheny improvement were started in the times when people knew little or nothing of the advantages of railroad communication, and believed, or tried to believe, that every mill-stream in the country could be made a navigable water-way to bring wealth to the inhabitants, and importance to the towns in its valley."* History of Fayette County, Pennsylvania.

If you walk down to the river at the Buena Vista trail head, you can see a long straight island across the river which is the remains of the lock wall of Lock and Dam No. 2, so this is a good place to talk about navigation on the Yough River. Lock No. 1 was between Boston and Greenock (see *Boston Map* in Chapter 2). Both 1 and 2 were built in 1850.

George Washington thought about building a canal on the Yough as early as 1784. Between 1793 and 1797, Isaac Meason and John Gibson of Connellsville removed obstructions from the river like rocks and logs, mostly by blasting them, under a state contract. But it only opened the river to one-way travel.

Two schemes to make the Yough navigable were put forth in 1816 and 1841, but neither amounted to anything. The first was really meant to be a bank; all the pro-moters wanted was the charter, but the state legislature wouldn't let them charter a bank, so they called it a navigation company. The 1841 bunch just spent a lot of state money with little result.

The route was also surveyed as an extension of the Chesapeake and Ohio Canal in the 1820s. This was at the height of "canal fever" following the success of the Erie Canal in New York when anybody with a stream wide enough for two carp to pass side by side wanted a canal of his own.

Why canals? At the time, it took a team of six horses about a month to haul two tons of freight from Philadelphia to Pittsburgh over roads which ranged from bad to horrible. By canal, two horses or mules could easily haul thirty or more tons. The drawback of the canals, though, was water: as often as not, there was either too much of it, not enough of it, or it was frozen.

It was estimated that the C&O extension from Cumberland to Pittsburgh would have to ascend and descend 1961 feet and would need 246 locks and 10 to 14 million dollars to do the job.

The other problem was that no one was clear where the water was going to come from on top of the mountain. Washington proposed that a portage road be built. Another canal engineer, Nathan Roberts, recommended in 1829 a four-mile-long canal tunnel through the mountain from Wills Creek to the Casselman River. He figured this would, according to B&O historian James Dilts, take "120 men working around the clock for thirteen years at a cost of $1.6 million." This was at a time when the longest tunnel in the country was less than a thousand feet long.

The Pennsylvania Canal was so sure that the C&O Canal would be built to Pittsburgh that they built an extension of their canal to meet it at the Monongahela River, including a tunnel under Grant's Hill (where the present U.S. Steel Tower and One Mellon Bank Center now stand), but that was just one more in a whole series of bad decisions made by the Pennsylvania Canal folks.

Without the canal, Yough River traffic was mostly downstream. Using the generous supply of local timber, flatboats were built and loaded with coal or produce or whiskey. Yough coal was sent downriver past Pittsburgh because the city was amply supplied by its own mines. The crew would wait for high water and start downriver to Cincinnati, Louisville, or even New Orleans. Once there, both the cargo and the lumber from the boat were sold and the crew walked home, provided they weren't drowned, sickened by malaria, or attacked by robbers on the way down or robbed and killed on the long walk home.

The Natchez Trace Parkway follows the route that the boatmen used to walk home.

When the locks and dams were opened in 1850, there was great celebration all along the Yough. Now, with the new locks and dams and steamboats, they could travel on the river both ways. New mines opened up and shipped coal in barges pushed by steamboats on the four-foot-deep channel. Packet boats—boats that sailed on a set schedule—carried passengers, freight and mail.

But the project, however praiseworthy, was a loser. Not only was there insufficient traffic to pay tolls, but the river refused to cooperate. Alternate floods and ice jams continually damaged the cheaply-built dams and locks and there was little money to fix them. The final blow came with a flood and ice jam that all but destroyed the dams in 1867. They were never rebuilt, but by that time the Pittsburgh and Connellsville Railroad was in operation and there was little or no need for river navigation. Mines on the opposite side of the river had to wait 16 years until the P&LE was built.

General William Larimer was the chief financier and engineer of the project, but it wound up costing him a great deal of money and he went west to found Denver, Colorado and make a fortune building railroads. Larimer was aided by the Markle family, who were important businessmen in the West Newton area.

There was one more Cumberland to McKeesport canal survey in 1875, a rumor of a federally-built lock and dam system to Connellsville in 1908 and a 1912-era survey to make the Yough navigable to West Newton, but no one took any of them seriously, especially since by 1912 railroads lined both sides of the river.

"No part of the Monongahela or Allegheny watershed is so nearly so destitute of wooded areas as the lower course of the Youghiogheny and Monongahela approaching Pittsburgh. The cleared land is poorly cultivated, and fully one-fourth is waste. The coal industry . . . occupies nearly the exclusive attention of the people . . . ." Report of the Flood Commission of Pittsburgh, Pennsylvania, 1912.

Mile 27.25 Elizabeth Township Sewer Authority
This is the sewage treatment plant for the Elizabeth Township Sewer Authority. 94 miles of line empty into this plant.

Mile 27.5 Bell Chapel United Methodist Church
Bell Chapel was built in 1892. The congregation was organized by people from Dravo, Scott Haven, and Buena Vista.

Mile 27.95 Industry, Frank and Scott Haven
These are all the same place. The town of Scott Haven is actually across the river on the B&O, but the P&LE decided to name its railroad station Scott Haven, too. It did the same thing at Jacobs Creek. There are two towns named Industry in Pennsylvania, the other is on the Ohio River in Beaver County, so they called the post office here Frank for what was, at the time, probably a very good reason. A story has it that the Post Office Department harassed the local postmaster until he came up with another name for the local post office and his first name was Frank so that's what he called the place to get them off of his back.

Today they call it Industry because there's no railroad and post office any more to give them any grief about it. That was its first name anyway. It was already settled in the 1870s before the railroad arrived, but most of the early inhabitants moved here after the Ocean No. 2 mine was opened.

The railroad had a station and a scale here for weighing loaded coal cars. Since the railroad charged by weight of the shipment, a scale was essential near major customers.

The First Baptist Church of Frank and the Merritt Primitive Methodist Church are the religious institutions in town. The Baptist congregation was organized in 1824 and built a church that lasted until 1861. The new church was built in 1863.

Merritt Primitive Methodist Church was named for Miss Ella DeMerritt, an evangelist who converted many of the local residents. The original building was completed in 1893, burned in 1941, and rebuilt in 1942.

There are two private clubs in town: the Industry Volunteer Fire Co. Social Hall and the Owl's Club. Should you have an uncontrollable desire to become an Owl, the membership is reasonable.

"The whole valley of the Youghiogheny River, from McKeesport to Connellsville, is almost a continuous hive of industry. It is filled with towns, villages and hamlets, and manufacturing of all kinds is carried on throughout the district. In addition to this, from also every hill, coal mines, shafts, tipples, etc., may be seen in every direction. Added to these are hundreds of coke ovens, which continuously send forth their volumes of smoke." Old and New Westmoreland, John N. Boucher, 1918.

Mile 28.27 The Red Waterfall

There's a bench across the trail from the Red Waterfall, so stop here for a bit and we'll talk about abandoned mine drainage or AMD. This is far and away the best example of it you'll see along the trail.

There was a complex of three mines here: Pittsburgh Coal Company's Ocean Numbers 2, 3 and 4 complex employed 708 men in 1907. By 1921, only Ocean No. 2 was working with 428 employees. It was still in operation in 1932, but closed soon after. All of these mines worked the Pittsburgh Coal seam. The Scott Haven Coal Company also had a small drift mine, the Spring Run Mine, up the hill here that worked the 48-inch Redstone Seam and employed 40 men in 1931.

The Red Waterfall runs out of the Ocean No. 2 mine.

Some sources will have you believe the water you see cascading down the hillside is highly toxic. It's not. Sitting here won't kill you, so you can relax and learn a bit of coal mine chemistry.

What's going on here is that the water has come in contact with coal. Coal has iron pyrite in it. Also known as "fool's gold," iron pyrite is a shiny compound of iron and sulfur that reacts to water. Through a series of chemical reactions, the iron and the sulfur in the coal become iron oxide (rust) and sulfuric acid. The iron oxide coats everything it comes in contact with, hence the red color; the sulfuric acid kills any marine life.

In a relatively short time, acid mine drainage will kill most aquatic life in a stream; because of it, thousands of miles of streams in Pennsylvania are "dead." But it can be treated.

So worry not. Sitting by the Red Waterfall isn't going to make your hair fall out or make you sterile. It's mostly just a fascinating reminder of the effects of coal mining.

The mine that caused the Red Waterfall, Pittsburgh Coal Company's Ocean No. 2. Empty cars were parked on the ramp on the right and drifted down one at a time to be loaded. The ramp is still visible. Courtesy Rivers of Steel Archives, Metzger collection.

Mile 28.85 Blythedale

Named for John Blythe, original owner of the Sarah Mine, the town was primarily a residence for local miners.

The big open lot on the river side as you come into town was a railroad yard for storing empty cars for the mines in the area. The picnic pavilion was built by Elizabeth Township and is available for trail use.

The red brick building on the bank side of the trail is the Workingmen's Beneficial Union Club. It was founded in 1913 by a group of Italian workers; almost all of the original settlers here were from the Italian region of Reggio Nell'Emilia.

The club built and moved into this building in 1915. They started a pension fund which paid $8.00 a month to "members with an incurable illness." They didn't have to pay out anything on the fund until 1926. Each member also had to serve as the unpaid bartender for a week.

It's still a functioning private club with about 200 members and owns and operates the ballfield in Blythedale. Most of the members are descended from the original "Reggiani."

Mile 29.5 Douglass

Colonel William Douglass was a local farmer and politician who operated a steam flour mill and a steam saw mill here in the mid-19th century. Douglass also owned the ferry at Boston.

In 1887 a man named Alex Chambers built 200 coke ovens in what is now the flat wooded area on the river side of the trail downstream from the bridge. These ovens were built for Andrew Carnegie and later operated by H. C. Frick, whom we'll talk about later. The Youghiogheny coke works closed in 1917.

The hollow here has been known at various times as Douglass Hollow, Mustard Hollow and Victory. About a half mile up the road is the site of the Warden Mine, one of the larger Pittsburgh Coal Company operations. It was opened in the late 1920s and closed in 1954. At its peak, 1,000 men worked there. The abandoned track up to the mine can be seen on the bank side of the trail about 50 yards up from the grade crossing.

The big deal in Douglass is the Tastee Freez, which wasn't here when the coke ovens were working—there was a company store then.

Be Careful On The Road Crossing Here!!!

For those who care about such things, the rails embedded in the red rubber grade crossing material are probably the last rails left of the P-Mickey east of Dura Bond.

Mile 29.5 Sutersville (Suterville)

Eli Suter had a ferry here from 1849 to 1896, and laid out the town in 1870, serving as its first postmaster. Suter was a farmer who also had a sawmill, built coal barges, owned a coal mine, and even built a steamboat.

The first bridge between Douglass and Sutersville. It was built as a toll bridge in 1896 and replaced the ferry. In 1910, Allegheny and Westmoreland Counties, due to popular complaints, agreed to take over the span and remove the charges.

Trolley tracks were built into the deck in anticipation of the line being extended from Frank, but the Suter family was so mad at the bridge company for closing down their ferry operation, they built a barn across the projected trolley right of way and refused to sell it. The trolley never did come to Sutersville.

The original bridge pier is just upstream from the new bridge. When the leaves are off the trees, close examination shows initials made by the stonecutters to mark their work. Courtesy Allegheny County Department of Public Works.

At the turn of the century there were four hotels here, a brewery and a distillery. This was the market town for the area and a place for the local men to come and get snozzeled in one of the many bars while the women shopped. It's said that the place really jumped on Saturdays.

The town faces on the railroad as it did when the trains were the source of much of its commerce. The hotels and many of the local merchants catered to the "drummer" trade. Drummers were salesmen who traveled by train, stopping at a town like Sutersville, where they stayed at one of the local hotels and rented a horse and buggy at a local livery stable to call on their customers. The town enjoyed frequent train service and the drummers took advantage of it.

The equivalent of a Sutersville today would be the commercial area around an airport.

Prohibition killed the brewery and the distillery and the automobile killed the drummer trade. The town became a bedroom community for other, more prosperous places.

Today there are a couple of restaurants and a post office here, but no other services.

You'll notice, as you go up the trail, that most of the towns are on the other side of the river, or, if the town's on both sides of the river, most of the population is on the other side.

Reason? The towns are built along the railroad and the Baltimore and Ohio not only got there first but offered the best passenger service.

You'll also note in the town histories that, before the coming of the mines, towns were built around ferries and later bridges.

 You may think that riding on the other side of the river for a while would be fun and decide to take the road between Sutersville and West Newton that's shown on the map as Sutersville Road. Don't. There's no shoulder and the locals drive like maniacs.

Mile 29.9

Riverview Coal Co. had a small mine here.

Mile 30.1

The concrete foundation in the hillside is the site of the Forest Hill Mine. It was a Pittsburgh Seam drift mine owned by Pittsburgh Coal Company and had 370 employees in 1921. It was still in operation in 1932, but closed soon after.

Mile 30.7 Smithdale

Originally called Taylor Town, Smithdale is not to be confused with Smithton.

Pittsburgh Coal Company's Ocean No. 5 mine located here was a drift mine that worked the Pittsburgh Seam. It employed 428 men in 1921 and 260 in 1951. There was a bucket line here to a gob pile up on the hill that Ocean shared with the Warden mine. The coal company closed the mine in 1954, but it was reopened by an independent company for a time in the 1970s.

Smithdale looking eastward in 1945. To the right is the Ocean No. 5 tipple and the bucket line that carried shale to a gob pile up on the hill. Several of the buildings on the extreme left still stand. Courtesy Pittsburgh and Lake Erie Railroad Collection, Archives Service Center, University of Pittsburgh.

Notice how we threw those two phrases in that last paragraph without any explanation? A "bucket line" is a continuous aerial tramway that carried cars of mine refuse out of the mine to a "gob pile," which is a pile of mine refuse (see the next chapter for more on gob piles).

Smithdale is the first of many company towns you'll encounter between here and Connellsville. A town like this is also referred to as a "coal patch." A patch was built by the coal company to house (and fleece) its miners. It was a closed system: the company opened a mine and built housing for the miners and a company store. Miners paid rent on the houses and were paid in "scrip" that was issued by the company instead of cash. Scrip could only be used in the company store, which sold the miners goods at a nice markup. The company made out all around.

Smithdale originally had a ferry over to Sutersville which consisted of a rowboat that held 6 to 8 miners. It was called Renner's Ferry and became a sky ferry in 1892. The 600-foot-long contraption lasted until 1962 when it closed for lack of needed repairs.

There are no services here.

Horses should take the paved road through Smithdale.

Mile 31.43 Allegheny/Westmoreland County Line

You're now in Westmoreland County, in land area the largest county of Pennsylvania. Crossing the line into Westmoreland puts you in the capable hands of the Westmoreland Yough Trail Chapter, a volunteer organization of about 200 members who maintain the trail from here to Fayette County.

WHAT IS IT?
The railroad calls this a whistle post. One was located on each side of a road crossing to tell the engineers when to blow the warning two long, one short, one long crossing signal, which is still used today.

CHAPTER 4: WEST NEWTON

Banning No. 4 mine in 1979. A huge gob pile is in the foreground. The round silo in the center to the left of the complex is part of the water treatment plant. The trail runs just to the left of the railroad cars.

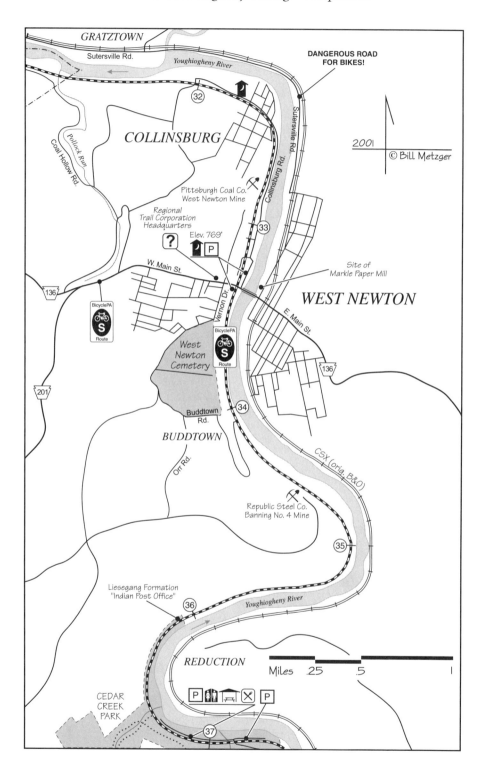

Mile 32.5 Collinsburg

Think of Collinsburg as suburban West Newton. It was a bedroom town for coal miners who worked the local mines—the West Newton and Ocean No. 5 mines were close by—and also for factory workers. Bear in mind that it was nothing for workers to walk a mile or two each day to go to work.

History doesn't record who Collins was, at least we haven't found it, but the town was settled largely by Germans. And the main cross street is German Street. There is also a German club—unmarked—here.

Mile 33 Feed Mill

The feed mill by milepost 33 is worth visiting for its ancient tub-style pop machine. It's not open on Sunday, though.

Mile 33.1 Church

The pretty white church on the corner belongs to the St. Paul A. M. E. Church, which was built in 1880.

Courtesy New York Central Historical Society, and John Carnprobst.

Mile 33.2 Station and Railroad Car

This old railroad passenger car is on its way to becoming the new environmental education center for the Yough Trail. It's called a combination car, or combine; half of the car was a baggage compartment and the other half a passenger coach. Often the passenger compartments on combines were used as the smoking cars on a train. It was built as P&LE's Number 148 in 1925 by the Pressed Steel Car Company of McKees Rocks, near Pittsburgh. As originally built it seated 48. Its last assignment was as a yard office for the Banning No. 4 mine at Buddtown. Railroads often used their old cars for offices and tool sheds because it was cheaper than building a new building. The combine was moved from Buddtown to its present location in 1999. The photo above shows sister car 147 as built.

The new building in front of the car is the re-construction of the West Newton railroad station, which will become headquarters of the Regional Trail Corporation (RTC), builders and operators of the Youghiogheny River Trail North. The new station is the same size and is on the site of the old one. It includes public restrooms.

If the station is open, forget that the RTC headquarters are in the basement of the Rite Aid building. Wherever they're located, stop in and say hi—they have all kinds of nifty trail information and will be happy to sell you T-shirts and stuff.

 The Route 136/Main Street Crossing is extremely dangerous. Walk your bike across.

Mile 33.3 West Newton

There are three stories about how the town got its name. Some say that Isaac Robb, who laid out the town, came to western Pennsylvania from Sussex County, New Jersey, where there is both a township and a town called Newton. He named it after his old home town.

The second story claims Robb named his town after Newtown (now Greensburg, the Westmoreland County seat) and called it West Newton.

The third version is that New Englanders named the place after the town in Massachusetts that Fig Newtons are named for. We prefer this last one if for no other reason that it's nice for a town to remind you of cookies.

No matter the origin of the name, history is clear on the fact that Robb laid the town out in 1796. Prior to being named West Newton, the settlement was known as Simrall's (or Semerall's) Ferry, then Robbstown.

Robb is said to have gotten really steamed when the army that George Washington sent to put down the Whiskey Rebellion marched by his place on the Glades Road and tore up his fences for firewood. He decided not to rebuild the fences and laid out a town which at first he named after himself. He sold the town lots and found a new line of work as a river trader. One night when the river was rising, Robb went to check his boat and drowned.

After Robb died, Robbstown became, for whatever reason, West Newton and was incorporated as such in 1842.

It became a transportation center because of the Glades Road and river navigation. Travelers came west over the road, built flatboats and headed downriver. Later, after the river was improved for navigation, they took the steam packet boats down to Pittsburgh. Because of the improved navigation, the Pittsburgh and Connellsville Railroad began construction here. They floated the rails and locomotives up the river on barges and began building toward Connellsville in 1854.

Good transportation also brought manufacturing.

The Markle paper mills at West Newton when they were in full operation around 1881. The building with the five smoke stacks to the right still stands, but without the stacks. History of County of Westmoreland, Albert, 1882.

There was a large paper mill here owned by the Markle family that began on Sewickley Creek in 1811, moved to West Newton in 1859 and operated until about 1893. The family built one of the first grist mills in the area in 1772. In 1779, General Joseph Markle took a load of flour down the river to New Orleans, one of the first to do so. It took him six weeks.

The paper operation grew in West Newton and the Markles opened a mill in Somerset County to supply pulp. The new mill was at Markleton along the trail (see Markleton, Chapter 18). Both the paper mill and pulp mill closed in 1893 because of the increasing pollution from the coal and coke industry. This mill was reputed to make excellent paper; it was highly prized by the Chinese and was also used for bank notes.

The paper mill was taken over by a factory that made radiators (the kind that go hiss in a house). One of the old mill buildings still stands. Other factories in town made railroad fusees (flares), chairs, coal stoves and even prefabricated houses.

There were at least two mines here: Pittsburgh Coal Company operated both the West Newton Mine, which employed 282 in 1921, and the Yough Slope Mine across the river, which employed 491 in 1907 but was closed by the early 1920s. Both worked the Pittsburgh Seam.

Up until the 1930s, the Baltimore and Ohio operated a commuter train to Pittsburgh that originated and terminated here. The engine for this train even had its own turntable and small roundhouse.

There are a lot of trail services clustered around the West Newton trail head. Across the river are several restaurants, the post office, banks, and a supermarket. The bridge here now is only the second on the site, the first being a wooden covered bridge built in 1833. The current bridge was built by Westmoreland County in 1906. It's 490 feet long and is in pretty good shape for being almost a century old.

Glades Road

The road you're crossing here (and you're walking your bike across, aren't you?) has been a road since at least 1772. It was called the Glades Road and ran from Bedford, PA to Washington, PA.

It was originally surveyed in 1755 by Colonel James Burd, who was with Braddock's ill-fated expedition and later with General Forbes' successful effort to rout the French from Fort Duquesne. A good case can be made that it was previously an Indian trail called the Glades Path.

The trail and road were named for the Glades, a large wetland in Somerset County they crossed. The road connected Forbes Road (now US 30) with the National Road (now US 40). Also referred to as the Great Road, it was organized as a turnpike in 1820, but revenues didn't pay the cost of maintenance and the state had to kick in some money to keep it going.

For a year or so it was a plank road while that particular fad was current. The theory was that paving a road with wooden planks would make it smoother, but the untreated boards warped and disintegrated under heavy use and they were thrown over and used for firewood.

During the Whiskey Rebellion, the middle column of Washington's army (there were three) used this road to march west. With the coming of the railroads it fell

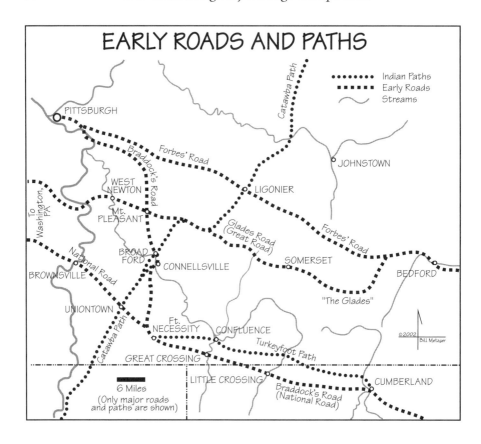

into disuse until revived by the rise of the automobile. Today the road is Pennsylvania Routes 31 and 136.

Northwest Caravan

One of the more notable enterprises to use the Glades Road was the Northwest Caravan, a group of Revolutionary War officers led by General Rufus Putnam, who had formed the Ohio Company of Associates. (This group isn't to be confused with the Ohio Company of George Washington's time.) The Company had purchased a million and a half acres in what was then known as the Northwest Territories—now Ohio—from the government at eight or nine cents an acre. The Caravan was on its way to take possession of the land when it stopped in West Newton in January, 1788.

By April 2, 1788, ten weeks after they arrived at the Yough, they had built a fleet of 8 boats, including one 50 feet long and 13 feet wide, having begun with just trees and working with hand tools. In the winter. After walking or riding horses all the way from Ipswich, Massachusetts—about 500 miles.

The boats carried the group, their goods, their families, and their livestock down the Yough, the Mon and the Ohio Rivers where they founded Marietta, Ohio, the first town in the new territory.

BicyclePA Route S

Going east, you'll see signs starting here for BicyclePA Route S. The Wheeling, West Virginia to Philadelphia route is one of a series of signed, cross-Pennsylvania bicycle touring routes that have been laid out take advantage of the best of the state's back roads and rail trails. Route S uses the Great Allegheny Passage from West Newton to Rockwood. There are presently three east-west and three north-south cross-state routes completed with more to come.

BicyclePA is an offshoot of the Pennsylvania Pedalcycle and Pedestrian Advisory Committee, known as PPAC, pronounced "peapack." It's an all-volunteer group that works with the state government to make Pennsylvania a more bike-friendly state.

Mile 33.38 West Newton Cemetery

The cemetery sits on a hill on the bank side of the trail. Among the notable decedents are Eli Suter of Sutersville and some of the victims of the Port Royal mine explosion. Bicycles aren't permitted in the cemetery.

From here to Buddtown, the railroad was four tracks wide to serve the Banning No. 4 mine.

Mile 34.04 Buddtown

This little settlement was named for Joseph Budd, who had a ferry here in the late 1700s. Problem was, it was easier to go west from West Newton because of the easier grade out of town, so it got the Glades Road, and Buddtown never developed much. For many years Buddtown was mostly known for the fact that a whole lot of people named Budd lived here on what was originally the large Budd estate.

Gob Piles

This is as good a time as any to talk about gob piles since the one you will see here is the first one you've really gotten a look at on your trek up the trail.

The Pittsburgh Coal Seam, like a lot of other coal seams, has a flaw: it's not pure coal. Throughout the seam are layers of "slate" (it's really shale), each an inch or two thick. Slate doesn't burn, so it has to be removed. Gob piles are where the slate is dumped along with whatever coal that escapes the cleaning process.

Since Banning No. 4 was built in 1959, it had a very efficient cleaning plant; the coal content of the gob pile is only about 8%. Gob piles can be economically cleaned up and the coal recovered *if* the coal content is high enough, usually about 20%.

To give you an idea of how much coal was taken from this mine, figure that the gob pile is about 10% of the total. This was a big mine.

Gob piles are also called "boney piles" and "slate dumps" but *never* slag heaps. Slag heaps are where the by-products of steelmaking are dumped. The environmental degradation is different but the ugly is just the same. You'll see some slag up the trail.

In the old days, when a gob pile caught on fire, and they often did, the slate would turn red in the fire and was called "red dog." Many, many roads and driveways in coal country are paved with red dog.

When Banning No. 4 mine was built in 1959, Buddtown became the location of the P&LE yard office where crews reported to work and got their assignments. West Newton's railroad car sat here next to the grade crossing.

Banning No. 4 was the newest and largest mine on the P&LE Yough Branch. It was also the last to close. The mine was originally built by Consolidated Coal Co. but was sold to Republic Steel. It was opened in 1959 and closed in 1982. At its peak it employed 500 miners. Republic Steel merged with LTV Steel in 1984.

The last of the No. 4 tipple was torn down in the winter of 2000-2001. Nothing remains but the concrete loading silo and the gob pile.

Mile 34.5 Banning Water Treatment Plant

The collection of white tanks and pipes on the river side of the trail is the water treatment plant for Banning No. 4 mine. The plant neutralizes the acid water with lime, which is first aerated in a settling tank. The plant is operated under contract by LTV Steel and treats 6 million gallons of water a day. Unlike passive AMD water treatment plants which use a series of settling ponds, this is an active plant which must be constantly maintained.

Mile 36 Cedar Creek Park Begins Here

Mile 36.25 Liesegang Structures

Geologist Jim Shaulis calls this the "best examples of these structures you're going to find in the East." They're called the "Indian Post Office" for their cubby hole appearance, and are weathered sandstone. The technical name is Liesegang structures, pronounced LISA-gang, named for R. E. Liesegang who first observed them in 1896.

According to Shaulis, "the cell walls of the honeycomb are made up primarily of iron minerals that have been concentrated there like rust on the inside of a pipe. The iron minerals are more resistant to the erosion of air and water and form cell walls up to eight inches deep."

This is one of those formations where you look and don't touch.

GEOLOGY

In the grand scheme of things, and we're talking really grand here, there have always been mountains to the east and a basin of some sort to the west. At least three mountain ranges have risen up and washed down in the last 450 million or so years. The first two are just about all gone and the third, the Allegheny range, is in the process of doing so.

Back in school your earth science teacher told you there were three kinds of rock: igneous, metamorphic and sedimentary. Igneous came from volcanoes—the bedrock; metamorphic was rock that has undergone some sort of change through heat, chemical reaction and/or pressure; and sedimentary was made of sediment.

So sedimentary rock is made from sediment. Fine. So where did the sediment come from? Those long-gone mountains to the east, is where.

Each one of those magnificent ranges were, in their turn, higher than the Andes, including our humble little Alleghenies. We Pittsburghers can honestly say we're sitting on top of a pile of old mountains.

What the sediments became depended on what was happening here at the time. An ocean floor became limestone; shale and siltstone washed down on land; coal formed in warm coastal swamps; and sandstone became river channels, dunes and beaches along the coastal plain.

Layer after layer built up; swamp, dune, river delta, ocean, seacoast, repeated again and again. You can see it in the rock. Seashells, plants, river bottoms, tree trunks, sand and even gravel are all preserved in stone, layer on top of layer, each one laid down flat in the great basin.

The most important time, economically speaking, was the Carboniferous age which ran from about 323 to 290 million years ago when Pittsburgh was 5-10 degrees south of the Equator and the area was a great steaming swamp overrun with plant life run riot. This was when the Pittsburgh Coal seam was formed.

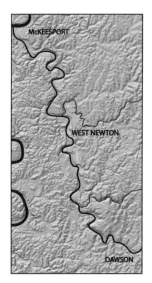

Western Pennsylvania topography.

About a million years ago, it got cold. A succession of glaciers covered the world and then retreated, most recently the one we call the Wisconsin Glacier which started retreating about 10-12,000 years ago. About 75 miles north of Connellsville, there was a glacier that was somewhere between a mile and a half and two miles thick and that, if you went straight north, would be solid ice clear to the North Pole and beyond, well into what is now Russia.

The land south of the glacier was arctic tundra; not much vegetation, soft soil that resembled Jell-o and vicious freeze-thaw cycles. When the glaciers melted, the weight of the ice was released and the land rose up. With all that formerly frozen water released from the glaciers, the land washed away. The valleys of western Pennsylvania were formed. Once you get west of Chestnut Ridge, there are really no hills, just valleys carved out of a plain.

So much for flat. A whole lot of western Pennsylvania is now somewhere down in Louisiana, Arkansas, and Mississippi or at the bottom of the Gulf of Mexico making more rock and trapping huge pools of oil. What we're left with is a landscape that's either up or down; a landscape with character. You want flat? Go to Kansas.

This is an example of a rail car used to haul coal from the mines. It held about a ton of coal.

Chapter 5: Cedar Creek Park/Smithton

Coal miners after a shift in 1898. Note the tallow lamps attached to their caps and the total lack of safety equipment. Bill Metzger collection.

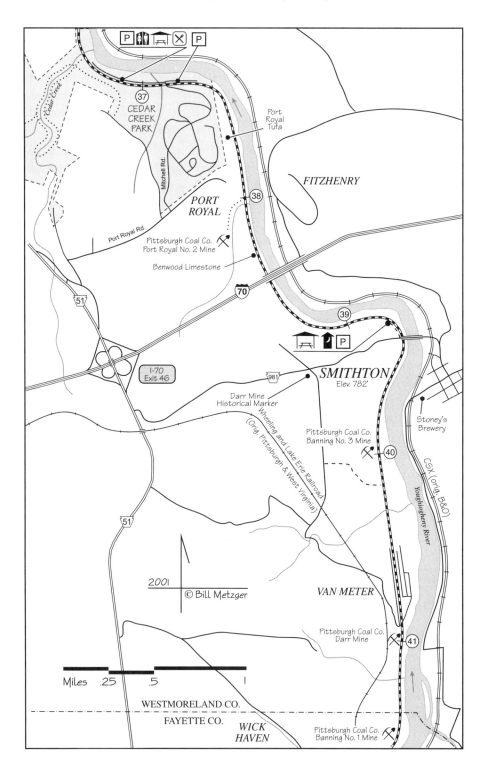

CEDAR CREEK PARK

Cedar Creek

37

Mitchell Rd.

PORT ROYAL

38

Port Royal Tufa

FITZHENRY

Port Royal Rd.

Pittsburgh Coal Co. Port Royal No. 2 Mine

Benwood Limestone

51

70

39

SMITHTON
Elev. 782'

I-70 Exit 46

981

Darr Mine Historical Marker

Wheeling and Lake Erie Railroad (Orig. Pittsburgh & West Virginia)

Pittsburgh Coal Co. Banning No. 3 Mine

40

Stoney's Brewery

CSX (orig. B&O)

Youghiogheny River

51

2001
© Bill Metzger

VAN METER

Pittsburgh Coal Co. Darr Mine

41

Miles   .25   .5   1

WESTMORELAND CO.

FAYETTE CO.

WICK HAVEN

Pittsburgh Coal Co. Banning No. 1 Mine

Mile 36.8 Cedar Creek Park

As soon as you pass Mile 36 coming up the trail you're in Cedar Creek Park, but aside from the bench, there's not much to the park until you cross the bridge over Cedar Creek. This is a popular park that's owned and operated by Westmoreland County.

Of immediate concern to happy trail users are the restrooms and the food concession offering what we hear are the best nachos on the trail.

But this is a full service park: there's all sorts of stuff on top of the hill, but first let's deal with what you can see from the trail. You may have noticed the hiking trail under the Cedar Creek bridge. This leads up into the Cedar Creek gorge, a cool shady spot replete with waterfalls and wildflowers. It makes a nice side trip if you have a lock for your bike. The trail features a suspension bridge up in the gorge that's well worth the walk just to see.

There are also picnic pavilions, water spigots and a boat launch ramp. The food concession in the replica railroad station also offers bike and cross country ski rentals.

Up above in the park proper there's an amphitheater that seats 2,500 for concerts in the summertime, baseball fields, basketball and volleyball courts, a playground and lots more picnic pavilions. It's a helluva climb up there on a bike.

What's That Sound?

So you're sitting at Cedar Creek Park taking a break and all of the sudden you hear a loud buzzing sound. You look around and convince yourself you're not in the middle of a cheap science fiction movie where you're being attacked by a swarm of radioactive killer tse-tse flies. But what is that noise?

You're hearing airplanes from the Mon Yough Model Airplane Club. They have a field in the park where they fly radio-controlled model aircraft. You may not be attacked by giant mutant insects, but you can relive the glorious days of World War II and see Hellcats, Spitfires, and Mustangs in action again.

Mile 37.7 Port Royal Tufa

Should you be willing to stand here long enough, you can watch rocks grow in a living, breathing rock formation known as a tufa. Think of a tufa as a fast-growing outdoor stalactite, the ones that grow from the roof of a cave. Rainwater percolates down through decaying vegetation and forms a stream which picks up carbonic acid which then dissolves the underlying limestone which then separates out a bit farther downstream as tufa which coats everything it comes in contact with.

The gray stuff under the moss in the photo on the next page is tufa. There are actually two different segments to the tufa about 100 or so feet apart.

This is one of only a few in the country and depends on a healthy ecosystem upstream to survive. The tufa was discovered because of the trail and is being preserved because of the trail. Geologist Bob Smith discovered the formation while doing a geological survey of the trail. The land upstream on top of the cliff, the forest that is vital for the tufa's growth, has been purchased by and will be preserved by the Regional Trail Corporation. The tufa will live on.

There are others of the tufa persuasion: Rome is mostly built on the stuff and the catacombs, burial place for centuries of Romans, are carved in it. The Roman

tufa is hydrothermal in origin and soft with a lot of encapsulated air. Mono Lake in California also has tufa deposits precipitated out from minerals in local hot springs.

Oh, and now that you know it's here, please don't disturb it. The moss that grows on the surface of the tufa in the image at left is easily damaged.

Mile 38 Port Royal

Port Royal was a court-house in Colonial times when Virginia claimed this part of the state. That being the case, Port Royal could have been named for the town of the same name in South Carolina or from Port Royal, Jamaica, once said to be the wickedest town in the world.

Whatever the origin of the name, Port Royal is now a ghost town on this side of the river. No sign is left of the coal patch town or the distillery that once was located here.

Mile 38 Port Royal No. 2 Mine Disaster

There were two mines here, one on each side of the river: Port Royal No. 2 was on the P&LE (trail) side and No. 1 on the B&O side. Both were originally owned by the Port Royal Coal & Coke Co. and became part of the Pittsburgh Coal Co. in 1899. Both were shaft mines; the coal seam is below river level and the mines were connected by three tunnels under the river.

On the morning of June 10, 1901, a small amount of explosive gas had been reported in sections of Mine No. 2 and those had been closed off. A section of the roof had also sunk and a crew of four men had been assigned to shore it up. Those four men worked during the day shift and went back into the mine to finish their work after dinner about 5 or 6 p.m. Two other miners went back to work to dig coal in another part of the mine about the same time.

About 6:15, the two men heard an explosion and thought there had been a roof fall. They continued working until their compressed air-operated machinery quit. The hoisting crew at the surface called a rescue party at the sound of the explosion who went to find the other four men. They found three of the four men's bodies, but several of their party were overcome by gas and left for the surface. A second group of rescuers went into the mine to assist the first. There was a second explosion at 10:05 p.m.

Everyone who was in the mine at the time was killed.

The dead included the superintendent of the mine and several foremen. They went in wearing nothing but work clothes, their way lit by little tallow lamps on their caps—they had no safety equipment whatsoever. In 1901 there wasn't any.

About 10:30 the next morning, a third rescue party had entered the mine when there was a third explosion. This group was burned slightly in the blast, but they successfully retreated.

In all, 19 men died as a result of the explosions.

The mine was re-opened in September and all the bodies but one were recovered. Port Royal Mine No. 2 was permanently sealed in October, 1901.

The site of the mine is up the path across the trail from Mile 38; it's only a hundred yards or so back in. It's a quiet little glade when the locals aren't running their ATVs up and down the hills.

Mile 38.3 Benwood Limestone

The cliff you are looking at here is Benwood limestone, named for Benwood, West Virginia. According to geologists, this rock is thought to be dolomitic calcium magnesium carbonate, and also layers of just calcium carbonate. Small animals with shells died and settled to the bottom of ancient Benwood Lake. Over hundreds of thousands of years these dead creatures started to pile up to form layers of calcium (from the shells) and other chemicals. The bottom layers of the dead creatures started to compress and turn the layers solid. As the sea levels changed the chemicals changed, more magnesium was put into the layers. If 15% magnesium is in the limestone they call it dolomite.

This rock is made of calcium, carbonate, calcite, and magnesium.

The recently rebuilt Interstate 70 bridge carries a road that runs 2,175 miles from Baltimore, MD to Cove Fort, UT.

Mile 38.37 I-70 Bridge

The bridge you're going under here and can hear for a mile or so is called the Smithton High-Level Bridge. It was originally built as Pennsylvania Route 71 and was designed to connect with the Pennsylvania Turnpike from New Stanton to Washington, PA at a time when Edward Martin was governor and later U.S. Senator. He just happened to be from Washington.

The bridge is 1,340 feet long and 165 feet high at its highest point. It was built in 1956-57. The bridge has recently undergone rehabilitation and the contractors used the trail as an access road which explains why the trail is so wide from here to Smithton. The rehab was finished in October, 2001.

Mile 39.25 Smithton Beach

A new picnic pavilion built with donations from the Belle Vernon Rotary and labor from the State Correctional Institution at Greensburg (sort of a jails to trails project) marks Smithton Beach, a great spot for swimming in the river and a place to put in a canoe for a float down to Cedar Creek or West Newton. The river's pretty calm through here.

Shirley Jones

What do "The Partridge Family," Stoney's Beer, and Smithton have in common? Shirley Jones, of course. Shirley grew up here—her dad was one of the Jones Brewery Joneses—graduated from high school and won a scholarship to the Pittsburgh Playhouse after coming in as first runner up in the Miss Pennsylvania contest in 1952. Her publicity says she is "America's Ultimate Lady . . . the embodiment of all that is right and wonderful about the American woman." There was some talk of erecting a statue to "the embodiment" in Smithton, but so far nothing has come of it. Rumor has it she comes to visit now and then.

Mile 39.3 Smithton, Population 369

To get to Smithton, climb up the road out of the parking lot, turn left on Route 981 and cross the bridge. The town is named for Joseph Smith (no relation to the Mormon), who settled here in 1800 with his wife, kids and in-laws. He dammed the river, built a grist mill and, like so many others of his time, operated a ferry.

One of Smith's sons operated a still house and one of the others ran a sorghum mill where sugar was made. There was also a paper mill where brown wrapping paper was manufactured. This lasted from 1868 to 1905 when it, like the Markle mills, closed because of pollution in the river.

When the railroad came to town, the original name of the station was Smith's Mills, but it was changed in 1882 when the first post office was established.

At the beginning of the 20th century, Smithton had an ice cream plant, a flour mill, a bakery and three hotels. But the biggest thing ever to hit the town was when William "Stoney" Jones, a Welsh immigrant and hotel owner, opened the Eureka Brewing Co. in 1907 and made Eureka Gold Crown Beer.

At the time there were breweries in every town of any size along the trail from McKeesport to Meyersdale: McKeesport had several, Sutersville had one, Smithton, of course, Connellsville had a couple, and Rockwood and Meyersdale each had one. This was the last one remaining.

Courtesy of Jones Brewing Company.

What Prohibition didn't shut down, economics did. In most cases, small breweries just couldn't compete against the big national brands. But Stoney's hung in there.

According to the company's publicity, immigrant miners couldn't pronounce "Eureka Gold Crown Beer," let alone spell it, so they asked for "one of Stoney's beers." So Stoney changed the name, which it carries to this very day.

Stoney's ceased brewing beer in Smithton January 10, 2002, the last brewery in the Yough Valley. But don't shed a tear quite yet. Under an arrangement with Pittsburgh Brewing Company, makers of Iron City and other brands, Stoney's will still be made using the original recipe and the brewing and bottling equipment will remain intact.

But the old brewery will now be essentially a beer distributor. They'll be happy to serve you a glass of Stoney's at the Long Horn in town. Smithton also has a grocery store and post office.

Whiskey Insurrection

"Our forebears suffered many hardships, but the want of whiskey was not to be reckoned among them." Smithton History, Ethelclaire Rhodes Smith.

Also known as the Whiskey Rebellion, the insurrection was the first to test the strength of the new United States Government and the resolve of President Washington.

Ever since 1760, the end of the French and Indian War, people had been moving into western Pennsylvania in droves; the majority of them were Scots and Irish who were fiercely independent, disdainful of taxes, and suspicious of government. They were farmers who cleared the land to grow grain and brought their whiskey-making skills and whiskey-drinking tastes with them.

After the Revolutionary War, the new nation was strapped for cash and had to increase taxes. The currency wasn't worth much and the folks here were living on what amounted to a barter economy. You couldn't give grain away—what didn't get milled into flour was tough to transport by pack horse—so the best thing was to make booze with it. A gallon of whiskey could be distilled from about three bushels of grain, weighed less, took up a lot less space and found a ready market. They traded their product for manufactured goods from over the mountains in Baltimore and Philadelphia and down the river as far as New Orleans. Most of the stills were small operations; a farmer with a still would often make whiskey for several of his neighbors.

When the federal excise tax on whiskey was imposed in 1791 at the behest of Alexander Hamilton, the Secretary of the Treasury, there were more stills in western Pennsylvania than anywhere else in the United States. To say the locals copped an attitude is something of an understatement. They had no money and no particular inclination to pay the tax if they had. The Feds appointed tax collectors and all hell broke loose.

The collectors and distillers who complied with the tax had their houses and barns burned; there were tarrings and featherings, torchlight meetings were held, and threats were made to secede from the state of Pennsylvania and the country in general. Most of the action was in Allegheny and Washington Counties, but there was plenty in Fayette and Westmoreland, too.

Congress, at the urging of Washington, who was one of the principal landowners in the area, reduced the tax in 1792 and eased the methods of payment, but that made matters worse. The rebels thought the Feds were giving in and escalated the foment. Things came to a head in 1794. The rebels burned the house of General John Neville, the chief tax collector (but rescued the whiskey stored in his basement). They then called a mass meeting of the local militia at Braddock's Field (now Braddock) with thoughts of attacking Pittsburgh. They did march on the town, but Judge Hugh Brackenridge managed to talk the boys out of it by letting them partake of libation from his own private stock. The tax collectors and sympathizers escaped from town and hightailed it to Philadelphia where they told harrowing tales of their travails at the hands of the would-be post-Revolution revolutionaries.

President Washington had enough. He called up the militias of eastern Pennsylvania, New Jersey, Virginia and Maryland, somewhere between 13 and 15 thousand men, and gave the rebels an ultimatum to cease and desist. They didn't and in came the Army. Washington himself led the troops as far as Bedford, but Alexander Hamilton made the trip out here and saw to it that all went well. One of the commanders was General Henry (Lighthorse Harry) Lee, father of Robert E. Lee.

The rebels held more meetings and did a lot of fuming, blustering, and posturing, but the insurrection ceased without a shot being fired.

Many of the resistors were arrested, but only 18 of the leaders were detained and held for trial in Philadelphia. They were forced to travel under guard on foot to Philly in the winter. When they got there, they were held for a while, then acquitted for lack of evidence; the march was considered punishment enough. Then they had to walk back home.

As rebellions go, this one ended well. Many of the soldiers liked western Pennsylvania so much they either stayed here when their hitch was up or came back with their families and settled here. The other good news was the government paid the soldiers in cash while they were still here. This brought a needed infusion into the local economy because the lads spent a lot of money on slaking their thirst. This time the locals paid taxes on it.

Mile 40.0 Banning No. 3 Mine.

This was a slope mine that worked a coal seam 80" thick and employed 176 men in 1920. It was operated by the Pittsburgh Coal Company. Foundations from the mine are on the bank side of the trail; gob piles are on both sides. Coal from this mine was cleaned at Banning No. 3 Mine.

 Be careful of the dirt bike and ATV riders who cross here. Remember the equation: $IQ = 1/rec\ hp$, or intelligence is inversely proportional to recreational horsepower.

Mile 40 was also the beginning of Jacob's Creek Yard, which ran between here and Mile 41.5. The purpose of the yard was to distribute empty coal cars to the mines and to weigh and dispatch loaded cars.

The Banning mines were all named for Colonel A. R. Banning, who was a coal and coke operator after the Civil War. As is typical of Yough Valley naming patterns, the town of Banning is across the river from the mines.

Mile 40.25 Campbell's Run Bridge.

Just east of this point, the railroad widened out to six tracks on the east side for the loaded cars and five tracks on the west side for the empty cars.

The Jacobs Creek yard office sat in the town of Van Meter near where the road crossing is today. Engine 5731 is a 1500 h.p. GP-7 road switcher diesel locomotive built by the Electro-Motive Division of General Motors in 1953. Judging from the car next to it, the photo was taken sometime after 1956. Bill Metzger collection.

Mile 40.8 Van Meter

The town was named for John Van Meter who operated a ferry here in the 1790s. The railroad called its station Jacob's Creek, even though the town of Jacob's Creek is across the river. Most of the houses in the town are company houses built by the Pittsburgh Coal Company for the miners of Banning No. 3 and the Darr Mine. The yards and gardens along the trail here are built on the old railroad yard.

The low stone house on the hill side of the trail was originally the Jacob's Creek railroad station. It's only one of two P&LE stations left on the Youghiogheny River Trail North. The other is at Connellsville.

Like the rest of the stations on the P&LE Yough branch, this was originally a frame building. This is a private dwelling; do them the courtesy of not trespassing. The big building on the hill side is the Van Meter company store.

In the railroad days, there was no grade crossing here. Residents crossed the tracks on a foot bridge. The yard office, scale for weighing loaded cars and steam locomotive servicing facilities were located here. There was also a turntable here at one time for turning locomotives.

Mile 41.0 Darr Mine

On the river side of this milepost is the gob pile for the Darr Mine, scene of one of the worst mining disasters in Pennsylvania history. The mine itself was on the hill side near here. At 11:30 a.m. on December 19, 1907, the Darr Mine exploded, killing 239 men instantly. The headline in the *Greensburg Morning Review* said, "The Earth For Miles Around Was Shaken As By An Earthquake."

A combination of a buildup of mine gas (methane produced by the coal), the use of black powder, an accumulation of coal dust, and poor ventilation was blamed for the disaster, but the main cause, according to the *United Mine Workers Journal*, was "management neglect."

In fact, the superintendent and the fire boss (the man in charge of safety conditions) of the mine had recently resigned due to bad conditions which Pittsburgh Coal Company, the owner of the mine, had failed to correct. At the time of the explosion, the mine employed 1,907.

The death toll could have been much, much worse. Because of a Greek Catholic holiday, St. Nicholas Day, many miners who would have ordinarily been at work were at church. Only one miner working in the mine at the time survived.

The Darr disaster established 1907 as the worst year in Pennsylvania coal mining history. 1,400 men were killed in coal mining accidents that year.

Darr mine was closed after the bodies were recovered. Many of the victims are buried at the Olive Branch Cemetery on Route 981.

Mile 41.31 Westmoreland/Fayette County Line

This section of trail is maintained by the Whitsett-Fayette Yough Trail Chapter, a group of about 30 volunteers. Fayette County is named for the Marquis de Lafayette, who was instrumental in bringing the French to help the colonials in the Revolutionary War.

Company Stores

"I owe my soul to the company store" wasn't just a catchy tag line in Merle Travis' enduring hit song "Sixteen Tons." Many miners literally owed everything to the company store.

It started with the best of intentions by Henry Clay Frick. Coal mines were often located in remote locations, so the miners couldn't easily travel to buy groceries and other supplies. The remote mine towns also made it difficult for the coal companies to bring in cash to pay the miners.

Frick set up the stores to satisfy the miners' needs, then set up a system of "scrip" to pay the miners in lieu of cash. It was also meant to tide the miners over through hard times. The scrip was only redeemable in the company stores and for paying rent on company houses. At a lot of mines, miners were prohibited from purchasing from anywhere but the company store, but a lot of merchants in the Connellsville coke region would take scrip, but only at a discount.

The mine owners quickly realized that the company store/scrip system was another way to make a profit and the system became institutionalized. In 1891, the Pennsylvania General Assembly passed a law prohibiting the coal companies from owning company stores. The companies easily circumvented the law by setting up their stores as separate subsidiaries. (Pittsburgh Coal Company called their chain of stores, like the one here, the Federal Supply Company.)

After scrip was abolished in the 1930s, miners were paid in cash. They and their families could charge purchases against the miner's check number. (Ask any miner what his check number was and he'll rattle it off without thinking.) At payday, contents of the pay envelope was what was left after the debt to the company store and rent on the company house were paid.

It was quite conceivable that you could work for a week and still owe the company money. But heating was no problem. "The coal you got extra," one miner said. "We stole it from the railroad. When we were kids and the trains stopped for water, we'd climb up on the cars and toss some coal off." But if you did have to buy coal, the company would be happy to sell it to you at a reduced rate. And deduct it from your pay.

In most cases, the company store lasted only as long as the mine did.

CHAPTER 6: WHITSETT

Banning No. 1 Mine in 1933. The concrete wall to the right, the concrete silos and the foundations of the building in the center still stand. The cables in the upper right are the bucket line between here and Banning No 2 at Whitsett. Courtesy Pittsburgh and Lake Erie Railroad Collection, Archives Service Center, University of Pittsburgh.

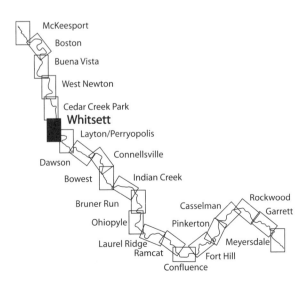

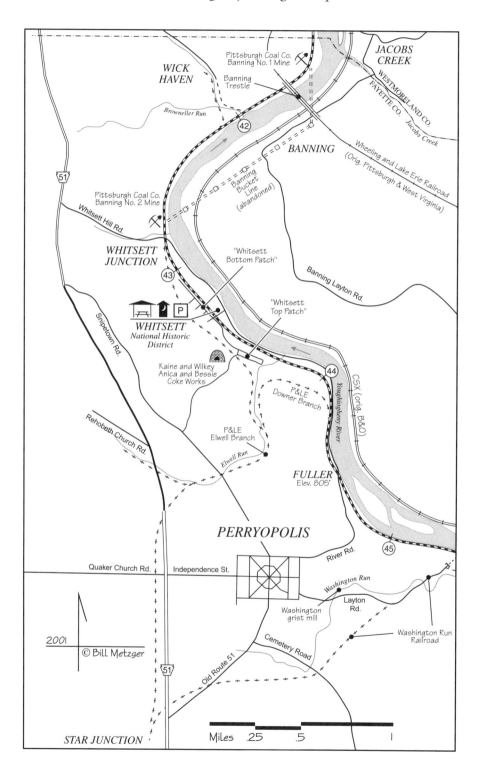

Mile 41.48 Banning No. 1 Mine

The foundations, concrete wall and silos are what's left of Banning No. 1 Mine. This was a big operation that employed 500 in 1951 and pulled 500,000 tons of coal out that year. Republic Steel bought this and the other three Banning mines from Pittsburgh Coal Company in 1947. This one closed in 1956.

There were a row of company houses in the complex on the hill side and a bucket line—an aerial tramway—to a gob pile across the river that was shared with Banning No. 2.

Pittsburgh Coal Company also called this the Champion No. 2 Coal Cleaning Plant. Champion No. 1 was on the Montour Railroad, now the Montour Trail. The Champion coal cleaning plants cleaned "run of mine" coal from other mines. Run of mine coal was everything that came out of the mine, slate and all.

THREE OF CREW HURT IN WRECK NEAR WEST NEWTON

Special to the Pittsburgh Press
CONNELLSVILLE, Pa. Jan. 6
One man was killed and three others were hurt today when a Pittsburgh & Lake Erie freight train, East bound, ploughed into a work train at Van Meter, a few miles from West Newton. The work train, which had been unloading debris, was standing still and the crew was not aboard at the time. Both freight cars and a caboose, making up the work train with an engine behind, were splintered, the wreckage piling up beside the track and fatally crushing a section hand. Crew of the freight engine remained at their posts and were finally able to check the speed of their locomotive, which, however, became locked with the engine pushing the work train. The dead man was identified as Daniel Burla, 56, of Whitsett. G.E. Heinbaugh, 32, of Dawson, brakeman; Frank M. Goldsboro of Dawson, engineer, and G.P. Stevens, fireman on the freight train escaped with minor injuries. Mr. Heinbaugh, riding in the locomotive, leaped before the crash. He was brought to the hospital here.

Pittsburgh Press, January 6, 1937. Photo courtesy Pittsburgh and Lake Erie Railroad Collection, Archives Service Center, University of Pittsburgh.

Coal was screened and graded by size from "slack" which wasn't much more than coal dust, to "lump", which was big chunks six inches or better. Each size had a different use.

Mile 41.64 Banning Trestle

The great bridge overhead here is the Banning Trestle of the Wheeling and Lake Erie Railroad. It's 1,582 feet long and 160 feet high, and was finished in 1930, just in time for the beginning of the Great Depression and therein lies the tale.

The trestle was built by the Pittsburgh and West Virginia Railroad as part of the long dreamed-of extension of that line from Pittsburgh to Connellsville and connection with the Western Maryland Railway.

Both lines were the brainchildren of George Jay Gould (see page 68) as part of his scheme to build a transcontinental railroad empire.

The Pittsburgh and West Virginia was often called "the High and Dry." It was built across the tops of the hills of western Pennsylvania simply because all of the good valley routes were taken up by railroads that had gotten there earlier.

Because of its route, it was a tremendously expensive venture, made more so when Gould decided to build an ornate and ultimately useless passenger terminal in downtown Pittsburgh.

To no one's surprise, and undisguised glee on the part of his numerous business enemies, the whole Gould empire collapsed in 1908. Under new management, the P&WV finally extended its line into Connellsville in 1930. With good leadership, the line managed to make a profit up into the 1960s, when it was leased to the Norfolk and Western Railroad as part of another empire-building deal. Norfolk and Western became Norfolk Southern, which sold the line to the Wheeling and Lake Erie in 1990, but traffic had already declined with the abandonment of the Western Maryland, its big connection at Connellsville.

The Pittsburgh & West Virginia Railroad's Banning Trestle was only 5 years old when this picture was taken in 1935. You can see the piers for the Banning Mine's bucket line behind the bridge. Carol Anthony collection.

Today, the line sees maybe one train a week, but that's due to change with the completion of a new intermodal terminal at New Stanton.

Mile 41.9 Wick Haven

The road here leads back to Wick Haven, a coal patch town that was built for Pittsburgh Coal Company's Wick Haven Mine. This early mine was gone by 1920, but in 1907 it had 297 employees. Later, the Wick Haven Coal Co. and Biggie's Coal Co. had mines here. The Wick Haven Coal Co. worked the Redstone Seam and Biggie's Coal Co. was working the Pittsburgh Seam at its Betty Mine in 1951.

The P&LE had a short branch line that served these mines.

There was a sky ferry here across the river to Banning.

Mile 42 Browneller Run

By now you've probably noticed that the streams along this section of the trail don't amount to much. That's the case from Boston to Connellsville. The reason is that none of the streams on this side of the river drain much territory. The Yough and Mon rivers form a fairly narrow peninsula so the longest stream you'll encounter is only about three or four miles long.

Mile 42.66 Whitsett Junction/Banning No. 2 Mine

Just before the stream now known as Banning No. 2 Run was the point of departure for the P&LE's Elwell Branch, which ran from here up to the huge coke making and mining complex at Star Junction and across the ridge to Fayette City. At the beginning of the 20th century there were 999 coke ovens in the Washington No. 1 and No. 2 complex at Star Junction.

The branch was built in 1894 and abandoned from Fayette City to Star Junction in 1946, and from Star Junction to Whitsett in 1964. The branch ran through the Elwell family's farm, hence the name.

There was a prodigious climb up to Star Junction, but the rule for building a coal branch has always been "empties up, loads down."

The original tipple for Banning No. 2 Mine at Whitsett. The gob pile is to the right. Note the difference in dress between the young men (probably managers) at the left and the boys next to them. It wasn't uncommon for young boys to be working as "slate pickers," cleaning the coal as it came out of the mine. Paul Dudjak collection.

Mile 42.8

Whitsett Hill Road up to Route 51. This road becomes River Road and is a good paved alternative to the trail for a bit, if you're so inclined.

Mile 43.6 Whitsett

Whitsett is a National Historic District and is a classic coal patch town. There are two sections to town: the "top patch" and the "bottom patch." The top patch is largely settled by African-Americans who came up from the South, and the bottom patch is largely Eastern European. Hungarians, Czechs, Yugoslavians, Austrians, Italians and Poles settled here to work the mines. Pittsburgh Coal Company originally had a company store here, but that burned down in 1938.

The large brick house on the north end of town toward the river is the original Whitsett home, built in 1873. It is reasonably intact and has also been a hotel for bachelor miners. The Whitsett family settled here in 1845, and operated a pick and shovel factory on the site, as well as a grist mill, a brick yard, and a general store.

The house was built on what was originally called Rainbow Island. The back channel was filled in when the railroad was built in 1883. Rainbow Island got its name from Joseph Finley, the original owner of the land, who called his farm "Rainbow," after the custom of the time to name one's property. Finley sold the property to the Whitsetts.

Banning No. 2 mine was purchased from the Whitsett family by the Pittsburgh Coal Company and began mining in 1902. In 1910 the mine employed 659 and was said to be the most productive in the Yough Valley. The area around Banning No. 2 site is still known as "the buckets" for the bucket line that ran from here to Banning No. 1. The line carried slate from both mines to a gob pile across the river. The grassy mound on the river side of the trail was the original gob pile for the mine, which was closed in the late 1950s.

The Kaine and Wilkey Company had a bank of coke ovens, the Anica Coke Works, up along the hillside between the top patch and the bottom patch. The operation started in 1901 and had 40 ovens. The remains are still visible when the leaves are off the trees.

The porta-potty at Whitsett is the last trailside toilet you're going to see until you get to the campground store at Adelaide. There are no other trailside services between here and Adelaide, 12 miles away. Be governed accordingly. Rental on this particular potty is paid by the Whitsett-Fayette Yough Trail Chapter, and it's kept up year round, so be grateful.

Whitsett also marks the end of the Pittsburgh Coal Seam. It disappears until Rainey up at Mile 54. There were mines in this next section, but they worked the smaller Redstone Seam.

Mile 43.8

The cliffs along here are marine fossil bearing. They're embedded in soft claystone and siltstone. It's trail property so you can feel free to poke around a bit.

Fuller Station.
Courtesy Pittsburgh and Lake Erie Railroad Collection, Archives
Service Center, University of Pittsburgh.

MILE 44.5 FULLER

The station at Fuller was the junction of the Downers Run Branch which formed a "wye" with the Elwell Branch up to Star Junction. The road crossing here is where you get back on the trail if you decided to take a break and ride along the river from Mile 42.8. This is also the easiest way up to Perryopolis.

Perryopolis

A short ride up the hill will take you to the delightful little town of Perryopolis. The town was named for Oliver Hazard Perry, hero of the War of 1812 ("We have met the enemy and he is ours . . ."), but was built on land that was owned by George Washington. The town was laid out in a unique hexagonal pattern with a town square in the middle.

The local historical society is quite active and has completely rebuilt George Washington's grist mill and distillery. It's open on summer weekends. They also offer a walking tour of the town that's well worth doing. It includes the oldest bank building west of the Alleghenies and a rare wooden blacksmith shop.

 If you're pausing in Perryopolis, read on about two men who had an enormous impact on Western Pennsylvania. If you're in a hurry to get on down the trail, skip to Chapter 7.

GEORGE WASHINGTON

Western Pennsylvania wasn't real hospitable for George Washington on his first three trips out here from his home in Virginia. On his first trip, he was patronized by the French, shot at by his Indian escort and barely survived drowning and hypothermia when he tried to cross the half-frozen Allegheny River on a makeshift raft. On his second trip, he started the French and Indian War (if he hadn't started it, the French would have), and lost a battle with the French at Fort Necessity where he was forced to surrender. He and his troops had to walk home in defeat and then explain how he started this war to the folks back home in Virginia.

The third trip was the kicker. He was sick for most of the journey out on General Edward Braddock's ill-fated expedition to capture Fort Duquesne from the French. Then General Braddock up and got his stupid self ambushed. Washington survived the battle with four bullet holes in his coat and two horses shot out from under him. Battle-wise, George was 0 and 2 with the French. The marvel is that he survived them.

In 1758, he marched with General John Forbes on the successful campaign to rout the French from Fort Duquesne and helped build Forbes Road, now US 30. Though ailing, Forbes was a better general than Braddock ever was, and won the fight with the French at Fort Duquesne after the French decided to boogie in the face of overwhelming odds.

Next time Washington visited these parts, it was to buy land. In 1769, he bought 1,600 acres in the Perryopolis area that Colonel William Crawford of Connellsville had picked out for him. Crawford was also the first person to show Washington the Pittsburgh Coal Seam. Washington called the farm "Meadow," which later became known as Washington's Bottom.

He had a grist mill and a distillery built on the property at considerable cost for the time and hired a Mr. Gilbert Simpson to run it and the surrounding property. Simpson was a poor manager with a wellspring of excuses for why he couldn't get his work done. Washington said in a letter, "I never hear of the mill under the direction of Simpson without a degree of warmth and vexation at his extreme stupidity." The relationship with Simpson ended with Washington's last trip out here in 1784 when he put the property up for lease to the highest bidder.

Eventually the mill was a success and worked for over a century.

GEORGE GOULD

Remember this name. George Gould is the reason there is a Great Allegheny Passage. Were it not for George, the Western Maryland would never have been built and later abandoned and there would be nothing to build a trail on.

George was the son of the 19th century stock manipulator and financier, Jay Gould. The Goulds had a dream to build a transcontinental railroad, one that truly crossed the country, not like those other "transcontinental" lines like the Union Pacific that only went from Omaha, Nebraska to Ogden, Utah. The Goulds scoffed and sneered and thought they could do better.

When Jay died in 1892, he left a huge fortune, said to be the largest ever amassed at the time. He willed it to his four sons, the oldest being George. George decided to make Dad's dream come true and set to work buying and building himself a real transcontinental railroad.

The Goulds already owned a sizeable piece of what they needed. Their empire ran from Salt Lake City, Utah to Buffalo, New York, a network that touched almost every major city in the Midwest, and they also owned Western Union, the telegraph company.

Problem was, the Goulds had managed to make some powerful enemies on the way. In the West, they were hated by E. H. Harriman, who owned the Southern

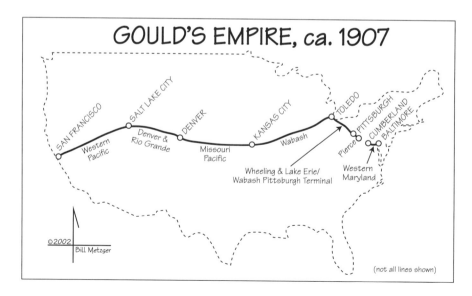

GOULD'S EMPIRE, ca. 1907

©2002 Bill Metzger

(not all lines shown)

Pacific and the Union Pacific Railroads, to name a few. Jay had pulled a fast one in the 1880s that had netted him $10 million in two years at Harriman's expense. Harriman held a grudge.

In the East, the Goulds were hated by the Vanderbilts, of the New York Central and our P&LE. In the 1860s, Jay controlled the Erie Railroad. Old Commodore Vanderbilt wanted the Erie and started buying stock. As fast as Vanderbilt bought Erie stock, Gould printed more. The scam was going great guns until someone discovered the ink on the new stock certificates was still wet. Gould hit Vanderbilt for about $7 million. Another grudge against the Goulds.

Problem was, George wasn't the sharpie his father was.

> "... George, according to his contemporaries, was equipped with few of the qualities needed for success in business; he was described as shy, unaggressive, rather unprepossessing, a trifle dull-witted .... All in all, he was splendidly endowed for one role in life, that of the rather arrogant dim-witted New York clubman, the late Victorian playboy with a dashing actress on his arm and a gray topper on his brandy-fumed head.* Richard O'Connor, Gould's Millions.

Nevertheless, in 1901, George started building his transcontinental railroad. The Gould enemies had other ideas; they blocked him at every turn. First, he bought the Western Maryland, which was at that time a little railroad owned by the City of Baltimore. It ran from Baltimore west to Big Pool, Maryland (where the paved portion of the Western Maryland Scenic Trail ends today). Gould bought the city's stock and promised the city fathers a lot of expensive improvements to the Baltimore terminal which he made good on. The Pennsylvania Railroad howled, but Gould won this round. He then started extending the Western Maryland to Cumberland, where he bought two coal-hauling railroads. Coal from these lines would help pay for the project. In the West, Gould started building the Western Pacific from Salt Lake City to San Francisco. Harriman fought the project every step of the way to the point of sending out gangs of workers to beat up the Gould crews. The Western Pacific also cost a lot of money to build.

George Gould and his wife, the former actress Edith Kingdom Gould. Their estate, Georgian Court, was a 400-acre extravaganza that was towered, turreted, statued, and gilded in the grand manner. It's now a Catholic girls' school. Lyndhurst, a National Trust Historic Site.

Gould bought the Wheeling and Lake Erie Railroad that ran from Toledo to Wheeling. He used it to get closer to Pittsburgh, where the big money was. Gould secured an agreement to haul Andrew Carnegie's steel traffic. Carnegie was perpetually steamed at the Pennsylvania Railroad and welcomed the opportunity to beat them. Agreement in hand, George started building the Wabash Pittsburgh Terminal Railroad (later the Pittsburgh and West Virginia). But, because the WPT was being constructed over the hills and valleys of western Pennsylvania, the line was enormously expensive to build.

Then, while the Wabash Pittsburgh Terminal was spending money by the bucketsful, Carnegie sold his whole steel operation to J. P. Morgan, who created United States Steel. The agreement for Gould's new railroad to haul Carnegie's Steel went out the window. Chances are good that Carnegie just used Gould to raise the price of his mills.

The WPT, with its showy, expensive, and useless passenger station in downtown Pittsburgh was a loser almost from the start—a super railroad to nowhere. The big money was in freight and without the Carnegie agreement, Gould didn't get much.

The Western Maryland Cumberland Extension also cost a bundle. Huge bridges and tunnels had to be built. You'll see these when you go down the towpath. When coal started flowing out of Cumberland from West Virginia, A. J. Cassatt, president of the Pennsylvania Railroad, worked a deal that closed all of Gould's outlets for the coal to Philadelphia, New York, and the rest of the East Coast. Gould couldn't move the stuff, let alone sell it. The Western Maryland was forced into receivership and things started to fall apart for George Gould.

About this time, Cassatt also forced Gould to tear up 1,500 miles of Western Union telegraph lines that were on Pennsylvania Railroad property. This cost Gould about $5 million. One by one, his railroads went into bankruptcy. He eventually lost control of all of them.

A lot of Gould's financial woes were self-inflicted. He liked to build railroads but didn't much care for operating or maintaining them. Gould's lines were well-engineered and built but had a reputation for shoddy operations and bad equipment, if, in fact, there was equipment at all. Gould wanted to be a social lion holding great parties and a railroad magnate controlling a nationwide railroad empire. He looted the railroads to pay for the parties and it caught up with him.

His enemies won and George got out of the railroad business. He died in 1923, just 59 years old, but we'll leave him in 1908 with the dream dead and a 126-mile gap between Pierce, PA and Cumberland still missing from the great transcontinental scheme. But worry not. There's more to the story and we'll tell it up the trail.

 Trail guide continues next page.

CHAPTER 7: LAYTON

A Washington Run Railroad passenger train poses on the bridge to Layton that's now the road. The Washington Run had a total of three engines, which they owned one at a time. This is engine No. 2. Bill Colbert collection.

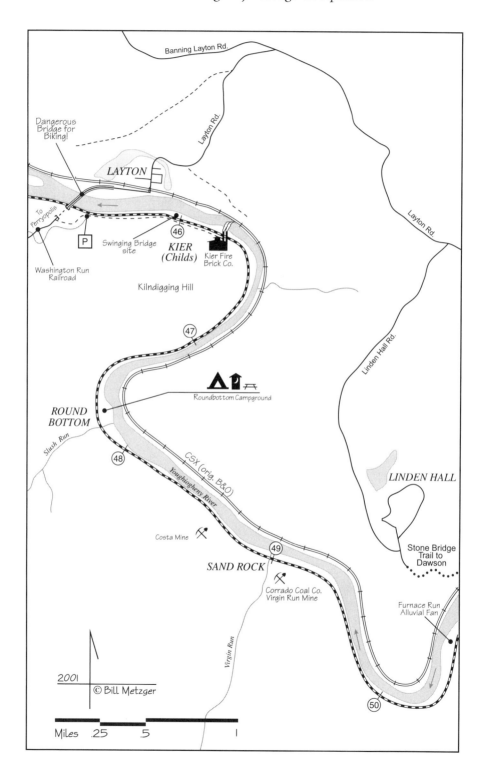

Banning Layton Rd.

Layton Rd.

Dangerous
Bridge for
Biking!

LAYTON

Layton Rd.

To
Perryopolis

P

Swinging Bridge
site

46

KIER
(Childs)

Kier Fire
Brick Co.

Washington Run
Railroad

Kilndigging Hill

47

Roundbottom Campground

ROUND
BOTTOM

Slush Run

48

CSX (orig. B&O)

Youghiogheny River

Linden Hall Rd.

LINDEN HALL

Costa Mine

Corrado Coal Co.
Virgin Run Mine

49

SAND ROCK

Stone Bridge
Trail to
Dawson

Furnace Run
Alluvial Fan

Virgin Run

2001
© Bill Metzger

50

Miles   .25   .5   1

Mile 45.3 Washington Run Railroad

The highway bridge you cross under here was originally built for the Washington Run Railroad, which was completed in 1900 and ran from Layton to the mines and coke oven complex at Star Junction. At its peak, the four-mile long line ran three passenger trains a day each way and hauled about 2,000 tons of coke a day to its interchange with the B&O.

Bill Metzger collection.

The railroad was owned by the Cochran Coal and Coke Co. and made money throughout its existence. (You'll hear more about the Cochrans when we get to Dawson.) The Pennsylvania Department of Highways took over the line for a road when the railroad was abandoned. The last train ran on March 12, 1931.

The bridge is 884 feet long and the tunnel is 218 feet long.

The big mystery here was why the railroad was built in the first place. The P&LE Elwell Branch ran up to Star Junction already. The Washington Run Railroad ran to within a few yards of it and certainly wasn't cheap to build with the bridge and tunnel. Plus, it had a pretty stiff grade up the hill.

 A word of caution: If you decide to ride your bike across to Layton: Be Careful!!! The bridge and tunnel are very narrow and the visibility is really bad.

Why, then, would the Cochrans spend all that money to build a duplicate railroad? Two guesses: the first is cheaper freight rates from the competition between the P&LE and the B&O. The second is that the P&LE went west and north and in 1900 had no eastern connection. Maybe Cochran gained access to the B&O as an outlet to the east.

Mile 45.4 Layton

Having just told you to be real careful going to Layton, now we'll tell you that some of the movie *Silence of the Lambs* was shot there. There's a yellow brick house in Layton where the bad guy lived and did all his misdeeds. The big local social item was that star Jody Foster stayed in Sarah Cochran's bedroom in Linden Hall. Supposedly she was the first person since Sarah herself to have done so.

Mile 46

The locals call the area here Bareass Beach. There was a suspension bridge that crossed from Layton to here to carry workers to the brick plant. You can still see the bridge foundations in the trees on the river side. As suggested by its name, there's some good swimming here.

Fishing

Some of the best fishing in western Pennsylvania can be found in the Yough from Sutersville upstream. Record-breaking muskies and trout are regularly caught. A reminder: you need a license to fish this and every other stream in Pennsylvania.

Mile 46.3 Childs

The factory you see on the bank side of the trail is what's left of the Kier Fire Brick Company's plant. There were three brick works in the Layton area for good reason. There was a ready availability of "fire clay" suitable for making furnace brick, a ready availability of coal to fire the clay brick and a ready market in the thousands of coke ovens in the Connellsville area and the blast furnaces in the Pittsburgh area. Fire clay was dug in Kilndigging Hill right behind this plant.

This particular plant was originally owned by the Childs family. Not coincidentally, Henry Clay Frick's wife Adelaide's maiden name was Childs.

Fire brick is made from clay that's high in aluminum, silica, or quartz making it capable of withstanding the high temperatures of furnaces and ovens. Ordinary building bricks would crumble in these heats. Aside from coke ovens and blast furnaces, fire brick, or "refractory" as it's also called, was used in the fireboxes of steam locomotives, steamships, and power plants.

In a world where there are no new steam locomotives, steamships, beehive coke ovens, or blast furnaces being built, the refractory business is a shell of its former self. Just like the coal mines, there were brickyards all along the Yough and Casselman valleys. And just like the coal mines, they're all gone.

Some railroad maps also call the place Kier.

Mile 47.8 Round Bottom

The stream bottom (Slush Run) underneath the bridge is lined with about five courses of brick, probably to protect the bridge from eroding away. The P&LE also had housing here for track repairmen due to its remote location and a small station. In the late 1930s, the flats on the river side were still being farmed. There's also supposed to be beavers in these parts.

Mile 48.9 Sand Rock/Virgin Run

The Costa Coal Company's Lucy Mine was located here. This was a small operation that worked the 36-inch Redstone Seam and only employed 10 miners in 1922. You can easily see the foundations and grades from the mine.

This is a great place to stop on a hot summer day. The "cool pool" on the river side of the bridge is about 10 degrees cooler than the water in the river.

Corrado's Virgin Run Mine was on the other side of the stream. It, too, was a small mine that worked the Redstone Seam and only had 15 employees. Remains of the mine are visible along the trail.

As the name Sand Rock implies, the outcrop here is sandstone, which is acid. Mountain laurel likes acid soil, which is why the stream bank is lined with it.

Mile 50.67 Furnace Run/Ironmaking and Coke

The run is named for the Little Falls iron furnace, which was built near here. It was an unsuccessful operation that operated around 1800. This is a good place to talk about ironmaking and coke in Fayette County, unless you're eager to get on down the Trail, in which case, skip ahead to the next chapter.

Iron ore was discovered in Fayette County at least as early as 1780 by George Washington's friend Colonel Crawford; the first furnace operation to make iron in the area was in 1789.

P&LE TRAIN PLUNGES INTO YOUGHIOGHENY

Several trainmen narrowly escaped death last night when a locomotive of the Pittsburgh & Lake Erie Railroad plunged into the swollen Youghiogheny River at Round Bottom, near Connellsville, Pa., last night, derailing nine freight cars. Engineer F.M. Goldsboro, of Dawson, Fireman J.P. Peebles of Liberty, and Head Brakeman C.J. Gaal of Dawson, crawled from the cab of the locomotive only slightly hurt. Conductor H.B. Shallenberger, of Vanderbilt, and Flagman J.Colbert of Connellsville, leaped from the caboose as the train crashed. Mr. Shallenberger said the train was going 29 miles an hour when it hit a spot in the tracks over a culvert which had been washed out. Uprooted trees and other debris were piled high against the wreckage. Mr. Shallenberger described the escape of the three men in the cab of the locomotive as a "miracle." Mr. Gaal was under water nearly two minutes, Mr. Shallenberger said. The conductor said thousand of tons of fill would have to be dumped in the river before it would be possible to recover the locomotive and the derailed cars. Pittsburgh Press, Thursday June 5, 1941.

There's a complete steam locomotive buried in the pile on the right. The river's still high from the recent rain storm.

Courtesy Pittsburgh and Lake Erie Railroad Collection, Archives Service Center, University of Pittsburgh.

Iron ore is basically iron oxide, or rust. To make iron, the oxygen has to be removed in a furnace. Three things are needed: iron ore, a source of heat (carbon in the form of charcoal or coke), and a flux (limestone) that makes the chemical reaction possible. A source of power is also needed to blast air into the furnace. All four are present in Fayette County.

Iron ore exists in varying quantities and quality all over the county. The iron-masters of the time gave some wonderful names to the local ore beds such as the Little Honeycomb, the Big Honeycomb, the Kidney, and the Big Bottom.

The source of heat was originally charcoal from the abundant forests in the area, but an iron operation exhausted the local forest at the rate of an acre a day. It so happens that Fayette County sits on some of the best coking coal in the world and after about 1830 coke began to be substituted for charcoal.

Just as charcoal is wood burned in a minimum of air, coke is coal burned with a minimum of air. The result in both cases is carbon but coal contains more carbon than wood and is more efficient in ironmaking.

Limestone is everywhere in the county, so that wasn't a problem either.

Power to run the furnaces came in the form of swift-running streams.

With all the necessary ingredients in place, there were at least 20 iron furnaces operating in the county in the 19th century. Only a few lasted into the 20th century; the most successful was the Dunbar Furnace Company which grew into a steelmaking concern and stayed in operation into the late 1940s.

Ironically, Connellsville coke made the big new integrated steel mills in the Pittsburgh area possible. An integrated steel mill is one that starts with raw materials and turns out finished steel products, keeping all the steps in between in house.

By the way, the difference between iron and steel is that steel is iron with the impurities, mostly carbon, removed. Cast iron is brittle; the brittleness is caused by carbon. Early blacksmiths and armorers removed the carbon by beating it out; keep hammering on a piece of hot iron and eventually it'll become steel. That's how swords are made: a piece of iron is heated, beaten flat, folded double, and beaten flat again, then the process is repeated again and again until the brittleness is gone.

There is nothing left of the Little Falls Furnace or the rolling mill that succeeded it but a small pile of slag—yes, this is real slag—along the side of the hill. The original name for Furnace Run was Arnold's Run, in case you hear that name.

 We hear this area is a hotbed of copperheads. Be governed accordingly.

Connellsville Coke

Furnace Run is also alleged to be the site of the first coke ovens in the area. According to the *History of Fayette County*, several ovens were built here sometime between 1830 and 1836. An Englishman was said to have told the locals about cokemaking using ovens in his country, so they tried it. It took a great deal of experimentation, but the result was a fine grade of coke and beehive cokemaking began in earnest.

Coke was used at a furnace in Blair County in central Pennsylvania at least as early as 1811 and at various furnaces throughout the state in the 1830s and '40s. The process by which the coke was made was called "ground ricking." The coal was piled on the ground, dirt was piled around it and the coal was set on fire. It was an inefficient and dirty process at best and charcoal was still the preferred blast furnace fuel.

Coke is a contraction of the words "coal and cake." Or, if you prefer, "cooked coal." The archaic spelling is "coak." It's coal with the impurities removed, especially sulphur, which makes iron brittle. Pittsburgh Seam coal in the Connellsville District is about 65% carbon. Coke after burning is almost pure carbon. The rest is all sorts of nasty organic chemicals like naphtha, nitric acid, benzene, and cyanogens, among many others. When recovered in a by-product coke plant, coke chemicals go into useful things like paint solvent, perfume, laxatives, and TNT. But in a beehive operation these chemicals were either burned off or washed away when the coke was quenched. Needless to say, the air and water pollution created by the beehive process was monumental.

Beehive ovens were so named because they were dome-shaped, like domestic beehives of the day. Coal was fed in through a hole in the top by "larry cars," a corruption of the English word lorry, or truck. The coal was set on fire and a door at the front of the oven was bricked up just enough to let in a controlled amount of air. After 24 or 48 hours and temperatures that reached 2,500 to 3,000 degrees, the hot coke was pulled out and quenched with water.

The first beehive coke put on the market met with something of a yawn. John Taylor was a stonemason who had a farm with a small coal mine on the property. He enlisted two carpenters, named McCormick and Campbell, to build a couple of flatboats and commenced cokemaking. They worked the fall and winter of 1841 and into the spring of 1842 and finally made enough coke to load the boats, which they floated downriver to Cincinnati when the water was high. Nobody in Cincinnati knew what coke was and, according to the *History of Fayette County*, "regarded it with suspicion, calling it cinders." They finally got rid of about half the stock, trading it or selling it at eight cents a bushel. They traded the other half for the machinery for a gristmill, which turned out to be worthless when they got it home.

But their story ends well. The half that sold wound up with a foundry owner who was originally from Fayette County. He used the coke, found out how nifty it was, came back to Connellsville, found McCormick and Campbell, and told them he'd buy all they could make. The lads were "disinclined to repeat the experiment." However, Taylor rented his ovens to the Cochran brothers, Little Jim and Sample, who went on to make a fortune on the stuff. Their uncle, Big Jim Cochran, handled the transportation downriver and is credited with the first successful sale of Connellsville coke.

Beehive coke ovens in operation. The men on the lower level are pulling finished coke from the ovens. The "larry cars" on the upper level fill the ovens with new coal. Note the quality of the air. Courtesy Rivers of Steel Archives.

The coke business started to grow when the Pittsburgh and Connellsville Railroad was completed between its namesake towns in 1860, just in time for the Civil War to start. However, there were still less than 200 ovens in the Connellsville district by 1871. This was the pivotal year when things really started to jump. There were 3,000 ovens on line in 1876, 4,000 in 1879 and 8,000 ovens in 1882 that were producing over four million tons of coke a year.

It can be truthfully said that Connellsville Coke fueled the Industrial Revolution of the late 19th century. It was easy to mine—all you had to do was dig into the side of a hill where it outcropped—and the coal seam was 6 to 8 feet thick. It was cheap to ship and the distance downstream to Pittsburgh by river or rail was less than 60 miles. A whole infrastructure of railroads grew up to ship it. It was of excellent quality—historian Frederick Moore Binder described it to be of "a silvery lustre and cellular, with a metallic ring." It was strong enough to withstand the weight of a charge of iron ore and limestone in a blast furnace.

Every new blast furnace in the Pittsburgh area in the 1870s and '80s—and there were at least 20 of them—was built to handle Connellsville coke. It was also shipped to steel mills all over the country and out west to smelt gold and silver ore.

Beehive ovens gave way to by-product ovens that recovered the organic chemicals for reuse. By-product ovens were somewhat cleaner and were built in larger, more efficient coke plants, like the Clairton Coke Works. The new ovens were also built near—or even as a part of—new steel mills, making them an integral and more efficient part of the steelmaking process. Gas from by-product ovens was used to heat the blast furnaces.

At the peak of the beehive era about 1900, there were about 40,000 ovens blazing away in the Connellsville Coke District. Contemporary accounts almost invariably described the coal supply as "inexhaustible" and of course it wasn't, but beehive cokemaking went on as though it was.

All told, the Connellsville cokemaking boom lasted less than 75 years. For every boom, as a legion of dot.com "millionaires" have recently and painfully rediscovered, there's a bust. Today, there are no working beehive coke ovens anywhere in Pennsylvania and Fayette County is one of the poorest in Pennsylvania.

Chapter 8: Dawson/ Dickerson Run

This was Galleytown, which was razed or moved to build the new Dickerson Run Yard in 1910-12. With the exception of the hills in the background, everything else in this picture is gone. The railroad cars in the foreground are empty coke cars, some of which are being repaired in the shop area at the right. Bill Colbert collection.

McKeesport
Boston
Buena Vista
West Newton
Cedar Creek Park
Whitsett
Layton/Perryopolis
Connellsville
Dawson
Bowest
Indian Creek
Bruner Run
Casselman
Rockwood
Garrett
Ohiopyle
Pinkerton
Laurel Ridge
Meyersdale
Ramcat
Fort Hill
Confluence

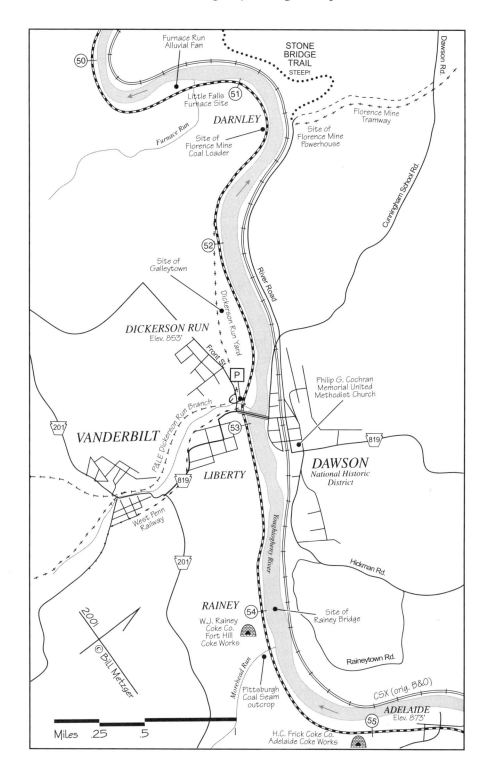

Mile 50.67 Furnace Run Alluvial Fan

Just about every stream flowing into another body of water leaves an alluvial fan. It's the stuff that has washed down the stream and gets deposited into the river. Geologist Jim Shaulis calls it a "deposit of boulders, cobbles, pebbles, sand, silt and clay."

The big deal about the Furnace Run fan is that it's accessible; you can go down to the river and take a look at it. The fan has grown up with vegetation which makes it erosion resistant. Since the river can't flow through it, it flows around it, which narrows the river, deepens its channel, and makes it run faster. Boulders washed down from Furnace Run created rapids.

Mile 51.1 Darnley

This is the site of a little-known but interesting coal loading operation. The Youghiogheny Coal Co. from Dawson operated the Florence Mine, about 2.5 miles back from the river on the B&O side, but they didn't like the B&O. So they built a tramway to haul their coal down Laurel Run to the river where they transferred it to aerial cable cars to cross over to the P&LE for loading. Not much is visible from this side of the river, but the site of the powerhouse is quite clear across the river up on the hill where River Road ends and the Stone Bridge Trail begins.

Mile 51.6 Dickerson Run Yard

When the Pittsburgh McKeesport and Youghiogheny Railroad was completed in 1883, the original railroad included a branch line up Dickerson Run. There was a nice flat alluvial fan from the run which made a fine place to build a little railroad yard and roundhouse. Dickerson Run Yard was born. Its purpose was to handle traffic from the branch and traffic to and from Connellsville, five miles east. The line connected with the Pennsylvania Railroad at Connellsville, but little traffic was interchanged between them.

The community of Galleytown grew up around the yard. There was a bridge across the river to Dawson and that's the way things were until 1910 when the Western Maryland began building its Connellsville Extension. The new interchange traffic between the two railroads had to be handled somewhere and Dickerson Run was the place since there was little available land around Connellsville.

The yard had to be expanded and Galleytown had to go. The houses were either torn down or moved up the hill to Vanderbilt and Liberty.

A new larger roundhouse was built along with a power house, offices and a railroad YMCA where crews could lay over. There were also railroad car repair shops. They called it "D Run" for short.

The new facility included a hump yard where trains were sorted by gravity from an elevated track called a hump. A train was pushed up to the crest of the hump and cars would be cut off and allowed to drift down the other side where they were switched to different tracks that were classified by destination. For example, Track 1 could be for cars destined for Connellsville, Track 2 for West Newton, etc. Early hump yards like this one were dangerous affairs as each car or group of cars that went over the hump had to be ridden down and hand braked by a brakeman.

Every car on an incoming train was entered on a switch list which gave the car's number, destination, and track where it was to be classified. Everybody working that particular train had a copy of the list. When a given car got to the top of the hump, a rider would climb on and stand on the small platform that's either on the leading or trailing end of each car. The car would be uncoupled and start rolling. The rider would then hold on with one hand and work the hand brake wheel with the other, slowing the car down to the right speed to couple to the cars already on the destination track and insuring that he wouldn't be knocked off.

His route would be set by switchmen hand-throwing switches according to the list.

A myriad of hazards awaited a man riding a car in a hump yard, from hand brakes that didn't work, to ladders on the cars that were loose or missing, to darkness, snow and ice. To survive in a hump yard, you had to be strong and nimble. Injuries were an almost everyday occurrence.

An old switchman told me that when a guy got hurt or killed, the first thing everybody would do was see where he stood on the seniority roster. If he was below you, you felt bad. If he was above you, you moved up a notch on your way to a better job.

Hump yards today have computer-aided retarder equipment that measures a car's weight and speed and slows it to a smooth coupling and no one is permitted to ride a loose car in a hump yard. Dickerson Run was never that sophisticated.

The new improved Dickerson Run started handling Western Maryland traffic on August 1, 1912. It closed in 1970, when the remaining business was moved to Connellsville yard.

Today the trail skirts around the edge of the old yard; the yard itself is private property and dangerous to enter. There's no trace whatsoever of Galleytown.

Mile 52.9 Dickerson Run Trail Head

The trail head is the site of the Dickerson Run station and the junction for the branch up to Vanderbilt and Juniataville. West Penn Railways had a branch of their trolley line that ended here. If you rode the trolley and wanted to go to Dawson, you walked across the bridge.

The present bridge is the second on the site. The first was an iron truss that crossed the railroad at grade on its way to Dawson. When Dickerson Run Yard was expanded, the grade crossing became too congested with railroad traffic and a new span was built across the tracks. The bridge was sloped up to meet it.

Dawson, Population 524

Little Jim Cochran was Big Jim's Cochran's nephew. Little Jim begat Philip G. Cochran who married Sarah B. Cochran. These are the Cochrans of Dawson and these folks are where the money came from.

Big Jim was a tough, enterprising Irishman who came to this country as a laborer and helped build the National Road. He hung around to make a buck flatboating sand downriver to the glassmaking factories in Pittsburgh. His claim to fame is selling the first boatloads of coke downriver for real cash money.

Cochran and crew took 6,000 bushels downriver in boats that had no shelter— they had to sleep on the coke—and they had to borrow money in Pittsburgh for provisions. They sold their coke to the Cincinnati foundry owner who had bought

The Washington Bank Building in Dawson has changed little from the days when Cochrans ruled their coal and coke empire from here.

some of the first Connellsville coke that had come downriver. That was the start of what became a sizeable fortune.

The Cochrans owned several coke works right in the Dawson area and, as the firm of Brown and Cochran, built the huge operation at Star Junction and the Washington Run Railroad. Little Jim built up the business and passed it to his son, Philip G., who died at age 50. Sarah and her son James inherited the fortune. The lad was going to carry on the family business but died of pneumonia in 1901 while away at college. In memory of her husband, Sarah built the beautiful Philip G. Cochran Memorial United Methodist Church in 1900. She had the church that was already on the site torn down to build the new one. The church alone is worth the trip across the river to Dawson.

But other treasures await you when you come to town. There are several Victorian mansions of the wedding cake variety and the original Washington Bank Building built by the Cochrans that was the center of their coal and coke empire. Little Jim's humble little abode is the confection directly across the street from the bank.

The town was named for George Dawson, who, according to the *History of Fayette County*, "used it for purposes of cultivation." That is, he farmed. The railroad called it Dawson's Station, but when the town was laid out, it got called Bloomington for some reason. It was changed back to Dawson after the locals protested and petitioned the court to do the changing. The court obliged.

This is another National Historic District that hasn't changed appreciably since the glory days at the beginning of the 20th century. It's unique in that it's one of the few places in the valley where owners and workers lived side by side.

 Don't even think about riding the Stone Bridge Trail on a road bike and be real cautious on a mountain bike. It's steep and rutted. But once you get up there, it's something to behold.

Linden Hall

After her husband died and left her a fortune and her son died prematurely, Sarah B. Cochran looked around for something to do. She toured Europe and the Orient and got the idea to build a real mansion, so she came home and built Linden Hall.

Sarah spent about $2 million to build the place at a time when a million bucks really meant something. She brought Italian stonemasons in to do much of the masonry using stone quarried on the property. European woodworkers did much of the interior. The stained glass windows are from Tiffany, of course. There's a pipe organ in the Great Hall and the carriage house alone is bigger than most of the McMansions being built today. Construction of Linden Hall was completed in 1913.

The place passed through several owners after Sarah went to that Great Hall in the sky, most of whom couldn't keep the place up. It wound up being owned, irony of ironies, by the United Steelworkers, who now operate it as a resort.

The resort has the usual resort stuff like rooms (not in the mansion), a restaurant, and all sorts of recreation including a place where people play at something called "golf," whatever that is.

But you can tour the mansion by appointment and it's worth the trip. Just be careful on the trail if you decide to go that way.

Mile 52.9 Vanderbilt/Liberty/Dickerson Run

These three towns are all on top of the hill from the Dickerson Run trail head.

Liberty, then known as East Liberty, is said to the first town settled in this section of the Yough valley. Vanderbilt once made *Ripley's Believe it or Not* as having the crookedest main street in the country It was named for William Henry Vanderbilt who financed the building of this end of the P&LE.

All three places were jumping when the P&LE was running and the mines and ovens were working, but now they've fallen on hard times. There are no services worth climbing the hill for and no particular points of interest to hold your interest if, for some perverse reason, you decided to climb the hill anyway.

Our advice: go to Dawson.

 Read on if you want to learn a little about the Pittsburgh Coal Seam. If you're continuing along the Trail, you may want to skip ahead to page 86 (look for the hiker & bike symbols).

"Coal has always cursed the land in which it lies. When men begin to wrest it from the earth it leaves a legacy of foul streams, hideous slag heaps, and polluted air. It peoples this transformed land with blind and crippled men and with widows and orphans. It is an extractive industry which takes all away and restores nothing. It mars but never beautifies. It corrupts but never purifies." Harry M. Caudill, Night Comes to the Cumberlands.

Mile 54 Pittsburgh Coal Seam

The Pittsburgh Coal Seam outcrops here; this is where it reappears along the Yough after being absent for about 12 miles. Geologist Jim Shaulis and friends cut away the brush so this is a good spot to take an up close and personal look at the coal that fueled the Industrial Revolution in Pittsburgh. You'll see veins of shale running through the coal. This is the stuff that gob piles are made from.

The Pittsburgh Seam, like all the coal in western Pennsylvania, is bituminous, or soft coal. Anthracite—hard coal—is mined in the eastern part of the state, one of the few places in the world where it can be found.

Native Americans called coal "rocks that burn." It was easy enough to come by. It outcropped from almost every stream bank.

British soldiers stationed at Fort Pitt dug it out of the side of what they called Coal Hill. Some of them had probably come from coal mining districts in England and joined the army to get out of the mines. Today, we call the hill Mt. Washington. The tourists who flock to the mountain to gawk at the view of downtown Pittsburgh are blissfully unaware of the maze of old coal mines that give the hill the consistency of a mound of Swiss cheese.

When it was first settled, the town of Connellsville had a public coal mine that hardly anybody used because they could buy it so cheaply. Colonel Crawford of Connellsville showed the coal seam to his friend George Washington who looked at it approvingly but never showed any interest in mining it.

Because of where it outcropped, it came to be known as the Pittsburgh Coal Seam. Many writers added the adjective "fabulous" in front of it and indeed it was. It was called the most important geologic formation in the history of the world.

> *"From the Pittsburgh coal bed in the four states of Pennsylvania, Ohio, Maryland, and West Virginia has been produced an output that, at mine prices, represents a greater value than any other single material deposit in the world has yielded."* The Pittsburgh Coal Bed—Its Early History and Development, Howard N. Eavenson, 1938.

It kept that status until the development of the Middle East oil fields and the Wyoming coal fields. Think about this: the Pittsburgh Coal Seam produced more wealth than all the gold, silver, lead, and copper mines out west combined. And it's still being mined.

> *"The value of the gold and silver production of the country in the year 1904 was: gold, $84,551,300; silver, $53,603,000; total, $138,154,300 . . . .The value of the Pennsylvania production of coal . . . for the year 1904 was about $550,000,000."* Report of the Pennsylvania Department of Mines, 1904.

Generally speaking, the Pittsburgh Seam is deeper to the south. Up north, it's almost at the surface. In northern Washington County, it's shallow enough to strip mine. In Greene County, just 50 or so miles to the south of Washington, it's about 400 feet below the surface. The mining pattern runs from north to south and inward from the rivers.

The early mines were drift mines, that is, they just dug into the side of a hill and followed the "drift" of the coal. Just about anybody could start his own coal mine, and many did. As the older mines played out, the deeper, bigger, more expensive and more productive mines were opened.

Pittsburgh Seam coal is good stuff: relatively low in sulfur, high in heating potential, and producing relatively little ash when it burns.

But the human cost of mining coal, even coal as rich as the Pittsburgh Seam, as Henry Caudill so eloquently put it, was more often than not "hideous."

> *"Since 1870, Pennsylvania's Annual Report on Mining Activities has recorded 51,483 deaths from mining accidents—31,113 deaths in anthracite mines and 20,370 deaths in bituminous mines."* PA Department of Environmental Protection.

You've passed the scene of the major mine disasters at the Port Royal and Darr Mines. And while the death toll at these mines was significant, that was only a small part of the picture. Men were killed or injured practically every day in the mines from roof falls, explosions, electrocution from the trolley wires that powered locomotives in the mine, and a myriad of other causes.

And the statistics don't include the slow lingering death from Black Lung, the aptly-named disease acquired from a lifetime of breathing coal dust.

Today, underground coal mining is vastly safer than in the bad old days, but men still die underground and there's another insidious plague attached to deep mining today: mine subsidence.

Longwall mining is the order of the day underground. That is, a continuous mining machine grinds away the coal in passes a couple of hundred feet wide. When the mining machine is finished, the roof is allowed to fall behind it. Pittsburgh Seam coal runs 6 to 8 feet thick, and the rock between the mined out area and the surface 400 feet or so above drops accordingly. Foundations crack, roads buckle, streams and wells go dry.

And there are still the gob piles, but now, they're huge monstrosities that fill in whole valleys. The coal companies are careful to keep them away from public view, but they're still an environmental nightmare.

So note well the black rock you see exposed here and keep this in mind: the most productive deep mine in the United States is in Greene County, Pennsylvania. And Greene County is one of the poorest in the state.

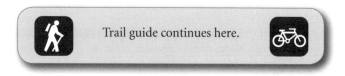

Trail guide continues here.

Mile 54

You'll notice a "bag wall" here. Its purpose is to protect Texas Eastern's pipeline from erosion. The bags are filled with a mixture of cement and water that hardens nicely into a wall.

Mile 54.1 Rainey

Back in the bushes along here are the remains of the Fort Hill Coke Works that was operated by the W. J. Rainey Company of Cleveland. Rainey was an arch-competitor of Henry Clay Frick, but never achieved Frick's wealth and power.

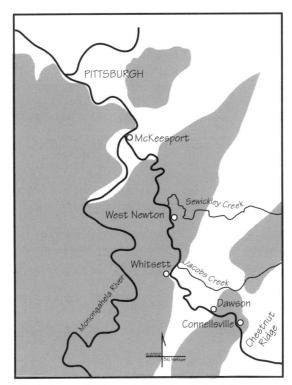

Shaded areas indicate the Pittsburgh Coal Seam.

The Fort Hill works was Rainey's first acquisition in the area; he became the second-largest coke producer in the Connellsville coke district. Fort Hill was opened in 1880 just as the P&LE was being built and was the first coke works on the new railroad in Fayette County. It started with 36 ovens and grew to 186 beehive coke ovens in tiers up the hillside. Rainey also operated banks of newer rectangular ovens that lent themselves to mechanized loading and unloading. Seventy-seven employees worked the ovens and adjacent mine.

Rainey had a coke works (called the Rainey Works) directly across the river from here and there was a bridge to connect them. The piers were laid in 1882 for a railroad bridge from the B&O side of the river to access the coal on what's now the trail side. The building of the P&LE negated the need for a railroad bridge, but it became a dedicated mine railroad to take coal from the Fort Hill works to the Rainey works across the river when the mine played out. The piers are still visible, and there's a footpath down to them.

This Fort Hill is not related to the Fort Hill on the trail in Somerset County; it was named for A. J. Hill who sold the property to Rainey and was the works' first manager. But the P&LE called the station here Rainey even though the Rainey works was across the river.

Fort Hill closed in 1920.

The interpretive sign was an Eagle Scout project done by a local lad.

CHAPTER 9: CONNELLSVILLE NORTH

Crawford Avenue in downtown Connellsville was still the *place to shop when this shot was taken about 1945. The automobiles wait while the shoppers board the trolley which is going to Scottdale, Mt. Pleasant and Greensburg, according to the sign on the front.* West Penn Railway. Photo courtesy of Pennsylvania Trolley Museum.

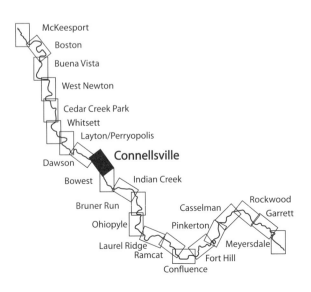

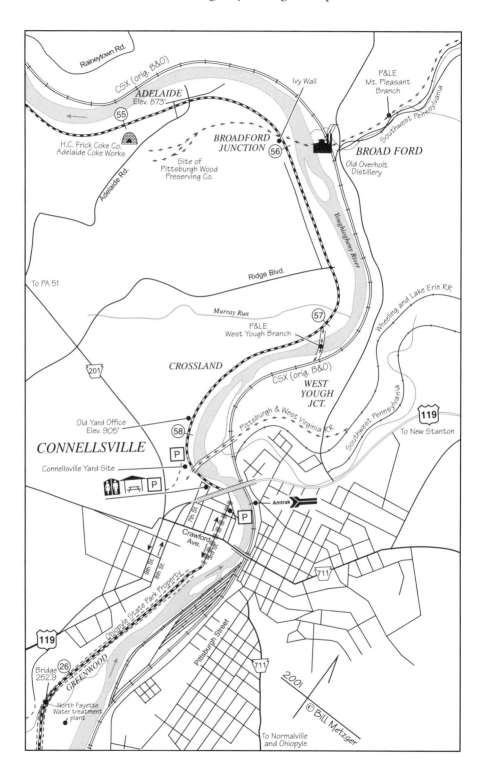

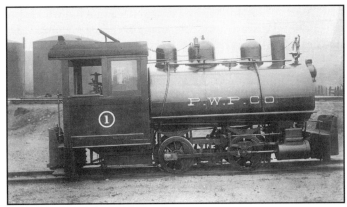

This little locomotive, which was built by the Porter Locomotive Works in Pittsburgh in 1920, worked at Adelaide pushing carloads of railroad ties around the creosote plant. Bill Metzger collection.

Mile 55-55.5 Adelaide

Both the town and coke works were named for Adelaide Childs Frick, wife of Henry Clay Frick. Adelaide Coke Works (also known as the Cupola Works) opened in 1888 and closed in 1923. It operated 375 beehive coke ovens and employed 230. It worked the Pittsburgh Coal Seam.

Unlike most of the mines along the Yough, the Adelaide mine was a shaft mine that dug down about 100 feet before it reached coal. (The argument could be made that given how they treated their miners, all these mines were shaft mines.)

Pittsburgh Wood Preserving Co. built a creosote plant here about 1920. It was sold to Koppers Co. and lasted until the early 1960s. Just as the name implies, the purpose of the plant was to preserve wood, mostly railroad ties, with creosote. The ties were loaded into special railroad cars and placed in an autoclave where, at high temperature and pressure, the creosote was impregnated into the wood. A creosote-treated railroad tie lasts about 10 times longer than an untreated tie.

The campground store and snack bar here has toilet facilities, but don't be a jerk and use them without buying anything.

 Take a break here to learn about a local industry titan, or resume following the trail guide at Mile 55.9 below.

HENRY CLAY FRICK

Since we're at the town named for his wife, it's time you learn about Henry Clay Frick, arguably the richest—and often the most hated—man to ever come out of the Yough Valley. Henry Clay Frick's grandfather, Abraham Overholt, was a well-to-do Mennonite farmer, businessman, and distiller. His father, John, was a ne'er-do-well from Ohio who got Frick's mother in a family way and married her, much to the chagrin of Granddad. The old man, to show his disapproval of the union, gave the young couple the two-room springhouse on the property to set up housekeeping. This is where H. C. Frick and his sister were born.

Young Clay, as he was called, was by all accounts a frail kid who contracted just about every childhood disease known to man, including rheumatic fever, which plagued him throughout his life. The other thing which plagued him all his life was a desire to live up to the expectations of his grandfather. Even though Frick's father eventually became a wealthy man, John Frick never measured up as far as his father-in-law or son were concerned. Clay was a hard working young lad, though, when he wasn't laid up with some ailment or another, and went clerking in a store when he was 14. At 17, he went to work at the Broad Ford distillery just when the beehive coke business was starting to get rolling, as luck would have it, just across the railroad tracks.

Frick saw the potential for coke and traded the booze business for beehives. He asked Judge Thomas Mellon, founder of Mellon Bank, for a loan to build his first 50 ovens. Impressed with young Frick's attitude, Mellon gave him the loan. When Frick realized the economies of scale that building 50 more ovens would bring, Mellon gave him an additional loan against the advice of his loan officer.

Young Frick worked hard at the coke business, and was doing well when the Panic of 1873 hit hard in the new coke region. Frick worked a deal to sell his uncle's railroad that ran from Broad Ford to Mt. Pleasant to the B&O and talked them into giving him a commission. The uncle was in financial trouble and the railroad deal bailed him out, but lost him his properties.

Frick had cash at a time when most people didn't and used the money to buy up coal properties in the Connellsville area at rock bottom prices. When prosperity returned, Frick was in an excellent position to sell coke to the booming Pittsburgh steel market. And sell he did, making a fortune in the process.

During the Panic, Frick set up a company store for the convenience of his employees and a scrip system so they could buy goods when there was no cash. Somewhere along the line, he realized the money that could be made from a company store in addition to mining coal and coking it. As a result, his stores generally accounted for 20% of a coke works' profits. Other coal companies also saw the potential and the hated company store/scrip system was born.

He made his first million by the time he was 30 and celebrated by smoking a five-cent cigar and moving out of his two room house in Broad Ford for more posh digs in Pittsburgh. The country pup from West Overton started running with the big dogs in the big city and befriended Andrew Mellon, son of the judge. Frick and Mellon did

Some of the crew from Frick's Adelaide Works stood on the hillside to get their picture taken. The tipple and powerhouse for the mine are to the upper right and a locomotive and larry car are to the upper left. Bill Colbert collection.

Henry Clay Frick.
Courtesy West Overton
Museum.

a turn around Europe in 1880. Returning home, Frick met the fair Adelaide Childs, of the manufacturing Childses, wooed and wed her, and on their honeymoon, took her to meet Andrew Carnegie.

Meeting Carnegie was a turning point in Frick's life, one that many would argue was a turn for the worse. The Carnegies—Andrew and his brother Thomas—were Frick's best customers for coke and through a series of machinations, the H. C. Frick Coke Company was formed with Andrew Carnegie as the majority stockholder. In many ways, it was a deal with the devil.

Carnegie, for all his later philanthropy, was a ruthless businessman who stopped at nothing in his almost pathological quest to make steel at the lowest cost, then make a 200% profit on it. Carnegie "was making 25 million dollars a year when his workers were making 15 cents an hour," said Martha Sanger in her book *Henry Clay Frick, an Intimate Portrait.* Frick became Carnegie's partner in the steel business as well as the coke business. And he was Carnegie's hatchet man.

It was a partnership that was stalked by death.

In 1891, 131 coal miners were killed in an explosion at Frick's Mammoth Mine in Westmoreland County. Also in 1891, striking workers rioted at Frick's Morewood Coke Works. Official reports say eleven strikers were killed by guards protecting the property. Unofficial reports say probably twice that were killed.

Frick's daughter Martha died that same year of complications from swallowing a pin, and he spent the rest of his life mourning her.

In 1892, steelworkers went on strike at Carnegie's Homestead Works. Frick closed the mill and ordered in replacement workers (scabs), hiring agents from the Pinkerton Detective Agency to protect the property. The resulting Battle of Homestead left seven workers and three Pinkertons dead. Frick, by then the chairman of Carnegie Steel, did the dirty work while Carnegie was staying at his castle in Scotland.

Between them, Frick and Carnegie set the tone for management-labor relations for half a century. The dictum was profits first always, people were nothing more or less than economic units; pay them as little as you could get away with, work them for 12 hours a day, and fire anybody who dissents.

It wasn't until the 1930s that the United Steelworkers finally won an 8-hour day in the steel mills.

Frick and Carnegie had a monumental falling out in 1899-1900 and characteristically, Carnegie tried to cheat Frick. Frick called Carnegie a "God damned thief," according to Sanger, and that was the last time they ever spoke to each other.

Both men went on to become philanthropists, Carnegie building libraries, museums, and schools, and Frick endowing hospitals, parks, and art museums. Before Frick died, Carnegie sent a mutual friend to ask if Frick would shake his hand one last time. Sanger relates that Frick told the friend he would "see Carnegie in Hell which is where we are both going."

At his death in 1919 at the age of 70, Frick had amassed a fortune worth $150 million and willed 5/6 of it to charitable works. But all that charitable giving never erased Frick's memory as a tyrant among miners and steelworkers.

His daughter Helen lived well into her nineties and devoted her life first to caring for her father while he lived and to protecting and nurturing his legacy after he died.

Today tourists visit the Frick Art Museum in Pittsburgh and Frick's house Clayton that Helen preserved exactly as it was when her father died. They marvel at the art displayed and the gracious living of what has been called the Gilded Age. But in the Mon and Yough valleys, where the backbreaking toil of thousands of workers paid for all that graciousness, Frick is still more often than not, a dirty word.

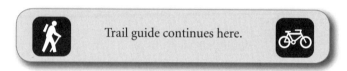

Mile 55.9 Broadford Junction

Broad Ford was an old river crossing so named because, well, it was a broad ford across the river on a branch of the Catawba Trail. There's an island in the stream made by the outwash from Galley Run that made crossing easier.

If you go down toward the river here, you can see the bridge piers from the abandoned P&LE Broadford Branch. It was originally the Youghiogheny Northern Railway and was built to tap the coke ovens across the river. It opened in 1883 and was abandoned in 1945, but the last train is said to have run over it in 1921. It ran through the Overholt Distillery on a steel trestle and up the valley of Galley Run to a place called Summit Transfer, about five miles away. The valley was a busy place when this line was built—there were coke ovens, two railroads, a road and the Run in an area that wasn't more than 100 yards wide at most spots.

A footbridge was built under the railroad bridge so distillery managers who lived across the river could walk to work. It stayed intact after the rest of the bridge was torn down.

On this side of the river, the P&LE called it Broadford. The B&O called it Broad Ford. They both pronounced it the same, though.

Overholt Distillery

The yellow brick buildings and chimney across the river belong to the Overholt Distillery, makers of Old Overholt whiskey. Local wags often referred to the stuff as "Old Overcoat" from the way you felt the morning after you drank it. The Overholt in question was Abraham Overholt, grandfather of Henry Clay Frick. Although he belonged to a religious sect that was by design teetotaling, he didn't mind making booze or imbibing a glass of the stuff first thing every morning.

> *Rye whiskey, rye whiskey, rye whiskey I cry*
> *If I don't get rye whiskey,*
> *I surely would die*

Traditional folk song

This serving tray from the West Overton Museum collection shows the Broad Ford distillery at its peak. The train in the foreground is on the Baltimore and Ohio tracks. It's crossing under the bridge for the P&LE's Mt. Pleasant Branch. The broad boulevard in the foreground is somewhat fanciful. Courtesy West Overton Museum.

Abstinence then wasn't the big issue that it became later. Whiskey often served as legal tender in Western Pennsylvania in the early years of the 19th century. It was certainly more valuable than a pack of Federal "greenback" paper money. Aside from its obvious use, it was valued as a disinfectant even before the notion of bacterial infection was understood. It had use not only in treating wounds but in treating dubious drinking water; a quart of whiskey in a couple of gallons of water made it safe (and fun) to drink. It also made a fair anesthetic.

Abe Overholt purchased the family farm as a young man in what's now West Overton about five miles from the trail, and the property included a still, like many farms in the area at the time. He promptly increased the size of the still and prospered making "Old Farm" whiskey.

Needing more space, Overholt built a new distilling operation at Broad Ford in 1853. At Broad Ford they made Monongahela Rye and Youghiogheny River Rye. After Abe died, they made Old Overholt in his honor.

The new distillery passed to his sons, then one of his grandsons, Abraham Overholt Tintsman. Enter Henry Clay Frick, another grandson, who hired out as a clerk in the distillery when he was still a kid.

Frick used the experience he gained in the whiskey business to good advantage in the coke business and through some slick maneuvering wound up owning the Broad Ford distillery. His friend Andrew Mellon bought a one-third interest in the operation and then another third after Frick died. The operation kept expanding with major renovations in 1899 and 1914.

During Prohibition, which started in 1919, the distillery continued in operation producing whiskey "for medicinal purposes" and doctors would write prescriptions for the stuff.

Bear in mind that Mellon, the two-thirds owner, was Secretary of the Treasury from 1921 to 1932. Prohibition lasted until 1933.

The Overholt Distillery closed in the late 1950s and was bought out by Jim Beam, who still makes "Old Overholt 4 Year Old Straight Rye Whiskey" with old Abe's picture on the label. We hear from those who know these kind of things that it's "zesty and cheap as blazes." But now they make it in Kentucky.

Mile 56

The English ivy wall on the bank and the accompanying steps led up to the home of John Overholt, nephew of Abraham Overholt. He used the railroad bridge to cross over to the distillery.

There was a small railroad yard here called Mayville Yard that served the coke works and the creosote plant. Why it was so named is lost in the mists of history.

Mile 57 Crossland

It's named for either for Colonel A. J. Crossland, a coke operator who managed a coke works across the river, or his cousin Greenbury Crossland who was a landowner with extensive holdings in Fayette County. There used to be an ornamental iron gate here mounted on the concrete posts, and just to add to the confusion, there was another Crossland in Fayette County just east of Uniontown which was an H. C. Frick coke works.

Mile 57

The railroad bridge across the river here carried interchange traffic between the P&LE and the B&O. The station on the B&O side was called West Yough Transfer; the P&LE called the line the West Yough Branch, all 0.19 miles of it. The bridge is owned by the Regional Trail Corporation, but as of now there are no plans for it, and they'd just as soon you didn't walk on it.

The nicely-done picnic shelter was an Eagle Scout project.

Mile 57.5

The mysterious concrete foundation built into the side of the hill held up a signal bridge that governed the entrance to Connellsville Yard.

Mile 58 Connellsville Yard

The green block building was the Connellsville yard office where the yardmaster gave orders to switching crews, the crews reported to work and clerks kept the records. The sign says "Connellsville Station," but it's not a station and never has been. The building was heavily vandalized after the railroad was abandoned; local thugs even cut a hole in the roof and stole all the plumbing.

The Fayette County Horse Owners Association rode to the rescue and completely rebuilt it. Today, the horsemen use it as a meeting room and make it available for meetings to other civic groups.

The steel shed was built by the Yough River Trail Council to house their equipment. You're now in the Connellsville Yard and just about at the end of the P&LE Yough Branch. Here's where the passenger trains tied up between runs, local freight traffic was loaded and trains from the Western Maryland were received and dispatched. There was also an interchange here with the Pennsylvania Railroad.

The P&LE officially ended at Crawford Avenue. Conversely, the Western Maryland started at the same point, but we won't talk about the WM until the trail is officially on it.

You may notice a bridge to nowhere over Route 119. This is what's left of the Connellsville Viaduct that connected the two railroads in 1912. If you look at the tower in the Yough Glass building, you'll notice a door way up there. This was at track level.

Most of the Viaduct was torn down about 1995.

 Be advised that this area isn't a particularly safe place to park, as car break-ins occur regularly.

Pittsburgh and West Virginia Bridge

The bridge that crosses the river here marks the eastern end of the Pittsburgh and West Virginia Railroad (see map page 9). It's 1,499 feet long and, like Banning Trestle, was opened in 1930. George Gould would have loved to have seen this bridge because this finally completed the missing link of his transcontinental railroad scheme. But the empire had long since collapsed and so had George.

As railroad bridges go, this one was relatively short lived—it was only in service for 45 years. It became redundant when the Western Maryland was abandoned in 1975 and a connection was made across the river with the B&O, by then the Chessie System. Today the Wheeling and Lake Erie, the successor to the P&WV, still connects with CSX here, but only runs one train or so a week.

Connellsville Park

The bottom of the paved ramp (which has a handicapped-accessible 5% grade) marks the end of the Yough River Trail North.

Colonel William Crawford. The caption under this rendering says it's "*from a portrait of doubtful authenticity.*" Centennial History of Connellsville.

The trail now runs through Connellsville's Riverfront Park. There are restroom facilities, water, picnic pavilions, and a stage where, should you be inclined, you can show off your prowess at the Frug and the Hustle or do a heartrending rendition of *Feelings*.

When the trail leaves the park, it's separated from traffic on Third Street. The red light at Crawford Avenue is activated by bikes on the trail, so if you go real, real slow as you approach the intersection, the light will change and you won't have to stop. Or just let somebody else go ahead and let them trip the light so you can ride through.

Colonel William Crawford (1752-1782)

The little cabin tucked away by the Route 119 bridge is the re-creation of the home of William Crawford, one of Connellsville's first residents. Crawford was born in Berkeley County, Virginia, now West Virginia. His family was visited often by George Washington. Washington taught him surveying and

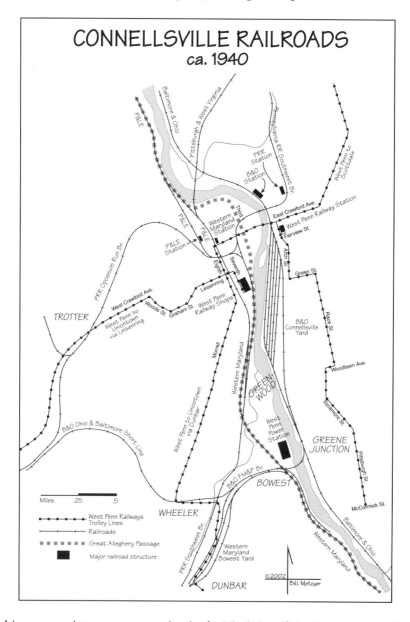

CONNELLSVILLE RAILROADS
ca. 1940

got him an appointment as an ensign in the Virginia militia. He came west for the first time in General Forbes' campaign, where he attained the rank of captain, and returned bringing his family in 1765 after the Indian wars were over in this area.

Crawford built his cabin here and started a farm on the meadow land along the river. He was known to have brought several slaves with him to help with the work. His wife Hanna and four children moved here in 1766. He originally farmed and made his living as a surveyor. The cabin sat within a few feet of Stewart's Crossing on the Braddock Road, and the Crawfords' frequent visitors included some of the most noted people of the time.

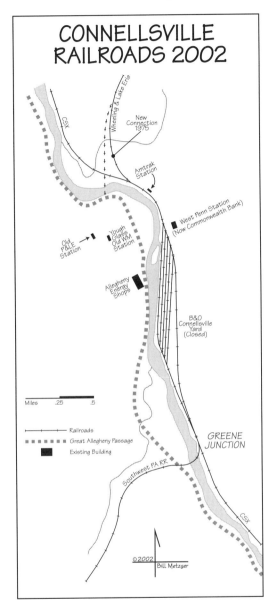

CONNELLSVILLE RAILROADS 2002

Wheeling & Lake Erie

CSX

New Connection 1975

Amtrak Station

West Penn Station (Now Commonwealth Bank)

Old P&LE Station

Yough Glass Old WM Station

Allegheny Energy Shops

B&O Connellsville Yard (Closed)

Miles .25 .5

——|—— Railroads
■ ■ ■ ■ ■ Great Allegheny Passage
■ Existing Building

GREENE JUNCTION

Southwest PA RR

CSX

©2002 Bill Metzger

On one of George Washington's visits, so the story goes, some local yahoos proposed a wrestling match and cast some aspersions about Washington's abilities. George took on all comers, beating each one of them and almost killing the last one of the bunch.

Crawford served as a justice of the peace for three different counties, but made the mistake of siding with the Virginians when they claimed this part of Pennsylvania in Lord Dunmore's War. The locals didn't look kindly upon this and booted him out of office in 1775.

He joined the Army in 1776, rising to the rank of colonel in the Revolutionary War, and was respected as a leader. After he returned home, he was asked to go to Ohio and fight against the Indians at Sandusky. The mission was to destroy a couple of Indian villages. The Indians had other ideas and captured Crawford. To show their displeasure, they burned him at the stake.

Hanna lived in the little cabin until she died, well into her nineties, living on a pension from her husband's military service.

One of the Crawfords' daughters, Ann, married Zacharia Connell, who was the founder of Connellsville. "But wait!" you say. "Wasn't Colonel Crawford here first?" And you'd be right, of course, but the Crawfords didn't live in Connellsville—the town on this side of the river was originally named New Haven. Crawford today is remembered for the county in northwestern Pennsylvania that bears his name.

Connellsville

There's a story that's been going around for years that Fayette County had more millionaires per capita at one time than any place in the world or the country. It may even be true; there was certainly a lot of money here, but it's one of those things that "everybody knows."

The Western Maryland station in Connellsville, the building that now houses Yough Glass, as it looked in 1917. Both P&LE and WM passenger trains stopped here. The tracks ran through town on the "high line." Courtesy Western Maryland Railway Historical Society.

However many zillionaires per cubic centimeter there were, one just needs to amble down Pittsburgh Street ("Millionaires Row") in Connellsville to view the extent of the conspicuous wealth. There are churches—many of them—that would be the pride of cities twice this size; there's the hulk of a once-grand opera house and mansions with stained glass windows by the acre. Connellsville *was* once twice this size: 22,000 people lived here in 1909. Today, 9,146 do.

Speaking of grandeur and gilt, the Carnegie Library on Pittsburgh Street should also be mentioned. If you've never seen an original Carnegie Library in the grand scale, this is the place to visit one. Carnegie loved to build libraries—he built 2,507 of them—but he usually didn't provide for books or maintenance.

A cynic would say that the Pittsburgh Street churches were no mere expressions of piety but an attempt to regain the good graces of the Almighty after committing the multitude of sins against the land and humanity necessary to strike it rich in the coal and coke business. But to be fair, the money didn't just come from the mines and ovens.

Connellsville once was home to two steel mills, a railroad car manufacturing company, a pump manufacturing company, two breweries, two distilleries, the largest lock factory in the world (Slaymaker), a safe manufacturing company, a brickmaking company and several glass manufacturing concerns, not to mention a myriad of smaller manufacturing companies including, of all things, a cigar maker. There was even a fledgling movie industry for a while.

That's in addition to the West Penn Railways' repair shops and the B&O's yard and shops. Altogether, five railroads and the trolley line came together in Connellsville.

The grand bank buildings along Crawford Avenue are ready proof of the big bucks that once earned their compound interest here. Crawford Avenue was the Wall Street of the Connellsville Coke District. The lifeblood of the *Daily Courier*, which still publishes, was news of the coal and coke industry. Commodity prices, mine openings and closings, strikes, accidents, and happenings on the railroads were all front page news.

In the glory days from the 1880s to the early 1910s, there were in the neighborhood of 40,000 beehive coke ovens at work in Fayette County alone. One history book shows a photo of the door of a beehive coke oven with the caption "gateway to wealth." Which it was, if you owned the oven.

Crawford Avenue was also where everybody from miles around shopped, brought in by the West Penn Railway's big orange trolley cars.

In many respects, Crawford Avenue, like so many similar main streets in the region, is now sort of like a period movie set, frozen in time from the coal and coke days. Downtown has changed little because there's very little economic incentive for it to change. Most of the retail business is in the strip malls along Route 119.

The big businesses still left in Connellsville are the Crown Cork and Seal Co., which makes lids for baby food jars, and the Anchor Hocking Glass Co., which makes Rolling Rock Beer bottles. The West Penn Railways became West Penn Power which became Allegheny Power. They still maintain their transformers and equipment here in the old trolley shops. The B&O became CSX and the yards, what's left of them, are used to store surplus railroad cars. The repair shops are closed. Some railroad crews still work out of Connellsville, but railroad employment is a mere fraction of what it once was. The rest of the mills and plants just up and died.

The good news for happy trail users is that Connellsville has welcomed the trail with open arms. Crawford Avenue is festooned with trail banners and a section of Third Street has been turned over to trail use. New trail-related businesses like restaurants and B&Bs are doing well in town. Should you be hungry for junk food, Connellsville's the last time you'll see any on your way up the trail to Meyersdale. There are junkerias on both sides of the river, so feed your grease and salt jones now.

The place that's now Connellsville was important before it was ever a town. It's where the Yough became "navigable," if you could call it that. When the water was high, you could float down to the Forks of the Ohio and points west and south. When the river was low, which was most of the time, you walked.

But more than that, this is where the Catawba Path crossed the river on its way from Olean, New York to the Carolinas, Kentucky, and Tennessee. Paul A. W. Wallace, author of *Indian Paths of Pennsylvania*, says this trail was " . . . one of the most important Indian highways in North America. It was known by many names as it passed through Pennsylvania: the Great Catawba War Path, the Iroquois Path, the Iroquois Main Path, the Iroquois Main road, the Cherokee Path, the Tennessee Path. With the connections it had at each end, it extended from Canada to Florida and west into the Mississippi Valley." This, folks, was an Indian Interstate and Connellsville was sort of an aboriginal Holiday Inn.

A branch of Nemacolin's Path that ran from Cumberland to Brownsville took off from near what's now known as Jumonville on the top of Chestnut Ridge, and joined the Catawba Path. This is the path that was made into a road by General Braddock's troops on their way to Fort Duquesne. They crossed here both on their way to what they thought was imminent victory over the French and back from what proved to be a humiliating defeat. Braddock's Crossing was about where the old stone bridge pier sits out in the river.

There was another ford here known as Stewart's (or Stewardt's) Crossing for William Stewart who lived here for a time, then left when Native Americans started uprising. It was also known as the Second Crossing of the Yough; the first was the Great Crossing at Somerfield on what's now the Yough Lake. It was about where Crawford Avenue crosses the river today.

Boatbuilding was a flourishing industry for about 50 years in Connellsville before the railroad came, just like West Newton downstream, and for the same reasons: a road crossing, good (sort of) navigation and plenty of timber. Flatboats carried immigrants to the west and shipped iron ingots to market downriver when the water was high. (See Yough River Navigation back in Chapter 3)

The old bridge pier in the middle of the river by the Riverfront Park boardwalk supported three bridges between 1816 and 1860, all of which either fell down or washed away. The river's shallow here because it runs over the outwash from both Mounds Creek to the north and Opossum Creek to the south.

It was laid out as a town in 1793 by Zacharia Connell, son-in-law of Colonel Crawford.

New Haven

The trail runs today through what was originally the town of New Haven, where Colonel Crawford lived until he was toasted by the Indians. Crawford's farm wound up in the hands of the Isaac Measons, father and son of the same name, who laid out a town in 1796. The Measons were ironmasters who had a furnace near here and were in their time the wealthiest family in Fayette County.

There are streets named Meason and Crawford in Connellsville.

Meason's home, which he called Mt. Braddock, still stands south of Connellsville. It's private property, but you can go up the drive and take a look at it.

There was, early on, a dam across the river between New Haven and Connellsville that powered a gristmill and a woolen mill operation that passed through a series of owners, all of whom met with financial disaster. The mill building became the National Locomotive Works, which also went belly up in 1878. The mill was torn down after that. It sat on the corner of First Street and Crawford Avenue.

New Haven and Connellsville merged in 1906.

Yough Trail South

As soon as you cross Third Street and go by the blue building and through the gate here, you've entered the Youghiogheny Trail South, owned and operated by Ohiopyle State Park. This particular section of trail was opened in 1995 up to the bridge.

The railroad grade you're riding on here was originally the Pennsylvania Railroad's Southwest Secondary, a line that ran from Greensburg to Fairchance, PA. It was first and foremost a coal- and coke-hauling line, and was built by the Pennsylvania as direct competition to the Baltimore and Ohio. There were places in Fayette County where a five-year-old could throw a rock from one railroad and easily hit the other.

This piece of the Southwest Secondary was abandoned in 1976 when it was not included in Conrail. You're only on this piece of railroad for about 0.4 mile, but this being a complete guidebook, it's worth noting.

West Penn Railways

The complex of buildings on the bank side of the trail belong to Allegheny Power, successor to West Penn Power. It's their main transformer and equipment shop now, but at one time it was the heart of West Penn's extensive trolley empire that connected Connellsville to the coalfields and the rest of western Pennsylvania.

By 1890 the science of electric propulsion was pretty well figured out and electric-powered railroad vehicles, commonly named trolleys for the little wheel that ran along the wire and powered the cars, came into vogue. There were several reasons for the trolley's popularity: roads were terrible; railroads were expensive—a normal railroad passenger train required a crew of five to operate—and, being propelled by steam locomotives, were dirty; trolleys didn't pull anything but themselves, so the track could be built to looser (and cheaper) standards of sharper curves and steeper grades. Since they were clean, people didn't mind having a trolley line run down their street and since they were cheap to operate and only required a one- or two-man crew, they could run more frequently.

Like Canal Fever and Railroad Fever before it, Trolley Fever hit the country hard. Everybody wanted their own trolley line. And, like every other Fever that has ever hit, there were fortunes made on trolley lines and, more often than not, fortunes lost.

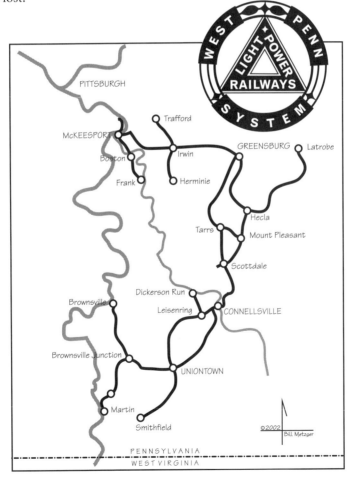

Generally, electric railways fell into two categories: street railways and interurbans. Street railways were the city lines and interurbans ran between cities. At first, Connellsville had both; they merged into West Penn Railways who operated everything.

The big orange West Penn cars were a fixture in the coal fields from 1900 to 1950, bringing reliable transportation to coal patch towns that otherwise would be hopelessly isolated at the end of a rutted and muddy road.

The cars brought people into Connellsville, Uniontown, and Greensburg to shop and just see the sights of the big cities. If you wanted to see a really big city, the train took you to Pittsburgh, but you could take the trolley, too.

West Penn's system lasted longer than most; it survived until the Fifties, but like most every other electric railway line, it too died because of the automobile, paved roads, and television. The last West Penn cars ran in August, 1952. Nobody wanted to take the trolley into town when they could stay home and watch TV. And the trolley's leaving was the beginning of the end for the downtowns of Connellsville, Uniontown, and Greensburg.

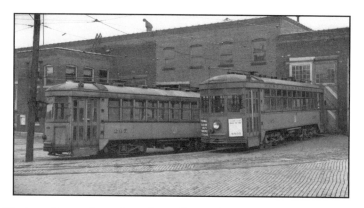

The Allegheny Power shops along the trail are where the West Penn Railways built and maintained their fleet of trolley cars. These two cars operated in the town of Connellsville. Remember how we told you about railroads being built to standard gauge of 4'8.5"? All the trolley lines in western Pennsylvania were built to what was known as Pennsylvania Broad Gauge, or 5'2.5", 6 inches wider than standard gauge. Near as anybody can tell, there was no good reason for it, but to this very day Pittsburgh's streetcars run on broad gauge track.
David C. Cope photo, courtesy Pennsylvania Trolley Museum.

CHAPTER 10:
CONNELLSVILLE SOUTH/
BOWEST

Train crews used to change at Bowest. Here, a Western Maryland crew from Cumberland is getting off the train and a Norfolk and Western (formerly Pittsburgh and West Virginia) crew is getting on to run to Pittsburgh. The jitney, technically called an auto-railer, made the run from Bowest Yard in Dunbar to the junction because there was no easy road access between the two points. It was numbered T-200 and is a product of the Kalamazoo Motor Company, which used the engine and hood from a 1940 Ford. T-200 is preserved at the Baltimore and Ohio Railroad Museum in Baltimore.

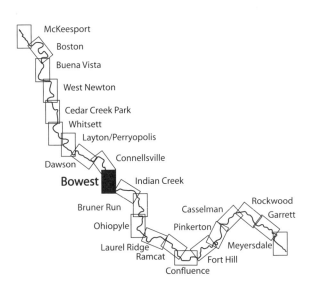

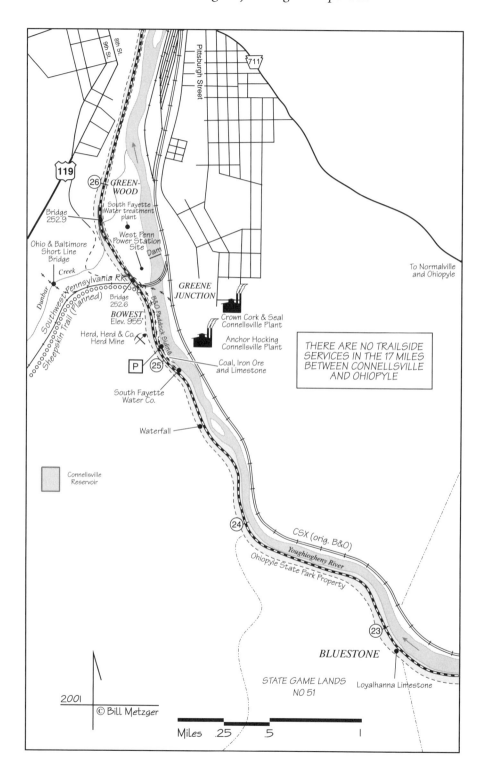

THERE ARE NO TRAILSIDE
SERVICES IN THE 17 MILES
BETWEEN CONNELLSVILLE
AND OHIOPYLE

Mile 26 Greenwood

This is one of those railroad-only names that denotes the spot where the Western Maryland and Pennsylvania railroads interchanged traffic. This is also where the Western Maryland and Pittsburgh & West Virginia railroads changed crews on their through freights. In 1956, the whole hillside collapsed and closed the railroad for almost a week—bad news for the railroad, good news for fossil hunters. The big boulders along the trail are fossiliferous. Say that out loud. Fossiliferous.

Mile 26 is the first you'll encounter on the Yough Trail South. Mile 0 is at Confluence.

Bridge No. 252.9, deck plate girder bridge, 731.5' long

Now we're on the Western Maryland Railway. It's time to talk about the bridges you're going to cross and how they're designated. This bridge was called No. 252.9 by the Western Maryland. That means it was 252.9 miles from Baltimore, Maryland. Remember, these are railroad miles, NOT trail miles. This is a plate girder bridge.

Steelmakers at the time the railroad was built (1910-12) couldn't roll long wide beams, so they made big girders by riveting a series of relatively small square plates together. It's called a deck plate girder because the railroad was built on top of the girders. The other type, through plate girder, means the railroad ran between the girders.

Like most of the bridges on the Western Maryland, the piers on this one were built to accommodate two tracks in anticipation of increased traffic which never came.

This particular bridge is built on a three degree curve. Civil engineers measure curvature in degrees. You really don't need to know how to figure degrees of curvature except to say that the fewer degrees, the wider the curve and the more degrees the tighter.

As we've seen above, some railroad bridges are girder bridges. Some are arches, be they steel, stone or concrete. Some are trusses—you'll go through one here in a couple of hundred feet—and some few are even trestles. And we've just hit on one of your author's pet peeves: somewhere along the line, somebody decided that every railroad bridge is called a "trestle" no matter what it's made of or how it's made. THEY'RE NOT ALL TRESTLES. You'll cross a trestle this trip, even though it's not called that. We'll be sure and tell you when we get there. So what should you call a railroad bridge? "Bridge" is just fine, thank you.

This bridge crosses Dunbar Creek, a stream which rises up on Chestnut Ridge. This particular stream had been despoiled by the Dunbar Furnace steel plant, but it's now becoming a respectable trout stream, with some native fish being caught.

The Pennsylvania Railroad Southwest Secondary also crossed under here on its way south to Fairchance.

Soon as we come off the bridge, we're on a high fill. The railroad built fills over areas like this because they were cheaper than building bridges.

Sit down on the bench here and we'll talk about the Western Maryland Railway for a bit or, if you're ready to move on, skip forward to Milepost 25.4 below (look for the hiker and bike symbols.)

Western Maryland Railway

By any account, this was a fine railroad—a good looking and well run company. It was a spit-and-polish operation that was old-fashioned bordering on quaint by the 1970s. Its locomotives were always clean and shiny, stations and wayside buildings always sported a fresh coat of gray paint with maroon trim, and the track was top notch. Some competing corporate weenie once called it "over maintained."

But it made money, at least before and after George Gould.

The Western Maryland began life officially in Baltimore in 1852, then spent the next five years figuring out where it was going to go, how it was going to get there, and who was going to pay for it.

Hagerstown, Maryland became the destination, although construction was stopped for a spell by the Civil War, then reached Hagerstown in 1872. The line played a vital role at the Battle of Gettysburg, bringing in thousands of men and tons of material, then evacuating the wounded and prisoners.

It experienced a growth spurt in the 1880s, but was still less than 100 miles from Baltimore. Much of its financing came from the City of Baltimore, who owned a

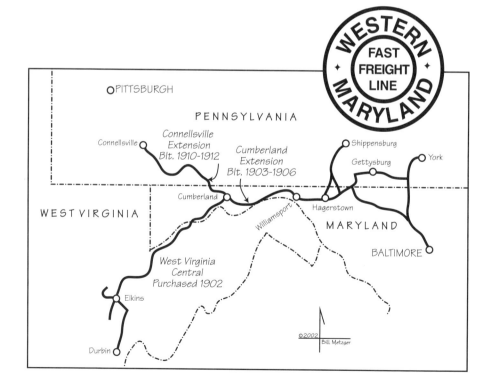

majority of its stock. The city put the railroad up for sale just in time for Gould to look upon it as the eastern anchor to his transcontinental system.

There were four bidders for the Western Maryland, but Gould and friends put in the winning bid of $8 million cash and a promise to build a tidewater terminal facility in Baltimore. Up to that time, the line ended on the edge of town. Gould made good on his promise; he built Port Covington near the site of old Fort Covington in Baltimore Harbor. This was a fine facility capable of loading grain, coal, and merchandise into oceangoing vessels. It was also quite expensive to build.

Soon after buying the WM, Gould purchased the West Virginia Central, a conglomeration of coal and logging railroads that ran north from the West Virginia coalfields into Cumberland. He was going to use coal from the WVC to finance some of his operations. To connect up with the WVC, Gould also set to building the very expensive Cumberland Extension from Big Pool to Cumberland. Even though the new line followed the Potomac Valley, it did so by a series of very pricey tunnels and bridges that straightened out the river's meanders. The scheme was dependent on being able to sell coal from the West Virginia Central in the Northeastern markets, but soon as Gould bought the WVC, that avenue was shut off.

The WVC had been sending coal to the northeast by way of the Baltimore and Ohio, the Western Maryland, and the Reading, a friendly arrangement that had lasted for years. But the Baltimore and Ohio controlled the Reading, and the Pennsylvania Railroad controlled the B&O. Word came from Pennsylvania Railroad headquarters to end the agreement *now* and a big chunk of Gould's income was cut off. Stifled from earning new funds, the WM went bankrupt in March, 1908. As

Judging from the cars in the train, this is a rare photo of Western Maryland Train No. 2, the Baltimore Limited, underway. It looks like it's approaching the west end of Salisbury Viaduct shortly after the railroad opened and the train was inaugurated in 1913. The steam shovel in the background is a clue the railroad is still new. The Baltimore Limited, and its companion the Chicago Limited, was, according to the railroad, a "solid electric-lighted train, vestibuled coaches and smoker, with Pullman drawing-room sleeping car." The service only lasted until 1917. The locomotive No. 203 was a Pacific type built especially for the new service.
Courtesy Meyersdale Public Library.

noted elsewhere, one by one after that, each of the Gould railroads went belly up and the empire collapsed.

But the new post-Gould Western Maryland had become a very valuable property. John D. Rockefeller recognized that fact, and bought heavily into the WM. Now reorganized as the Western Maryland *Railway* (it had been the Western Maryland *Rail Road*) with renewed (surprise) connections, the new management decided it still needed an outlet to the west.

Flush with Rockefeller money and an agreement with the Vanderbilts' P&LE to interchange traffic at Connellsville, the Western Maryland Connellsville Extension, the very railroad beside which you now sit, was built. It had already been planned in the Gould era. The railroads agreed to interchange traffic for 99 years. When the WM was abandoned, the agreement still had 36 years to go. Now they interchange people. Rockefellers, by the way, were on the boards of both railroads.

Maynard Sembower collection.

It took two years, from 1910 to 1912, to complete the 87-mile line at a cost of $10-12 million. It had already been surveyed by the Gould people, so the plans were ready to go.

The completed result was a fine railroad with great steel bridges, gentle curves and the easiest grades of any east-west line in the East. The ruling grade eastbound is only 0.8%. Westbound, it's 1.75%, but bear in mind that most of the heavy traffic—grain, coal and steel products—was eastbound, either for export or for the wealthy markets of the northeast.

You're sitting between two of the structures that the Western Maryland built. There are plenty more to come.

Western Maryland Passenger Service

It's a very safe bet to say that more people have ridden the Western Maryland's Connellsville Extension as a trail than ever did as passengers when it was a railroad. Passengers were never a big deal on this line. By the time the Western Maryland entered the picture, folks had been traveling merrily on the B&O for 40 years; the WM was the new guy in town. They tried their hand at pair of deluxe Baltimore to Chicago trains, the *Chicago Limited* and the *Baltimore Limited*, but these were no competition to the B&O's fleet of trains.

Western Maryland's *Limiteds* only lasted about four years. After that, a pair of local trains soldiered on until they were finally taken off in 1931. Even today, if you have a hankering to ride a passenger train along the Yough and the Casselman, all you have to do is call Amtrak. They'll be happy to sell you a ticket.

The Alphabet Route

Although the mainstay of the Western Maryland was hauling coal, it also enjoyed an excellent reputation as a mover of merchandise freight. In fact, it often billed itself as "the Fast Freight Line," competing successfully for business against the other bigger railroads in the Northeast.

It got the nickname "the Alphabet Route" when the P&WV was finished into Connellsville in 1931. A through route was set up from Chicago to New York using six different railroads. What made this routing successful was general heads-up railroading. Engines were used to their best advantage and crew changes were accomplished quickly. "The Alphabet Route" involved the Nickel Plate Road (New York, Chicago & St. Louis), the Wheeling and Lake Erie, the Pittsburgh & West Virginia, the Western Maryland, the Reading, and the Central Railroad of New Jersey. The poor clerks who had to type this routing on waybills typed: NYC&StL, W&LE, P&WV, WM, RDG, CNJ.

The nickname stuck and some marketing genius capitalized on it naming the fast trains the "Alpha Jets." These were the hottest trains on the railroad. The Western Maryland would pick up the trains at Connellsville and run them to Harrisburg, PA and vice versa. Everybody on the Western Maryland knew you didn't mess with the Alpha Jets.

If The Western Maryland Was So Great, How's Come I'm Riding My Bike On It?

The Western Maryland was redundant from the day it was built, but you have to consider the time. As we've discussed previously, the Pennsylvania Railroad had a virtual stranglehold on Pittsburgh traffic moving east and what made it worse was they controlled the B&O. Pittsburgh industrialists were desperate for relief and had been for decades. The Western Maryland was a godsend.

But times changed. The Rockefellers had been one of the major stockholders in the Western Maryland and played an instrumental role in financing the Connellsville Extension. But after World War I, they divested themselves of WM stock and the B&O, by then independent, purchased a 40% controlling interest in their most direct competition. To avoid problems with federal and state regulators, the B&O placed its WM stock in trust with the Chase Manhattan Bank and both railroads competed hotly with each other.

They also cooperated. There were emergency connections between the two lines at Ohiopyle, Confluence, and Sand Patch in case of derailment and they freely exchanged traffic at Hagerstown, while maintaining the fiction that they were independent railroads. But in the early 1960s, things started to change. Western Maryland management looked at the long term situation and saw themselves as a very small railroad in a world that was increasingly being populated by giants. Other railroads were merging and creating larger systems and the WM saw its costs increasing and projected revenues decreasing. Since it was already owned by the B&O, there was no prospect of merging with somebody else.

Western Maryland bit the bullet and went to the B&O and said that maybe it was time to consolidate the two operations. At first, things moved slowly, even imperceptibly, but after the B&O/C&O merger was successfully completed, management turned its attention to the Western Maryland. In the early 1970s the word went out that the Western Maryland was near the end. The WM's fine locomotive fleet started turning up all over the east coast and looked dirtier and more forlorn each day. Traffic was diverted and piece by piece, the Connellsville extension was taken out of service. The last through trains only used the old Western Maryland main line from Ohiopyle to Bowest, then it, too, was shut down in 1975.

A couple of coal mines around Rockwood and Meyersdale kept some of the track active for a few more years but Western Maryland was, for all intents and purposes, dead. The few trains that ran over what was left of its tracks were mere ghosts.

But weep not for the proud "Wild Mary." The track might be gone but the beautiful right of way and the fine structures got saved.

And you get to ride your bike on them.

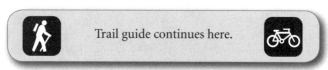

Trail guide continues here.

Bridge No. 252.6', deck plate girder and through truss bridge, 746.9' long

Both this bridge and the Greenwood bridge were rehabilitated by the Commonwealth of Pennsylvania in 1994 at a cost of $827,000. Rehabbing included new decks and railings.

You'll notice that neither bridge has been repainted. None of the old railroad bridges on the trail have been. Reason? They don't need it. The wooden decks will need to be replaced long before the steel will need to be repainted. A couple of things wear out a bridge quickly: weight and corrosion caused by salt. The couple of thousand pounds a day these bridges carry on a heavy day now is nothing compared to the thousands of *tons* they were designed for, and they're never exposed to salt, the killer of bridges.

Ohio & Baltimore Short Line

This graceful Romanesque arch belongs to the abandoned Ohio and Baltimore Short Line, which was once projected to run from Connellsville to Washington, PA, but only 3 miles were built.

If you direct your gaze southward as you stop and take in the scenic vistas from this bridge, you'll notice what appears to be an overgrown Roman arch. This is one of the tangible remains of the Ohio and Baltimore Short Line, another grand scheme in the grand tradition of railroad grand schemes that John Garrett (you'll come across a town named for him up the way), then president of the B&O, started to build in 1873 and again in 1881 to bypass Pittsburgh. Pittsburgh was becoming quite a bottleneck for railroads and this line would run from Connellsville here, through Washington, PA, to Wheeling, saving the B&O several miles and a lot of time.

Much money was spent, some grading done in both Fayette and Washington Counties, about three miles of actual railroad was built and that was about it. The three miles got abandoned in 1941, but the abandoned archway does make a great-looking ruin.

The "Sheepskin" Line

If, while you're stopped here, you gaze toward the river, you will espy Greene Junction, where the railroad crosses the river. The railroad here was originally the B&O's Fairmont, Morgantown and Pittsburgh Subdivision, aka the FM&P, aka the "Sheepskin" line, originally built as the Fayette County Railroad Company in 1860. It ran from Connellsville to Morgantown and Fairmont, West Virginia and served the coal and coke regions down there.

The Sheepskin moniker came about because supposedly a farmer called it a "sheep skinning railroad" after the first train over the line scared his sheep.

The line was abandoned as a through route in 1991 and cut back to Smithfield, PA. The remaining track was purchased by Fayette County and is operated by the Southwestern Pennsylvania Railroad under contract. The Southwestern Pennsylvania runs from Greensburg to Smithfield and does a thriving business on lines the bigger railroads deemed unprofitable. It runs down to Uniontown a couple of times a week, so the chances aren't real good you'll see a train on it. But if you do, it's considered good juju. Seeing a train on the SWP while you're crossing over it means the rest of your ride will be pleasant and scenic.

West Penn Railways Revisited

One of West Penn Railway's lines from Connellsville to Uniontown also ran under this bridge. The substation on the riverside marks the site of the old West Penn power station. The coal-burning station supplied electricity to the whole West Penn railway system and to other electricity users for 50 miles around. It was built in 1906, closed in 1954, reopened for a while in 1956 and dismantled in the early 1960s. Power House Dam still stands to supply the water intake for

The West Penn Connellsville Power Plant shortly after it was expanded. The Western Maryland bridges are in the background. The bridges and dam still stand. Courtesy Miller Library, Pennsylvania Trolley Museum.

the North Fayette Water District pumping station and is the last remaining dam on the Yough between Confluence and McKeesport.

Continuing to gaze to the north, you see a series of empty bridge piers upstream of the active bridge. These were also built for the Ohio & Baltimore Short Line and were only used for about 20 years.

> *"Remember about mountains: what they are made of is not what made them. With the exception of volcanoes, when mountains rise, as a result of some tectonic force, they consist of what happened to be there."* John McPhee, Assembling California.

State of the art 1911 railroad construction at Bowest. The concrete piers for the two bridges have been poured and the fill between them is almost done. The "dinkey" engine is pushing six dump cars full of rock across the spindly wooden trestle—this really is a trestle—to be dumped on the fill. By the time job is finished, the trestle will either be filled in or torn down. The view is westward toward Connellsville; the tracks in the foreground are the B&O "Sheepskin" Line and the tracks in the valley belong to the Pennsylvania Railroad Southwest Branch. Courtesy Rivers of Steel Archives.

Mile 25.3 Bowest

"Bowest" is a contraction of B&O and Western Maryland. This is where the Western Maryland branched off to the south to join with the Sheepskin line. The WM served several mines in the Fairmont, West Virginia area and used the B&O's tracks to get to them.

The Western Maryland had a railroad yard about a mile south of here named, oddly enough, Bowest Yard. The closest town was the old iron and steelmaking town of Dunbar, home of the Dunbar Furnace Company and currently home of '50s teen idol Fabian. Dunbar Furnace made steel from locally-mined coal, iron ore, and limestone. Portions of it lasted until the early 1950s. Dunbar Furnace owned much of the land along the trail for the next several miles. Fabian owns 20 acres near Dunbar.

Bowest was also a crew change point where Western Maryland crews from Cumberland would change with Pittsburgh and West Virginia Railroad crews from Pittsburgh. There was a telegraph office here and track maintenance buildings.

The grade that's presently blocked off on the bank side of the trail will become part of the planned Sheepskin Trail that will run from here to Morgantown, West Virginia. Construction should begin in the near future.

It's not often that you can stand at an exact spot and say, "a whole geologic province begins right here," but that's precisely what you can do at Bowest. As soon as you ride off the bridge you leave the Pittsburgh Low Plateau and enter the Allegheny Mountain Section. This is where the trail meets Chestnut Ridge, a mountain that runs about 90 miles in a north northeasterly direction from the Cheat River in West Virginia near Morgantown up to where it peters out in Indiana County, Pennsylvania.

The part of Chestnut Ridge you see across the river is about 2,100 feet high. On a clear day from atop the ridge, you can easily see the skyline of downtown Pittsburgh, 40 miles away. From on top the mountain looking west, you have no notion of the valleys and ridges of Western Pennsylvania. The horizon is so flat from atop Chestnut Ridge that you can see the curvature of the earth.

A traveler going due west from this point (roughly 40 degrees north latitude) will not encounter 2,100 feet again until Kearney, (CARney) Nebraska, a thousand miles from here. Our traveler wouldn't start seeing mountains—the Rockies—until 150 miles further west of Kearney at Julesburg, Colorado.

The abandoned brick building down along the riverside belonged to the Southwest Water Company.

Mile 25.2

The little AMD waterfall running out of the hillside is coming from the Herd Mine, owned by Herd, Herd and Co. Washington Herd was the president and Homer Herd was the vice president. The Herds didn't do business with the Western Maryland but loaded their coal on the B&O siding below. They employed 50 men at this mine and worked the 36-inch Lower Freeport coal seam. The mine was active in the 1910s.

Mile 25 Iron Ore, Limestone, and Coal

Stop and take a break at the bench by the gate where the access road comes up from the pumping station. Before the two bridges were finished, this was a trail head of sorts for the Connellsville end of the trail. The locals still use it.

But more importantly, you can sit here and see exactly why there was an iron-making industry in Fayette County. All the ingredients are right here within reach: iron ore, coal for coke, limestone for the flux, and good transportation.

The roaring noise you can hear from here is from the Crown Cork & Seal and Anchor Hocking factories.

There's also a gun club across the river. You can often hear them going bang bangity bang. Pay them no mind.

Mile 25 North Fayette Water District

The pumping station along the river belongs to the North Fayette Water District now, but it was originally built in 1880 by the Trotter Water Company, which was owned by H. C. Frick and supplied water for coke quenching at the Leisenring and Trotter coke works and for drinking water to the local communities. The road to the station was originally a spur of the B&O railroad called the Paddock Siding. It was used to bring in coal to run the steam-powered pumps.

The reason Frick put the pumping station here is that his various coke plants were busily polluting the water downstream. This is the last place where the water was good.

The station pumps water from the river up to a reservoir on the hill.

You will notice railroad rails driven into the roadbed on the bank side of the trail. This is the remains of a slide fence that protected the line from rockslides. The fence was wired to trip the signals to "stop" if there was a slide.

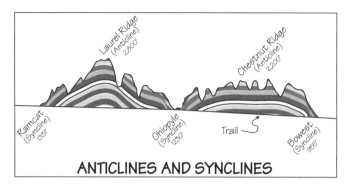

ANTICLINES AND SYNCLINES

Anticlines and Synclines

Take a bedsheet or a tablecloth and push it. You get a pile of wrinkles. That's exactly what happens to a continent when another continent pushes it. The top of the wrinkles are called anticlines and the bottoms or troughs are called synclines. You're traveling through the Yough Gorge which is a series of anticlines and synclines.

The tops of Chestnut Ridge and Laurel Ridge are anticlines and Ohiopyle and Confluence sit on synclines.

When you start into the gorge at Bowest, you're entering the Chestnut Ridge anticline. The big mountain-pushing effort ran out of steam right about here. West of here, the ripples get smaller and much less noticeable.

As you enter the gorge and the anticline, you're going back in time. Going west to east as we are, the layers of rock you pass through get older and older until you get to about Mile 20.6, then they start getting younger again. When you get to Ohiopyle you get to the top of the stack, then the process is repeated through Laurel Ridge and Negro Mountain.

It's important to remember that the river is actually older than the mountains. While the mountains were rising, about 250 million years ago at the end of what geologists call the Permian Period, the river stayed pretty much in the same place and cut through them. To the non-geologist, 250 million years is known generally as a "hell of a long time ago."

This was also 50 or so million years ago before the dinosaurs started roaming the earth, to coin a phrase, so chances are good that a triceratops or two moseyed through the Yough Valley.

But as the mountains rose, they were also being torn down by the river that became known as the Youghiogheny. At one time, the land was probably a mile higher than it is now.

Here's something else to remember about anticlines and synclines: anticlines fracture and synclines compress. When the anticlines fracture, cracks open up and begin the eroding process. The compressed rock in a syncline bunches together and is resistant to eroding.

To summarize your geology lesson: the mountains rose up, cracked and were worn down by the river over a really long time. What you ride through today is what's left.

Mile 24.5 Waterfall

Just off the trail is a beautiful little waterfall that makes a cool place to take a lunch break. It makes a musical sound like a Japanese garden. As far as I know, it doesn't have a name. But the water falls over Pottsville Sandstone.

Mile 24 State Game Lands

If you're doing this section of the trail in the spring or fall, don't be surprised if you see chaps riding mountain bikes or walking down the trail wearing lots of orange clothing and carrying guns or bows and arrows. They're hunters and they're making use of the State Game Lands that the trail runs through in this section of the gorge. They're allowed to be here.

State Game Lands in Pennsylvania are state-owned property where it's legal to hunt. In fact, it's encouraged. Hunters pay for the game lands through their hunting licenses. Other states call them wildlife management areas but that brings to mind images of bears and bunnies in business suits sitting behind desks.

It's legal to hike and mountain bike on trails in the game lands, but you're not allowed to camp or build a fire.

The immediate trail right of way is owned by Ohiopyle State Park, and it's illegal to hunt on the trail, but hunting is permitted in most of the rest of the park. Game Land No. 51 was purchased by the Western Pennsylvania Conservancy and turned over to the state at cost in 1978.

Oh, and nobody's allowed to hunt in Pennsylvania on Sundays and it's illegal to shoot bicyclists every day of the week, so don't worry. But during deer hunting season, it's a bad idea to wear a brown jacket and have a white handkerchief sticking out of your back pocket with a Walkman with antennas on your head. A real bad idea.

Mile 22.8 Bluestone

The Dunbar Furnace Company had a siding here that was given the name because this is where the Loyalhanna Limestone outcrops. Loyalhanna Limestone is serious good stuff—it's what the whole trail is surfaced with. It's a sandy limestone that packs well and sets up almost like concrete. Trail builders use it also because it's cheap—at least the screenings are. Limestone screenings or "fines" are what's left over when limestone is crushed. The big uses of fines are for rail trails and horse racing tracks.

The Loyalhanna Member of the Mauch Chunk Formation is about 50 miles wide and 500 miles long. There are several quarries along Chestnut Ridge that mine it for construction purposes other than rail trails, believe it or not.

Mile 20.6

The broken rocks in the small stream here mark the middle of the Chestnut Ridge Anticline. You have been going back in time. Now from here to Ohiopyle you're going forward.

Weather in the Gorge

"Since Laurel Ridge is oriented at right-angles to approaching weather systems, it forces the prevailing westerly airflows upward. As the rising air cools, the moisture it contains can condense. If the level of moisture reaches the saturation point, precipitation results. Additionally, the mountain can act as a barrier and slow the movement of storms, prolonging their impact on the local area." A Hiker's Guide to the Laurel Highlands Trail, Sierra Club, Pennsylvania Chapter.

What this means to you is that if it's going to rain here, chances are it's going to rain harder and longer than every place else. Be governed accordingly.

Also figure that it's 1.5 degrees cooler for every 500 feet you gain in elevation, so Meyersdale at the present east end of the trail will be about 5 degrees cooler than McKeesport.

Its hard to believe that monsters like this once traveled on the railroad that's now the trail. This engine, called a Challenger type, had 20 wheels and weighed, fully loaded with coal and water, over a million pounds. It was 121 feet long, one of a group of 12 built in 1940 and '41 especially for the Connellsville Extension. All of these engines were scrapped in 1953. Courtesy Western Maryland Railway Historical Society.

CHAPTER 11: INDIAN CREEK

In the 1870s, after the Pittsburgh and Connellsville Railroad was completed, William Henry Jackson (1843-1942) took a series of pictures of the scenic wonders of the new line. He paused here to photograph Indian Creek. Mouth of Indian Creek by William Henry Jackson, c. 1872. Courtesy Library of Congress, Prints and Photographs Division, Detroit Publishing Company Collection (LC-D43-T01-1736).

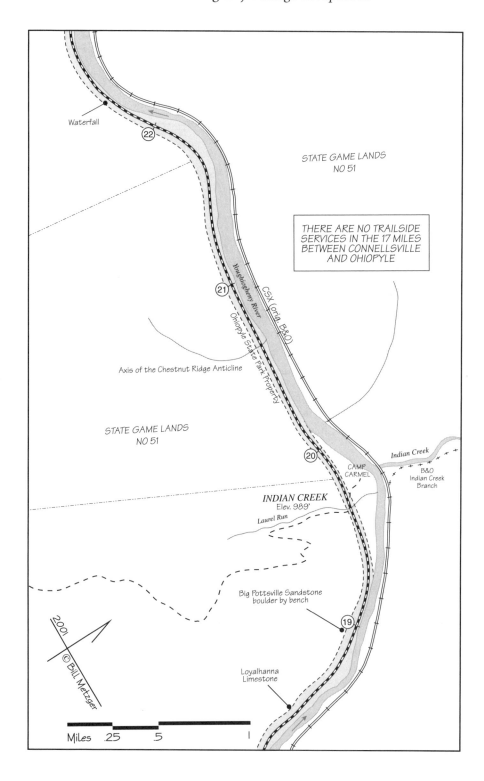

Waterfall

㉒

STATE GAME LANDS
NO 51

THERE ARE NO TRAILSIDE
SERVICES IN THE 17 MILES
BETWEEN CONNELLSVILLE
AND OHIOPYLE

Youghiogheny River

CSX (oria. B&O)

Ohiopyle State Park Property

㉑

Axis of the Chestnut Ridge Anticline

STATE GAME LANDS
NO 51

Indian Creek

㉔

CAMP
CARMEL

B&O
Indian Creek
Branch

INDIAN CREEK
Elev. 989'

Laurel Run

Big Pottsville Sandstone
boulder by bench

㉑⑨

2001 © Bill Metzger

Loyalhanna
Limestone

Miles   .25   .5   1

Mile 19.6 Indian Creek/Camp Carmel

The timber in this part of the Gorge is at least third growth. The first cutting of the old growth timber was to make charcoal for the local iron furnaces. There were two near here: the Old Laurel Furnace, and the New Laurel Furnace just upstream. They operated from 1797 to 1835. The cleverly-named New Laurel Furnace came second.

Some of the timber was also cut by small family operations and floated down the river in rafts to Pittsburgh. Some of it was cut to build flatboats for trade and western immigration.

The second cutting was for mine props and railroad ties. The McFarland Lumber Co. had a sawmill at Indian Creek across the river on the B&O side. They built a bridge to carry their railroad across the river and up Laurel Run before the Western Maryland was built. The operation lasted from 1900 to 1906.

The town of Indian Creek was across the river at the mouth of its namesake stream. The Western Maryland also called their station on this side of the river Indian Creek, even though the stream is Laurel Run. There are many Laurel Runs in Pennsylvania. This is merely one of them.

The Western Maryland had a telegraph office here and water facilities for the steam locomotives fed by a dam up Laurel Run. There were several houses for the railroad personnel.

Today Camp Carmel is a church camp owned by Christians for Camp Carmel, Inc., a non-profit organization affiliated with the Baptist Church. The camp was originally built by the McKeesport YMCA, which sold it to its present owners in 1953. It's private property.

Indian Creek across the river was famed by the B&O as a photo location to pose their trains. The stone bridge on a curve made for a great shot, but other than that, Indian Creek was the site of a B&O station, McFarland Lumber Company's sawmill, a junction for the Indian Creek Valley Railroad, and a town with 25 homes. The bridge still stands, but now it's a ghost town.

The Indian Creek Valley Railroad was 22 miles long and operated as far north as Kregar, which is on the other side of the Pennsylvania Turnpike. The line spawned a network of logging railroads that ran up every hollow on the west side of Laurel Mountain. At its peak, four passenger trains a day traveled the line and connected with the B&O. After the logging ended, several mines opened up along the line. It was bought by the B&O in 1926 and abandoned in 1972. A portion of the old line is now a rail trail between Champion and Indian Head. It's about 6 miles long and makes for a pretty ride if you ever get up that way.

Mile 19 Pottsville Sandstone

When you sit at the bench here, there's a huge boulder on the other side of the trail. This is Pottsville Sandstone. You can actually hear Pottsville Sandstone. This hard rock is what makes all the rapids in the river, including the Ohiopyle falls. The splashing noises are the persistent sound of the river trying mightily to wash the sandstone away. Some day, of course, it will, but the rock has been making the river really work at it for thousands of years. All the boulders you see strewn along the hillsides in the gorge are Pottsville Sandstone. It's the most important rock formation in the entire gorge. Rock strata (layers) are named for the place where they were first discovered to outcrop. This one was identified in Pottsville, PA, clear across the state.

It's hard rock with quartz crystals in it, which is why it's still around cluttering things up. It's also slightly acid, which makes it a favorite of mountain laurel. You can track the sandstone layer on the mountainside by following the laurel growth. A spring that rises in sandstone is generally "soft" water, because there's little dissolved in it. "Hard" water comes from limestone which dissolves easily.

Pottsville Sandstone wound up on top of the rock stack when the Alleghenies were washing down during the last several ice ages. Geologists estimate that erosion washed away 20 to 30 meters of rock every million years or so. When the land here heaved up to form Chestnut Ridge and its neighbors Laurel Hill and Negro Mountain, softer rock underneath the sandstone was eroded away by the river. The hard sandstone broke up into room-sized boulders.

During the Wisconsin Ice Age of 20,000+ years ago, there was freezing and thawing. Gravity kicked in and there was downslope movement, the big rocks sliding down on soil that was like Jell-o. When the climate warmed up, the boulders quit sliding. The big rocks you see are in pretty much the same place they were when Native Americans lived here.

Mile 17.9 Fossil Bearing Red Beds

The jumbled rock you see here is siltstone from the Mauch Chunk Formation. It's a petrified beach that bears ripple marks from a long-vanished seashore. There's also petrified worm tracks, and if you look closely, according an unnamed geologist, you can see petrified worm poop.

Mile 17.1 Pipeline

The little jog in the trail and the rocks where you can sit and enjoy the great view of the river valley are there because of Texas Eastern's pipeline. This particular line connects a pumping station at Berne, Ohio, with Chambersburg, PA, part of a network from Texas to the Northeast. It was built in 1993 before the trail was constructed. The woods across the river are owned by the Western Pennsylvania Conservancy and are part of the Fallingwater preserve.

Indian Creek on the B&O was a favorite spot for photographers. This shot shows the new Western Maryland grade in the background.   Paul Dudjak collection.

Chapter 12: Bruner Run

The J. B. Davis sawmill that was the reason for the settlement of Bruner Run.
R.A. Baker photo, Van Sickel Collection.

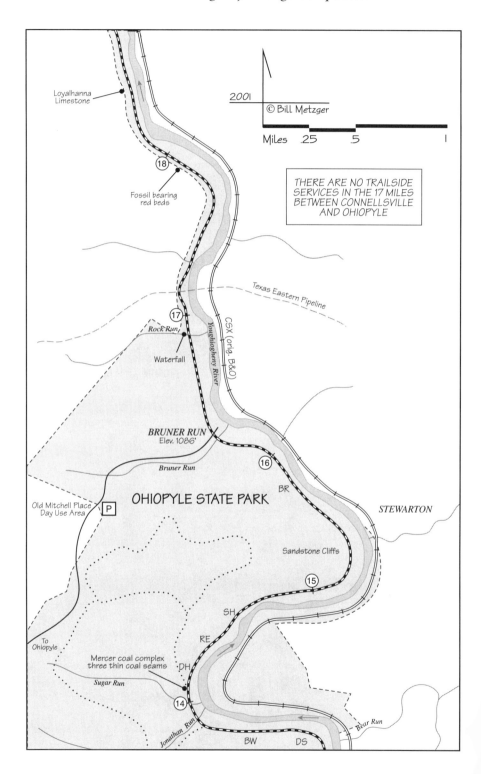

Loyalhanna Limestone

2001

© Bill Metzger

Miles .25 .5 1

THERE ARE NO TRAILSIDE
SERVICES IN THE 17 MILES
BETWEEN CONNELLSVILLE
AND OHIOPYLE

18

Fossil bearing
red beds

Texas Eastern Pipeline

17

Rock Run

Waterfall

CSX (orig. B&O)

Youghiogheny River

BRUNER RUN
Elev. 1086'

Bruner Run

16

BR

Old Mitchell Place
Day Use Area   P   OHIOPYLE STATE PARK

STEWARTON

Sandstone Cliffs

15

SH

To
Ohiopyle   RE

Mercer coal complex
three thin coal seams   DH

Sugar Run

14

Jonathan Run

Bear Run

BW   DS

Mile 16.4

Bruner Run is famous as the takeout point for Ohiopyle rafting trips, but from 1920 to 1925 it was the site of J. B. Davis' sawmill. Davis built a railroad that ran 7 or 8 miles up the stream and a sawmill on the flats where the takeout is. Supporting the sawmill were a boarding house, a store, and several houses. There was a cable suspension bridge across the river to get to the B&O station at Stewarton.

There was also a section house—a railroad track maintenance base—here.

This is yet another naming anomaly. The place name is Bruner Run, but the stream that flows down was originally Haney Run. And the Western Maryland originally called it Stewarton.

 The park people and the raft people would just as soon you didn't ride your bike down to the takeout. It just gets in the way. Also, be advised that the road crossing here is a bit dangerous.

As you go up the trail from Bruner Run toward Ohiopyle, you'll see a series of posts on the river side with two letters on each one. These mark the locations of emergency access to rapids on the river.

Here's what the letters stand for:

BR Bruner Run Rapid
SH School House Rapid
RE Rivers End Rapid
DH Double Hydraulic Rapid
BW Bottle of Wine Rapid
DS Dimple Rapids

This unsuspecting black snake was sunning himself on the trail when he was set upon by a geologist and a guidebook author with cameras. He is a harmless member of 11 species of snakes identified in Ohiopyle State Park. Two, the Northern Copperhead and the Timber Rattlesnake, are poisonous, but whether poisonous or not, leave them alone. It's illegal to kill them in the park and a bad idea everywhere else. Keep an eye out when you're riding the trail. That "stick" might have scales.

CHAPTER 13: OHIOPYLE

It's a pretty safe bet to say that this William Henry Jackson photograph from c. 1872 was one of the first taken of the Ohiopyle falls, showing the two old mills that used the falls for power. Courtesy Library of Congress, Prints and Photographs Division, Detroit Publishing Company Collection (LC-D43-T01-1741).

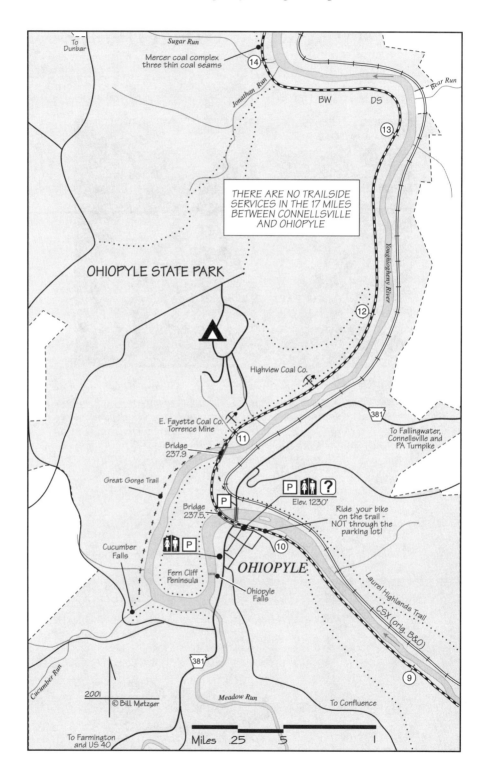

THERE ARE NO TRAILSIDE
SERVICES IN THE 17 MILES
BETWEEN CONNELLSVILLE
AND OHIOPYLE

OHIOPYLE STATE PARK

To Dunbar

Sugar Run

Mercer coal complex
three thin coal seams

Jonathan Run

BW   DS

Bear Run

Youghiogheny River

Highview Coal Co.

E. Fayette Coal Co.
Torrence Mine

Bridge
237.9

Great Gorge Trail

Bridge
237.5

Cucumber
Falls

Fern Cliff
Peninsula

Ohiopyle
Falls

OHIOPYLE

Elev. 1230'

Ride your bike
on the trail –
NOT through the
parking lot!

To Fallingwater,
Connellsville and
PA Turnpike

Laurel Highlands Trail

CSX (orig. B&O)

Cucumber Run

2001
© Bill Metzger

Meadow Run

To Confluence

To Farmington
and US 40

Miles   .25   .5   1

Mile 14

You can see three thin coal seams embedded in the cliff here across about a 30 foot interval. These are known as the Mercer Coal Complex, for Mercer, PA.

Mile 14 Waterfalls

In the spring and early summer when the streams are flowing briskly, both Sugar Run and Jonathan Run sport nice waterfalls.

Mile 11.5

This is the site of the Highview Coal Company's mine. Aside from the fact that it was working in 1921, nothing much else is known about it.

Mile 11

The Western Maryland had a spur on the downstream end of the high bridge that served several small coal mines. The old railroad grade is now the Great Gorge (hiking) Trail that follows the river. You can also see some foundations of the East Fayette Coal Company's Torrence Mine near here. It was a small mine that worked the Lower Kittanning Seam.

Mile 11 Bridge No. 237.9, Deck Plate Girder Bridge, 663' Long

This is known as the Ohiopyle High Bridge. It's about 100 feet above the river. When you cross this bridge, then the low bridge, you'll see how much the river drops in its trip around the Fern Cliff Peninsula. This bridge has been decked twice for trail service, first in 1989 and again in 1999.

None of the huge tulip poplars that grow around the east end of the bridge were here when the railroad was abandoned in 1975.

This is a good place to tell the story of the last passenger train on the Western Maryland. On May 21, 1975, the Chessie System, then-owners of the Western Maryland, ran a special train from Pittsburgh to Hancock prior to the abandonment of the line. Invited guests included conservation and government officials and some press from Pennsylvania and Maryland. The idea was to sell the soon-to-be-abandoned railroad as a recreation corridor of some kind. The rails to trails movement hadn't started yet.

Your author and a friend chased the train by car from Pittsburgh to photograph it because this was the last time we'd get a chance to see a train running on the WM.

We shot the train coming across the bridge at Greene Junction then high-tailed it to Ohiopyle where we set up at the high bridge. We got there in plenty of time.

"Oh boy," we said, "we're gonna have exclusive shots."

Here came the train, its headlight shining around the bend right before the bridge. Then it stopped.

The last passenger train on the WM Railroad.

Everybody got off the train and walked across the bridge ahead of it. And crowded around us. Then the train came across the bridge. Then everybody took their picture of the train coming across the bridge. So much for the exclusive shot.

We chased it as far as Deal and got a shot there. Then we got lost. We finally caught it sitting at the station in Hancock. We didn't even bother to shoot it there. It was already too dark.

There's a happy ending to this story. Out of that train trip came a commitment from the Western Pennsylvania Conservancy to purchase 10 miles of railroad in the Yough Gorge. And that was the beginning of the Great Allegheny Passage.

Mile 10.5 Fern Cliff Peninsula

The Fern Cliff Peninsula is not that big, maybe 120 acres, but it's been a National Natural Landmark since 1973 and with good reason. It's sort of a little world all its own: a mini-ecosystem.

It was created when the Yough River hit the Pottsville Sandstone at the top of the Ohiopyle (Ligonier) Syncline and was forced to make a hard left hand turn. It then dropped off the sandstone, creating the Ohiopyle falls.

It was last logged in 1911, but many of the original old growth oaks and poplars were left standing. It was scheduled to be logged again in 1951 but was not, through the efforts of Edgar Kaufmann, who purchased the peninsula and donated it to the Western Pennsylvania Conservancy.

A trainload of excursionists has just arrived at Ohiopyle on the B&O from Pittsburgh. The station and gazebo are located where the Fern Cliff parking lot is now, an area that was much more interesting then than it is now. A careful look at the picture will reveal three types of spans on the bridge: an iron truss, a wooden covered bridge and either an iron or wooden truss at the end. Courtesy Ohiopyle State Park.

Because the Yough flows north, it brought seeds up from southern Maryland and deposited them along the bank. Although the seeds don't come up here any more because of the Yough Dam, they thrived at Fern Cliff. Why? The steep banks create a mini-climate at the bottom. It's warmer down there, and southern species like Buffalo Nut do just fine.

True to its name, ferns cover the floor of the Peninsula and do well because of the dampness from the river.

The Fern Cliff Hotel was right by the falls, but its remains have pretty much disappeared. There was also a ball field near the trail that's growing up quite nicely. There were plans back around the end of the 19th century to subdivide the peninsula into town lots. Fortunately that never occurred.

The red pines with the red needles were planted by the Civilian Conservation Corps (CCC) in the 1930s. But the white pines, the ones with five needles, are native old growth trees.

The Baltimore and Ohio station stood where the parking lot is today and there was an emergency interchange track between the WM and the B&O here. The Western Maryland also maintained a telegraph office here.

 There are about three miles of marked *hiking* trails on the Peninsula. Don't ride your mountain bike on them and stay on the trails to protect the delicate ecosystem.

Bridge No. 237.5, Bowstring Truss Bridge, 621' Long

It's known as the Ohiopyle Low Bridge, but there's nothing low about it. As you may guess from looking at it, this is not an original railroad bridge. Part of the original bridge was removed in 1975 to improve clearances over Route 381 when the new highway bridge was built into Ohiopyle. And there the unused part of the old railroad bridge sat for years, looking like its sister up in Confluence that suffered the same fate.

Bridge No. 237.5, award-winning bowstring truss bridge at Ohiopyle.

The state park people, who owned it, tried all sorts of schemes to either adapt it or to get rid of it. They even advertised to try to get some movie maker to blow it up. No luck.

So finally they bit the bullet and designed and built the beautiful new bridge you see and cross today.

DCNR, the Pennsylvania Department of Conservation and Natural Resources, designed the bridge with remarkable sensitivity. They wanted the bridge to be functional of course, but it also had to blend in with its surroundings and provide an unobstructed view of the river. And they succeeded admirably. All told, the project cost $2.1 million and the universal opinion is that it was worth every penny. The experts agree. The bridge has won several national design awards.

When you stand on the bridge and look downstream, you'll see two blue ropes stretched across the river. These mean "don't go over the falls, you idiot."

One weekend a year, the state park lets kayakers go over the falls. The rest of the time, they're off limits to boating. So don't go over the falls, you idiot.

Ohiopyle, Population 76

It's almost axiomatic that any town in Pennsylvania that has "city" in its name isn't one. Case in point here is that Ohiopyle was originally called Falls City. Probably realizing that the place was never going to be even close to being a city, the non-city fathers reverted to Ohiopyle, the Native American name for "white frothy water," said to be derived from the word "Ohiopehhle" or "Ohiopehille." Then again, it might mean "Falls City" in a Native American language.

While we're on the subject of names, the B&O spelled Ohiopyle as one word and the Western Maryland used two: Ohio Pyle, just the opposite of what happened downstream at Broadford.

George Washington saw the falls in 1754 (see Confluence Chapter 16) and decided that it wasn't a real spiffy idea to take a canoe over them and went back upriver to Great Crossing (Somerfield) to start the French and Indian War.

There were bridges across the river here starting in 1854, but the place was still pretty isolated until the Pittsburgh and Connellsville Railroad (B&O) arrived in 1871 and Ohiopyle immediately became the place to be. Several hotels sprang up and the railroad ran special excursion trains up from smoky ol' Pittsburgh for folks to take the water and the mountain air. A round trip excursion ticket cost a buck.

At the peak of the railroad tourist era, there were five hotels in the area catering to a variety of tastes and income levels. Buildings lined both sides of Commercial Street, the main drag. The permanent population was estimated at the time to be about 400. Today it's 76.

The falls supplied power to a variety of mills and a thriving little community was built around tourism, flour milling, and logging. For a while the falls powered a small hydroelectric plant. Later in the 20th century, some coal mining took place, but it was never on the scale that took place downriver. The coal seams were small and hard to work. The water pollution they caused has long outlived them.

The Ohiopyle Company had a logging operation here that cut timber to the south. It worked from 1905 to 1920 and at its peak had a logging railroad that ran 26 miles up Big Meadow Run and through the hills.

After the big resort hotels went out of favor, the logging and mining played out and the excursion trains stopped coming, the town, like so many others in the Yough valley, went into decline and was headed for obscurity.

Enter Lillian McCahan, Edgar J. Kaufmann, and Mrs. Albert F. Keister.

Lillian McCahan was the spinster Western Maryland station agent at Ohiopyle. She is described as "a Jenny Wren of a woman, she was small, pert, hyperactive, extremely voluble, and fully capable of confronting opponents, especially male, of any size."

Kaufmann was heir to the Pittsburgh department store chain that bears his name and was the original owner and builder of nearby Fallingwater, the Frank Lloyd Wright-designed home.

Mrs. Keister was a socialite whose family owned property around Cucumber Run.

Kaufmann purchased the Fern Cliff peninsula and donated it to the Western Pennsylvania Conservancy. Mrs. Keister's family donated the Cucumber Run land. And Ms. McCahan, bless her heart, fomented and agitated for the preservation of the area, especially the peninsula, to all who would listen.

They were the leaders who set the stage. The Pennsylvania Department of Environmental Resources (now Department of Conservation and Natural Resources) and the Western Pennsylvania Conservancy began purchasing the land and receiving donations. All lands acquired by the Conservancy were turned over to the state at cost. After opening to the public in 1965, Ohiopyle State Park was formally dedicated in 1971. It has grown to encompass 19,052 acres.

> ⚠ The section of the trail from Ohiopyle to Confluence is somewhat problematic. To an experienced bicyclist, this section can be scarier than a highway with no shoulders full of people driving RVs. It's often full of inexperienced riders—folks on vacation who have never ridden a bike or never experienced the glories of a rail-trail. They often don't know the "rules of the road." Be very careful through here. The scenery, however, is wonderful. We strongly recommend riding this section during the week or early in the morning on a weekend.

Ohiopyle State Park

With the park, people came to Ohiopyle in droves. This little town now sees about 2 million visitors a year. They come to raft, kayak, canoe, swim, hike, ride bikes, camp, and to just hang out and soak up the scenery.

Besides the river and the bike trail, there are plenty of other reasons to come here. Ohiopyle State Park offers miles of hiking trails, great vistas from on top the hills, and Cucumber Falls. It's a prime spot for birding. The more than 40,000 acres of continuous forest make it a great migratory stop. Nearby are the two Frank Lloyd Wright-designed houses, Fallingwater and Kentuck Knob.

It can get crowded. On a nice summer weekend or in the fall when the leaves are at their peak, the way to get to Ohiopyle is to ride your bike in from Connellsville or Confluence. Forget driving in here and trying to park. Even getting off the Turnpike at Donegal can be a challenge.

There are all the necessary services in the town of Ohiopyle or the park. But, if you're through-biking on the trail, and want to camp, be advised that the Ohiopyle campground is at the top of a very steep hill.

Mile 10 Ohiopyle Visitors Center

Stop in the station and say "hi" to whoever is at the desk. They know all kinds of cool stuff like where the bathrooms are, where the trail is, and where the falls are.

Like so much of this trail, the fact that the Ohiopyle station still stands is remarkable. It was used as a maintenance base in the last days of the railroad and was saved from destruction by the park.

What this station has in common with thousands and thousands of other small town stations across North America is its layout. It's in three sections. The current information area was the waiting room. This is where you bought your ticket or picked up your telegram. There were usually benches lining the wall and one in the center to wait for your train. After 1931 when the last scheduled Western Maryland passenger train stopped here, the railroad turned it into a locker room for the local track maintenance crew.

The center section with the bay window was the agent's office. The town's transportation and information needs were handled from here: tickets were sold, mail was handled, telegrams were sent and received, waybills for freight were typed up and billed, and orders were taken from the dispatcher and given to passing trains.

The person who worked in this office *was* the railroad as far as the residents of the town were concerned.

The big doors are on what was the freight section. This is where you picked up your new stove from Sears or your crate of baby chicks. Bigger towns had their own freight houses, but this was Ohiopyle. One station and one agent—and for 27 years that agent was Lillian McCahan—was sufficient.

Ohiopyle Station.
Courtesy Western Maryland Railway Historical Society.

Laurel Highlands Trail

The Laurel Highlands Trail starts across the river. It's a hiking trail that runs for 70 miles along the top of Laurel Ridge in Appalachian Trail style complete with AT-type shelters. The northern end of the Laurel Highlands is at the Conemaugh River gorge near Johnstown.

Most of the land along the trail is owned by the state of Pennsylvania either as park, game land, or state forest, so hiking the trail is a pleasant wilderness experience. The trail even has its own bridge across the Pennsylvania Turnpike.

The Thousand Mile Club

From Connellsville to Confluence, the trail is patrolled by the Thousand Mile Club. They're volunteers who ride the trail and give assistance and directions, spot maintenance problems such as downed trees, and do minor repairs to bicyclists in trouble. They wear distinctive green T-shirts and are nice folks. If you see one, stop and say "hi."

Our Grand Canyon Is Grander Than Their Grand Canyon

When you leave Ohiopyle, you enter the Laurel Hill Anticline and the deepest part of the Yough Gorge and therein lies a tale.

In case you didn't know, there's a Grand Canyon of Pennsylvania. Technically, it's called the Pine Creek Gorge and it's in Tioga County near Wellsboro in the north central part of the state. It's the Grand Canyon of Pennsylvania only because they got the name first.

In truth, that canyon is number five in the grand scheme of Pennsylvania grand canyons. The Yough Gorge through here is the deepest in the state. In fact, according to Brad Clemenson who studied it, our gorge is deeper than theirs by almost double: 1,660 feet to their 840 feet.

Depending on how you measure it, theirs is longer; the Yough Gorge is 27 miles from Connellsville to Confluence, and it's 48 miles from Ansonia to Jersey Shore along Pine Creek. BUT if you add in the Casselman Gorge up to Garrett, we come in at 55. Both gorges have rail-trails—they have the Pine Creek Trail—but we have the Ohiopyle Falls.

So there you are. They have the name, but all things considered, we have the grander canyon.

> "... *an immense uninhabited wilderness, overgrown everywhere with trees and brushwood, so that nowhere can one see twenty yards.*" Brigadier John Forbes as quoted in *Montcalm and Wolfe* by Francis Parkman.

You're riding through some beautiful forest here, but it's far from the "forest primeval" that James Fennimore Cooper described with his turgid prose. The forest that Native Americans knew around here was made up mostly of white pine, white oak, chestnut and hemlock. With very few exceptions, such as Cook's Forest in the northern part of the state, there is no old growth forest left in Pennsylvania. The forest you see here has grown up since the mountains were logged off between the 1890s and 1920s. The Chestnut Blight killed practically all of the chestnut trees by the 1930s. They're now extinct.

When the forest went, the Pennsylvania whitetail deer herd went with it. At the beginning of the 20th century, the whitetail deer was practically extinct. Today, with the regrowth of the forest and good wildlife management practices, the deer herd measures in the millions. Many counties in Pennsylvania have more deer than people. Research is underway at Virginia Tech and elsewhere on genetic engineering to restore the chestnut trees.

In addition to this 8-point buck, whose horns are still in summer velvet, there are 24 other species of mammals in the park, including otter, mink, bats, raccoons, bobcats, and bears. If you ride quietly in the early morning or late afternoon, you may get lucky and spot some of them. Almost 1400 species of plants have also been identified.
Courtesy Ohiopyle State Park.

CHAPTER 14: LAUREL RIDGE

Two semaphore signals guard the east end of Ohiopyle siding. This is a nice reminder of what the railroad looked like when it was in operation and shows how quickly the trees grew up after it was abandoned. Courtesy Western Maryland Railway Historical Society.

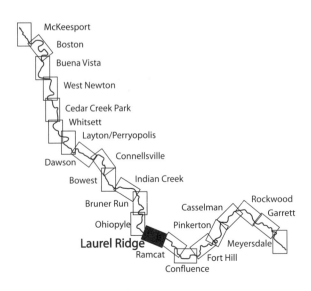

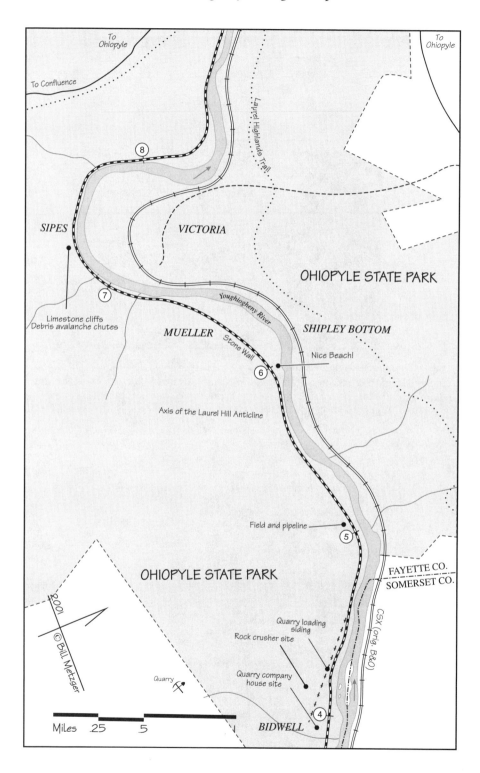

Mile 7.5 Sipes

You're riding along a steep cliff here. It's across the river from a flat area. A couple of significant things are going on here. Whenever a stream meanders, or makes a bend, on the inside of the bend is a bar, like sandbar, or "deposition," and on the outside of the bend there's a cut bank. Geologists love cut banks because the rocks are exposed.

The flat area across the river, called Victoria, was once home to a half dozen farms and orchards, the last of which was bought out in the '60s by the park.

The other phenomena here are the "debris avalanche chutes" which look like small dry streams until you stop and look up through the brush and mountain laurel. These go clear to the top of the cliff and carry all sorts of stuff down during a storm. Jim Shaulis calls each one of these a "valley in the making." He also cautions "you don't want to be standing underneath one of them in a storm."

Debris avalanche chute.

Mile 6-7

The area of the trail along here was farmed until the late 1940s. The stone wall, which is fully a quarter of a mile long, wasn't built for the sake of building a wall, but as a place to dump the rocks that kept coming to the surface of the fields.

Farming here was somewhat like farming in New England. Every spring the frost heaved up a new crop of boulders. Removing them was backbreaking work. So when you consider the wall, consider the poor shmoe who built it. An old railroad map shows Jonathan Mueller as being the landowner of record at the time the line was built, so he was probably said shmoe.

Railroad retaining wall at mile 5.5.

Mile 6

Right by the milepost is a picnic area and a trail that leads down to a nice beach.

Mile 5.8 Axis of Laurel Hill Anticline

Mile 5.5 Retaining Wall

This tie and rock retaining wall was built by the railroad in 1929.

Mile 5

We're told the field here is a pretty good place to spot deer.

Mile 4 Bidwell Station

Old railroad maps call this Bidwell then say the name was changed to Sang Hollow in 1925. The real Sang Hollow is in the Conemaugh River gorge, just downstream from Johnstown. The real Bidwell is across the river. Newer railroad maps settled on the name Bidwell, but other sources call it Bidwell Station. The station in question consisted of a small shelter.

Whatever the name, this is the area near Mile 4 that's the site of the Bidwell Lumber Company's logging railroad and loading area. Prior to the Western Maryland being built, the lumber company built a sawmill over on the B&O side in 1904 and an aerial cable that hauled logs across the river. After the advent of the Western Maryland, Bidwell Lumber loaded their logs on this side of the river.

There was a quarry here up on the side of the mountain. The workers lived in company houses on the high fill on the left side of the unnamed creek. The quarry worked the Pottsville Sandstone and manufactured millstones, among other stone products.

The old grades and loading areas are still visible.

The railroad tore out the siding to the quarry in 1926, so it's safe to assume the operation had gone belly up by then.

WHAT IS THAT?

Before the railroads used two-way radio communication, crews had to stop the train and get off and talk to the dispatcher using one of these handy telephone boxes.

CHAPTER 15: RAMCAT

At about Mile 2.5 right before Ramcat, the railroad ran through this cut of Pottsville Sandstone. Note all the mountain laurel growing out of the acidic rock. This is the east end of the Laurel Hill anticline.

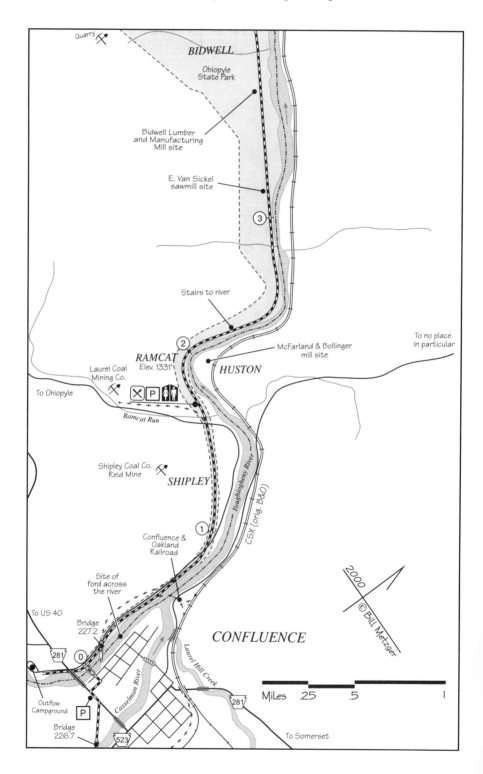

Quarry

BIDWELL

Ohiopyle
State Park

Bidwell Lumber
and Manufacturing
Mill site

E. Van Sickel
sawmill site

③

Stairs to river

McFarland & Bollinger
mill site

To no place
in particular

②

RAMCAT
Elev. 1331'

HUSTON

Laurel Coal
Mining Co.

To Ohiopyle

Ramcat Run

Shipley Coal Co.
Reid Mine

SHIPLEY

Youghiogheny River

CSX (orig. B&O)

①

Confluence &
Oakland
Railroad

Site of
ford across
the river

2000

© Bill Metzger

To US 40

Bridge
227.2

281

0

CONFLUENCE

Casselman River

Laurel Hill Creek

281

Miles   .25   .5   1

Outflow
Campground   P

Bridge
226.7

523

To Somerset

Mile 3.2

The E. W. Van Sickel Lumber Co. had a mill and logging railroad here about 1923. This operation didn't last long; the railroad had to climb the mountain with a series of six switchbacks that were expensive and dangerous to operate. Van Sickel quit and headed for West Virginia when his locomotive tipped over and several of the cars fell into the quarry.

Mile 2.5

This cut is one of the prettiest spots on the whole trail.

The wooden steps you see along here were built by the Chestnut Ridge Chapter of Trout Unlimited as an access for fishing. People walking down to the river were causing erosion on the trail because of the steep slope down. The trout people jumped in to fix the problem.

The Yough through here is prime trout fishing water. From Ramcat down to the Route 381 bridge at Ohiopyle is special regulation water where you can only keep trout 14 inches or longer and can only keep fish from the opening day of trout season, the first Saturday after April 11, to Labor Day and you can only keep two fish a day. So if you see fishermen, and the chances are very good that you'll see fishermen, they're after trout.

Ramcat

Depending on what map you look at, the place that today is known as Ramcat was also called Kephart and Shipley. Shipley came from the coal company that owned the Reid Mine. "Ramcat" is what the locals called bobcats. Ramcat is most famous for being the point where the first section of the trail that's now the Great Allegheny Passage was built toward Ohiopyle.

But before that, Ramcat Run was the site of a couple of industries. Starting in 1901 there was a big sawmill operation across the river at Huston owned by an outfit named McFarland & Bollinger. There was the usual town and railroad station and the operation included a bridge across the river and an 8-mile-long logging railroad up Ramcat Run. The original owners sold out to the East Brady Lumber Co. and the whole operation was over by 1911 when the Western Maryland came through.

After the WM opened, there was another railroad up the run, probably on the same grade, that ran to the Laurel Coal Co.'s Reed Mine. The Laurel Coal Co. was a small operation that had four company houses about where the parking area is now. There was a siding at Kephart that the railroad used to set out work cars.

Ramcat also marks the end of the Middle Yough Gorge and the Laurel Mountain Anticline. You're out of the mountains for a bit and into a nice little valley.

There's a restroom and snack bar here.

CHAPTER 16: CONFLUENCE

Western Maryland Challenger 1206 hammers by Confluence station on August 27, 1946. You'll see that timber cribbing wall in the photo of the station later in this chapter. R. A. Baker photo, Van Sickel collection.

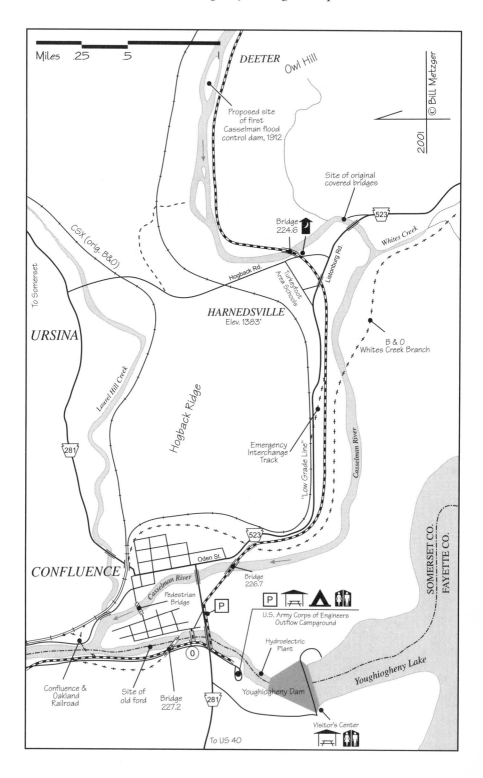

Mile 0.5 Confluence & Oakland Railroad

The section of trail from here to the old Route 281 bridge is built on the grade of the Confluence & Oakland Railroad, a branch of the Baltimore and Ohio. This line was built in 1890 and connected with the B&O main line across the river (see map). It ran 20 miles south to Kendall, Maryland and at its peak, operated a train a day down and back. The line was abandoned in 1941 in anticipation of the building of the Yough Dam. The bridge that crossed the river here was removed without a trace in 1960, after debris backed up behind it and caused flooding. Much of the grade of the Confluence & Oakland is now on the bottom of the Yough Lake.

Bridge No. 227.2, Deck Plate Girder Bridge, 715' Long

Just like a piece of the original Ohiopyle bridge was removed by PennDOT to improve highway clearances, this one had a couple of spans removed by our favorite state transportation department to improve clearances on the Confluence side. DCNR made a deal with the Turkeyfoot Fish and Game Club to swap property—the original right of way ran right through the club—and the bridge was bypassed. It's the only Western Maryland bridge that's not being used by the trail.

Old Route 281 Bridge

The nifty pedestrian bridge you're crossing here into Confluence didn't always look this way. It was originally a steel truss bridge that carried Route 281 across the Yough River. It had an open grate steel deck that scared the bejeezus out of bikers (including your author) and was slated to be demolished when the new 281 bridge—the one that you can see upstream from here—was put into service. The superstructure was seriously deteriorated and everything pointed to tearing down the old bridge. But the borough (that's what we call a town in Pennsylvania) of Confluence wanted to keep it open for trail use because of the heavy bike traffic that comes into town.

PennDOT did a safety analysis and it turned out to be cheaper to save the bridge than to tear it down. Girders that had been placed under the bridge in the 1930s to strengthen it were actually holding the whole thing up. They needed to be repainted but were otherwise in fine shape. With a $200,000 grant, the superstructure and offending deck were torn off, the bridge was redecked with treated Pennsylvania hardwood and observation platforms with benches were added. All in all, it's a vast improvement over the old bridge.

Here you can take the bridge into the town of Confluence—you'll have to anyway if you're going to Meyersdale—or you can take a side trip on the trail up to the Outflow Campground and take a look at the dam.

When you cross this bridge, you leave Fayette County and enter Somerset County.

Yough Dam and Reservoir

> "The Youghiogheny is a particularly troublesome flood-producing tributary.... Report of the Flood Commission of Pittsburgh, PA, 1912

After a series of disastrous floods in Pittsburgh in 1907 and 1908, the Pittsburgh Flood Commission was formed and studied the watersheds of the Allegheny, the Monongahela and the Yough/Casselman Rivers. One of the many suggestions was that a flood control dam be built at the bend in the Yough just upstream from

Youghiogheny Dam. The overflow spillway is to the left. The rectangular building to the right of it is the hydroelectric plant. The visitor's center is to the right at the top of the dam and the campground is in the foreground. Courtesy U.S. Army Corps of Engineers.

Confluence. That was in 1912. Nothing much was done on the report and the mother of all floods hit Pittsburgh on St. Patrick's Day, 1936. All of a sudden there was a flurry of action culminating in the building of the Youghiogheny Dam and Reservoir starting in 1938. The dam was officially completed in 1948.

The Yough Dam is 184 feet high, 1,100 feet wide at the base, and 1,160 feet long at the top. It is built of 3,060,500 cubic yards of concrete, stone, and earth and backs up a lake 14 miles long.

A hydroelectric plant generates electricity that goes out on the power grid. The plant is licensed to Seven Springs Borough and a common misconception is that it's exclusively for the resort, but there's no direct line. It gets its power off the same grid as anyone else.

The dam makes the river clearer because silt coming downstream settles out into the lake and it makes the river really cold because they draw the water off the bottom. Because of the dam, a flood at Pittsburgh will be 6 inches lower.

The big benefit of the dam, as far as recreation is concerned, is that it keeps the downstream river levels high enough for boating and fishing. Operators at the dam maintain the water level, but they get their orders from the U.S. Army Corps of Engineers District Office in Pittsburgh. Each flood control dam in the district sends in a morning report every day that includes rainfall, stream flow based on gauges in each river, and the lake level. The district then tells each dam what the flow should be based on the optimum lake level for the time of the year and downstream needs. The Corps works closely with Ohiopyle State Park and their needs for water not only for daily recreation but for special events.

There's a visitor's center at the top of dam with a restroom, picnic tables, and brochures.

Confluence, Population 825

On June 26, 1871, the Pittsburgh and Connellsville Railroad from Cumberland to Pittsburgh was completed; the line from Cumberland met the line from Pittsburgh at Fort Hill. The celebration was held in Confluence. One hundred and thirty years later, on August 24, 2001, the section connecting the first 100 miles of the Great Allegheny Passage was opened between Confluence and Fort Hill. A two-day celebration was held in Confluence.

The word "confluence" is defined as a coming together. They pronounce it CON-fluence. The town is well named. The Yough and Casselman Rivers and Laurel Hill Creek join here. Christopher Gist, the explorer and friend of George Washington, is said to have given it the name Turkeyfoot because the three streams flowing into one resembled a turkey's foot. It's more likely that Gist was the first to call it the Turkeyfoot in English, having learned the name from the area's Native Americans; several native settlements were located in the area. It was also called Crow Foot.

Whatever the bird in question, a look at the map shows that this fowl had really crooked toes. A Native American trail called the Turkeyfoot Path ran from here over the mountains to what is now Cumberland, Maryland. It was laid out as a shortcut to following the rivers, the rivers being more of an impediment to travel in that time than a convenience. The Ohio Company (the one started by George Washington's brother and friends) proposed to widen the Path in 1751 as a road and would pay anyone who did the work the sum of "twenty five pounds Virginia currency." A 1752 map showed the road, so they must have gotten the work done. There were roads that led in several directions from here and each was called "the Turkeyfoot Road."

Washington stopped here May 20, 1754. He wrote in his diary:

> " . . . we gained Turkey Foot by the Beginning of the Night . . . Tarried there some time to examine the Place, which we found very convenient to build a Fort, not only because it was gravelly, but also for its being at the Mouth of three Branches of small Rivers . . ."

He canoed down the Yough as far as Ohiopyle, looking for an easy water route west for his troops, and turned back when he found the falls. Washington estimated that it was about 10 miles from Confluence to Ohiopyle. Not a bad guess on his part; it's exactly that. After failing to find a suitable water route west, Washington came back upstream and took the Nemacolin Path. A week later, he ambushed and killed the French Lieutenant, Jumonville, and started the French and Indian War. It was just luck that Washington found the French first and ambushed them. The French were trying to do the exact same thing to him.

Washington's proposed fort at Turkeyfoot was never built.

William Tissue laid out a town here in 1800 and called it New Boston, but nothing much came of it. For a time, Turkeyfoot was a stopping place on the way west and cattle drovers continued to use the Turkeyfoot Road even after the National Road was paved—it was easier on the animals' hooves. The main route that carried the name Turkeyfoot Road ran from Shippensburg, PA to the east, through Turkeyfoot, south of Sugar Loaf Mountain to Dunbar and Uniontown (see map page 44).

Local citizens strongly resisted the coming of the railroad because of the loss of business from the roads, but when the Pittsburgh and Connellsville Railroad was completed, it brought more prosperity to the place than the roads ever did. The town of Confluence was laid out in 1870 as the railroad was arriving.

At the beginning of the 20th century, Confluence was a bustling burg, with lots of lumbering and coal mining, and railroad branch lines going off in all directions. There were several factories here that used the plentiful local wood. The biggest industry in town at the time was the Beggs Tannery, a large operation that was directly across the railroad tracks from the square.

Tanneries were common in Pennsylvania due to the abundance of hemlock bark. Hemlock is high in tannin, which is the principal ingredient in tanning leather. As the supply of hemlock dried up, the tanneries moved elsewhere; Beggs' tannery closed in 1920.

The B&O main line splits here; originally the railroad departed from the river and went up over the hill, saving three miles. In 1902 there was a need for a second line and the "Low Grade" was built. Both rejoin at a place called Brook, which is one of those places that has never been anything more than a name on the railroad. After the big trees were cut, the coal mined, the trains quit stopping, and the dam was built, Confluence was well on its way to drying up. River and trail recreation changed that. Today, there are a couple of quite good restaurants and B&Bs in town and the place is coming back to life. Confluence is unusual for a trailside town in that it's flat and it has a large town square, complete with gazebo. The benches in the square are a great place to take a break and watch the world go by very, very slowly.

You're now in Somerset County and have left the Pittsburgh accent, mostly. They definitely have their own way of talking here. Five miles becomes "fov molls." Sixty minutes is "a nar." A hamburger is a hamburg. The three meals are breakfast, dinner and supper. But things still need washed here and they drink pop. When something's finished here, "it's all." And the plural of "you" is "yous."

Allegheny Highlands Trail (Pennsylvania)

After you *carefully* cross Route 281 and start up the ramp, you're on the Allegheny Highlands Trail (Pennsylvania) on a section of trail that was opened to great cheering and thunderous and sustained applause on August 24, 2001. This 5.7-mile segment runs from Confluence to a mile or so west of Fort Hill. You have to climb a ramp up to the trail because the railroad grade has been removed here by PennDOT to make room for the new Route 281.

The Allegheny Highlands Trail Council is the oldest volunteer group in the Allegheny Trail Alliance. It was formed in 1987 and has about 300 members. The trail itself from here to the Mason-Dixon Line is owned by Somerset County. Mile 0 is the Mason-Dixon Line. The mileposts you see from 42 to 36 are experimental. They're made of recycled plastic.

Bridge 226.7, Deck Plate Girder, 478' Long

This is the first time you cross the Casselman River, so let's talk about it first, before we talk about the bridge. You'll follow this river the rest of the way to Meyersdale. It has also been known as the Little Youghiogheny and the Castleman. It was named for Jacob Castleman, a hunter and early settler who hailed from Hampshire County, Virginia. From the source of the Casselman near Bittinger, Maryland to its mouth at Confluence is only 17 miles by a straight line. By the river, it's about 53. It's a U-shaped stream that rises on the slopes of Meadow Mountain in Garrett County and flows around Mt. Davis. It starts flowing northeasterly, then turns left at Meyersdale and then turns left again at Rockwood and winds up flowing southwesterly.

On its way, the Casselman has managed to carve a very respectable gorge through Negro Mountain. Coal mining still takes place in the Casselman watershed and once in a while there's some pretty heavy acid discharge. You'll notice a decided lack of aquatic vegetation. There's not much life in the river to speak of, but, according to Gary Smith, a fisheries technician with the Fish and Boat Commission, the river is "a whole lot better than it has been." The Casselman suffered an acid mine drainage blowout in 1993 that killed most of the life in the river and it's still recovering. There's still some drainage south of Meyersdale in the Shaw Mines area and, according to Smith, "there's some pretty nasty stuff coming in." Coxes Creek is also problematic with pollution coming down from the Somerset area. The Commission stocked the Casselman with fingerling trout and smallmouth bass in 1999 and they're growing to "decent length," and there are some aquatic insects and forage fish, so there's hope for the river. But there's still strip mining going on in Somerset County, so things are still a bit iffy.

Now about the bridge. It was rehabilitated in only 6 weeks in the spring of 2000 with an innovative decking system that used prefabricated modular construction. The 10-foot-long sections were fabricated at a blacksmith shop in Somerset, then bolted into place on the original ties. The whole job cost $170,000 and was funded with federal and state money.

Western Maryland's Confluence station in 1951. The semaphore signal on the station is an order board telling the train crews if the operator here will give them orders from the dispatcher, and the two semaphores to the right guard the Confluence siding where trains could meet. Courtesy Western Maryland Railway Historical Society.

White's Creek Branch

The abutments of the next bridge you come to were built to carry the railroad bridge that crossed the Baltimore and Ohio White's Creek Branch. The branch was originally built in 1901 by the J. R. Droney Lumber Company using rails and ties leased from the B&O. In 1902, the B&O bought the branch. It ran about five miles up White's Creek to Unamis, where the lumber company built a town and sawmill. The area was logged out in 1911 and the last lumber was shipped in 1912. After that, the line served several coal mines. It was abandoned after the bridge over the Casselman washed out in the flood of 1936.

The new trail bridge was built in 2001.

Right after you cross the bridge, Luther Miller's fuel dealership sits on the site of the Western Maryland's Confluence station.

This section of trail, about two miles, is like riding down a country road without the traffic. It's wide and pretty flat. And your author thinks it's terrific. There was an emergency interchange track here (see map at the beginning of the chapter) between the B&O and the Western Maryland so that trains could cross from one railroad to another should the need arise. If you look up at the railroad toward the cleared area, you'll see a small concrete structure that was a phone booth. You can see one up close at Meyersdale station. It marks where the switch was for the B&O's side of the interchange track

Harnedsville

There are maybe 20 houses and the Turkeyfoot Valley Area Schools (Go Rams) in Harnedsville. All 494 students—K-12—in the district go to school in this one complex.

This is one of the oldest towns in the area; it was laid out and named in 1847 by Samuel Harned. Before that, the people of the Monongahela Culture had several communities near here.

Settlers from New Jersey came into the area about 1774. They are said to have built mud houses as their first dwellings. The place was first called Mudtown.

Harned arrived on the scene about 1821 and built a distillery. According to a recent article in the *Somerset Daily American*, Harned added "a gristmill and a tannery to the town, attracting a new settlement of people. He also operated one of the first stores in the town. By 1876, Harnedsville had a blacksmith shop, shoe shop, saddle shop, cabinet shop, church and about 17 houses."

The B&O built the Low Grade Line through town in 1902, the Western Maryland came in 1912, and the B&O White's Creek Branch was just across the creek, but even with three nearby railroads, there was no station. The B&O put theirs in Ursina just over the hill and the WM's was in Confluence, just two miles away.

You know you're in Harnedsville when you pass under Route 523 through the new box culvert.

Bridge No. 224.6, Deck Plate Girder Bridge, 302.7' Long

You're crossing the Casselman River for the second time on a bridge that was redecked in 1994. This bridge is on a 3 degree curve. Now you're on the left bank of the river, where you're supposed to be.

Here's where you start noticing you're climbing. The grade really isn't much—0.8% at the most, but it's steady until you get to Rockwood. Your only real break from climbing is the bypass around Pinkerton Horn. But it's a whole lot of fun riding back down the other way.

Flood Control Dams

The Pittsburgh Flood Commission of 1912 recommended a series of five dams on the Casselman. The first dam would have been 4.2 miles up from Confluence, the last was planned to be just upstream from the Pinkerton high bridge and would have backed the river up as far as Markleton. The dams were never built.

CHAPTER 17: FORT HILL

Monongahela village from the Late Woodland period (A.D. 900-1650.)
From "Prehistory of the Upper Ohio Valleys" by W. J. Mayer-Oakes, *Annals of Carnegie Museum,* 1955.   Courtesy Carnegie Museum of Natural History.

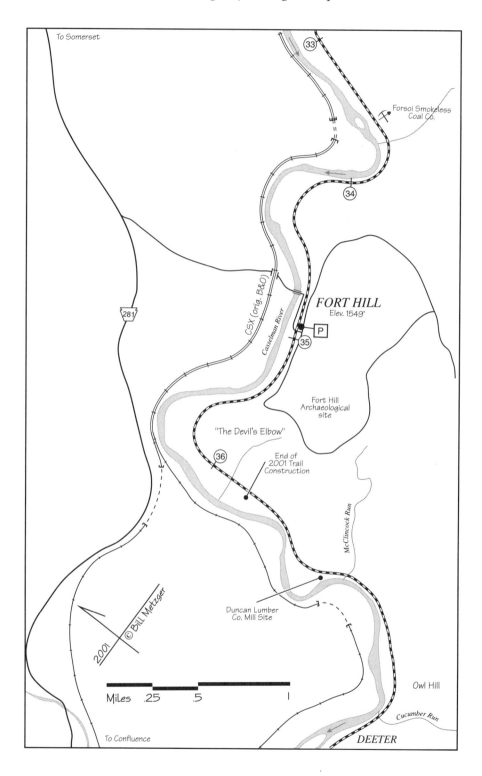

To Somerset

Forsoi Smokeless
Coal Co.

33

34

CSX (orig. B&O)

Casselman River

281

FORT HILL
Elev. 1549'

P

35

Fort Hill
Archaeological
site

"The Devil's Elbow"

36

End of
2001 Trail
Construction

McClincock Run

© Bill Metzger

2001

Duncan Lumber
Co. Mill Site

Miles   .25   .5   1

Owl Hill

Cucumber Run

To Confluence

DEETER

Fort Hill

The hill between Cucumber Run and McClintock Run was known as Owl Hill. The Duncan Lumber Co. had a mill on this side of the river and a logging railroad that crossed the river and ran along the side of the hill. Since they shipped all their lumber on the B&O they didn't connect with the Western Maryland when it was built. The WM had to build a wooden trestle over the line. When Duncan ceased operations about 1916 the trestle was filled in.

The Devil's Elbow, the next hill up the way, was notorious for its unstable rock strata, which sloped on the same angle as the side of the hill, so there was precious little to anchor a railroad to. The railroad had to be realigned in 1932 because of slides, and the trail contractor also had trouble in this part.

Duncan Lumber Company had a mill and mill pond at the mouth of McClintock Run. Floating logs in a pond made them easier to handle. Note the lightly constructed logging railroad, typical of such operations and the conveyer from the pond up to the mill. Courtesy Railroad Museum of Pennsylvania.

Mile 36.2

The open lot on the river side marks the eastern end of the 2001 trail construction. Heavy equipment and trail surfacing material were kept here.

Mile 35 Fort Hill

The town of Fort Hill, what there is of it, consists of a few houses and a post office on the side of a very steep hill. It's named for the flat-topped hill to the south that was the site of fortified villages built by the Monongahela People, who had vanished by the time Europeans made it on the scene. The site was excavated by an archaeological team in 1939. The excavation, which was undertaken as a Depression-era work-relief project by the Works Progress Administration (WPA), turned up numerous artifacts and defined the sites.

The WPA project is as much of a story as the archaeological sites themselves. Somerset County was hit hard by the Depression. Many of the coal mines had closed and the majority of the timber was logged off. There was little work to be had.

Unofficial inquiries over the years had identified the tentative locations of several prehistoric Native American sites in the county and archaeology was one of the WPA's approved projects. Edgar Augustine, an engineer from Addison, PA with an interest in archaeology, led the digging, which started in 1935 and ended in 1940. The crews were paid at the rate of 25 cents an hour for a laborer, assistants got 50 cents and supervisors hauled in a buck for an hour's work. Nobody could work more than 60 hours in a two week pay period. But it was work, and that was all that mattered in those lean years.

Among the sites that were identified and excavated were several around Confluence, the Fort Hill sites and a cluster near Meyersdale. Some consisted of simple rock shelters and others were fortified villages with dozens of houses. The problem with the WPA project was that until recently nothing was done with the artifacts that were excavated or the information that had been generated by the digs. Many of the artifacts have since disappeared.

Several groups and individuals in the last couple of years are finally making some sense of the work of six decades ago, among them the Somerset County Archaeological Society and Bernard Means of Maryland, who has published several manuscripts and articles on the area.

This is also where the Pittsburgh & Connellsville Railroad was completed in 1871.

The loading docks along the trail near the grade crossing were built by General Refractories to load fire clay from a mine on top of the hill. They were later used to load coal from local strip mines.

Mile 33.2 Forsoi Smokeless Coal Co.

You can see the grades from the loading track and the tipple from this small mine.

NATIVE AMERICANS

Paleo Period

As near as anybody can tell, people first came to western Pennsylvania somewhere between 11,000 and 12,000 years ago. Archaeologists call these people the Paleo Indians. Their projectile points were made with a signature single or double flute along the blade. The climate was cooler and wetter because the glaciers that had covered much of the northern hemisphere were starting to retreat, but were still less than a hundred miles to the north. They hunted caribou and other now-extinct species like hairy mammoths, but other than that, not much is known about them or their culture.

Archaic Period

The culture changed to the Archaic Period about 9,000 years ago. Thousands of artifacts from this time have been found on sites in the Youghiogheny River watershed. When the glaciers retreated, animal populations shifted. Hairy mammoths, saber tooth tigers and the other large mammals became extinct and modern animals that we know like bear and deer moved in.

People here gradually shifted to more specialized hunting and gathering and practiced woodworking, weaving and hideworking. Their tools have been found in their larger base camps and settlement camps where ceremonial and domestic activities occurred. Base camps were on major rivers. They engaged in long-distance communication with other groups, trading and hunting and exchanging marriage partners. The Woodland People, who lived from 1,000 B.C.E. to 100 B.C.E., made ceramic vessels, farmed, and lived in a more sedentary settlement system. Both Early Woodland and Late Archaic artifacts have been found on the same floodplains and terraces where they grew squash, pumpkin, gourd and corn and hunted and fished.

Woodland Period

In this general area there were two groups of Woodland people who built sacred burial mounds: the Adena people and the Hopewell people. The Adena people built conical mounds along the major rivers. The Hopewell people, with their cultural center in Ohio, continued to build large burial mounds in the region from 100 B.C.E. to A.D.E. 400. Burial mounds, stone tools, and ceramics from these cultures are found in the Youghiogheny River watershed. These people declined when the climate got colder and long distance interaction with other groups deteriorated.

A 3,000-year-old point from the late archaic period. Archaeologists call this a Meadow Wood point for the area in New York where points like this were first identified. It was used for hunting and was made of locally-found chert, a flintlike material. It was found in the Sewickley Creek area.

Late Woodland Period

During the Late Woodland period (A.D. 900-1650), what's known as the Monongahela culture dominated southwestern Pennsylvania and parts of Ohio, West Virginia and Maryland. The Monongahela people were farmers who cultivated corn, beans and squash along the floodplains and terraces of major rivers. They lived in small villages that varied in size, but usually consisted of one or two concentric rings of houses surrounding an open central plaza used for ceremonies and other community activities. Inside their round houses were sleeping platforms attached to the walls and central hearths for cooking and heating. Large pear-or petal-shaped storage structures attached to the back of the houses provided an area for storage. For protection they built wood palisades buttressed with mounds of earth surrounding many of their villages.

When the Monongahela abandoned a village, these large earthen rings remained and were described as "forts" by early European travelers. Monongahela villages stood on many of the high and dry terraces along the Youghiogheny River especially at stream junctures and near fords along the network of Indian paths. These prehistoric roads provided transportation routes necessary for trading beaver furs, marine shells, corn, and other commodities.

At the beginning of the 17th century, European trade objects began to permeate the Upper Ohio Valley, though it is unlikely that much direct contact occurred between the Monongahela and Europeans because trade was probably conducted through a series of middlemen, both European and Native American.

Among the important clusters of prehistoric sites along the Great Allegheny Passage associated with Indian paths was a group of sites near the Sewickley Creek, which is on the opposite side of the river from the trail between Sutersville and West Newton. The creek, also known as "sweet water" because of the many large and productive stands of sugar maple trees along its banks, is associated with dozens of archaeological sites from the Woodland period.

Another site cluster occurs at the mouth of Laurel Hill Creek (Confluence) where the Turkeyfoot Path crossed the three streams. This cluster is near the Fort Hill site, another multiple village site surrounded by a wood and earthen palisade. Other villages were known to exist in McKeesport, Meyersdale, Mt. Pleasant, and Connellsville.

In the early 1600s, Native American refugees, traders, or others who had been in contact with the Europeans passed diseases such as measles, whooping cough, smallpox, chicken pox, typhoid, and cholera to inland native groups like the Monongahela. One of the earliest and worst epidemics occurred during the period between 1616 and 1617 when thousands of Indians died. Decimated by disease, the Monongahela were dispersed as the Iroquois expanded their territory from the north into the rich mountains and valleys of western Pennsylvania.

With the Monongahela territory unoccupied, the Delaware (Lenape) and Shawnee, whose territories were sold or taken over by European settlers, sought permission from the Iroquois to settle in the region. These refugee groups, not the Monongahela people, were the "Indians" described by the earliest traders and explorers who ventured up the Youghiogheny River.

From information courtesy of Christine Davis.

Chapter 18: Pinkerton Neck/Markleton

The Markleton Sanatorium was a Victorian structure that used some of the buildings of the former Markleton pulp mill. Bill Metzger collection.

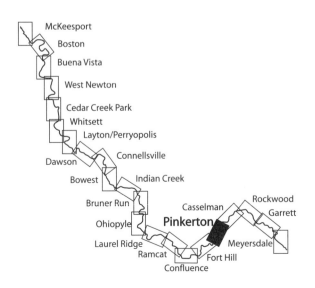

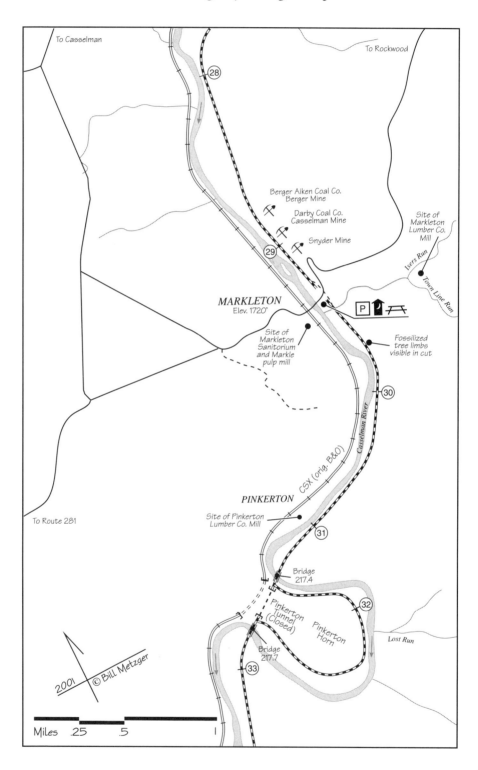

To Casselman

To Rockwood

28

Berger Aiken Coal Co.
Berger Mine

Darby Coal Co.
Casselman Mine

Snyder Mine

Site of
Markleton
Lumber Co.
Mill

Isers Run

Town Line Run

29

MARKLETON
Elev. 1720'

P

Site of
Markleton
Sanitorium
and Markle
pulp mill

Fossilized
tree limbs
visible in cut

30

Casselman River

CSX (orig. B&O)

PINKERTON

To Route 281

Site of Pinkerton
Lumber Co. Mill

31

Bridge
217.4

32

Pinkerton
Tunnel
(Closed)

Pinkerton
Horn

Lost Run

Bridge
217.7

33

2001 © Bill Metzger

Miles   .25   .5   1

Mile 32.8 Bridge No. 217.7, Deck Plate Girder Bridge, 543' long, about 100' high

Stop on the bridge and take a look at the river. The view from here is quite breathtaking. This is called the Pinkerton High Bridge. If you have a panoramic camera, break it out here.

Mile 32.7 Pinkerton Tunnel (Closed) 849' Long

The tunnel is currently closed due to unsafe conditions, but long range plans call for it to be rehabilitated and reopened. You'll notice that it, like the big bridges on the railroad, was built to accommodate a second track.

Mile 31.2—32.7 Pinkerton Horn

By the Western Maryland Railway, it's maybe a thousand feet across Pinkerton Neck from the Pinkerton high bridge through the closed tunnel to the low bridge. The river takes almost two miles to join those two points. It's like Ohiopyle without the falls and the millions of tourists. The peninsula formed by the river is called Pinkerton Horn. Matthew Pinkerton, who was supposed to have operated the first grist mill in the area, was probably the area's namesake. The Pinkerton Lumber Company took the name and established a sawmill and town here. But we get a bit ahead of ourselves.

Pinkerton Logging Co. train.
Courtesy Railroad Museum of Pennsylvania.

The B&O built a tunnel across Pinkerton Neck and to cut expenses, the tunnel was lined with timber rather than brick or stone. In 1879, the timber caught fire and the tunnel collapsed. Rather than rebuild it, they built a railroad around Pinkerton Horn that served as a bypass. This line (railroaders call a temporary track a "shoofly") is now the grade that's used by the trail.

Pinkerton Tunnel was rebuilt using brick and stone and reopened in 1885, but Pinkerton Lumber Co. also used the grade for a time for their logging railroad. It was used again as a haul road when Pinkerton Horn was logged again in the early 1980s. The Western Maryland built their own tunnel across Pinkerton Neck and saved more than a mile and a half of railroad and a lot of curves. The old grade came to the rescue again when it was found that Western Maryland's Pinkerton Tunnel was unsafe for trail use. A surface was put down and that's how you ride around Pinkerton Horn today.

The actual town of Pinkerton was about a half mile upstream from the tunnels on the B&O side of the river. You can see the site from the power line.

Logging operations began in 1879. According to logging railroad author Benjamin F. G. Kline, the town at its peak consisted of "a sawmill, hemlock bark storage sheds, numerous houses for the workers, a school, store and a picnic grove complete with a homemade horse-drawn merry-go-round." The B&O had a station there and Kline reports that the lumber company also erected a "clubhouse" at the top of Pinkerton Neck above the B&O tunnel. There was a bridge across the river at Pinkerton for the logging railroad that ran about 8 miles up Lost Run on the side of Negro Mountain. The bridge was abandoned after the Western Maryland was built and lumber was shipped out on the new railroad. Logging operations ceased about 1917. Today, on the flat spot along the CSX main line that was Pinkerton, there is no trace of the town.

Mile 31.2 Bridge No. 217.4, Deck Plate Girder Bridge, 242' long

There are some nice rocks near the bridge on the upstream side for swimming and sunbathing. The canoeists call this Lunch Rock. And yes, this is the Pinkerton Low Bridge.

Mile 31

The denuded area just across the bridge on the bank side of the trail was strip mined.

Mile 29.8 Worthington Sandstone

The sandstone in the cut here contains fossilized tree limbs.

Mile 29.3 Markleton

Today, according to Postmaster Jim Peters, Markleton has exactly 14 houses, not counting the post office. There's an access area built by the Pennsylvania Fish and Boat Commission with a changing area, a chemical toilet, and a couple of picnic tables, and that's it for the whole town. The only way you know you're even in the town when you're riding the trail is because the railroad overpass has been removed and you have to leave the trail and cross the road. This is a good place to take a break, since you've been climbing ever since you left Confluence. While you're here, take a look around and reflect on the fact that about a hundred years ago Markleton was a veritable boomtown.

The town was named for and by the sons of General Joseph Markle of West Newton. He became a general in the Indian wars out in Indiana, fighting under William Henry Harrison, who later became President for a month.

General Markle inherited a grist mill and paper mill in West Newton from his father and passed the operation on to his sons S. B. and Cyrus P. The boys purchased 5,000 acres of land in Somerset County and built a pulp mill to supply their West Newton operations.

The mill was, in 1881, said to be the largest of its kind in the world. In addition to the factory, the Markles built 15 company houses, a store, a church and a railroad station on the B&O. They built an 8-mile logging railroad across the river and up Town Line Run to access their timber lands.

Since this was a pulp operation, methods could be a tad more relaxed than those that were used logging for lumber.

> *"They do not use axes or cross-cut saws up there in cutting down trees. Such tools are too slow in performing the required work. They simply blow a tree up with dynamite. A specimen of this sort of thing was witnessed by (reporters). A few large spruce were selected as the 'victims' and the 'feller' who fells began to quickly bore a hole in the base of the tree with an inch auger. The hole was driven in about ten inches, the chips were removed and a dynamite cartridge*

was inserted in the hole. The dynamite used comes in sticks like a candle and resembles moist brown sugar. A fuse was attached to the charge, and after it was lighted the men sought a place of safety and waited. In a few seconds there was a mighty roar and the great tree was lifted up into the air about ten feet, then with a swoop and crash it came to the earth, splintered half way up the trunk . . . . "Dynamite is not cheap, but it may truthfully be said that a little of it goes a long way." History of the County of Westmoreland, Pennsylvania, 1882

After C. P. Markle died, the operation was sold to a man named Parsons from New York. Both the West Newton and Markleton operations closed around 1893 due to increasing river pollution from the mines and coke ovens, and the assets were sold off.

In Markleton, the timber lands and railroad were sold to gentlemen named McCune and Lytle who named their operation the Markleton Lumber Company. The pulp mill site was sold as a sanatorium.

The art of advertising copyrighting not being what it is today, they called the Markleton Sanatorium or "The Markleton" the "Little Switzerland Under Turkeyfoot Plateau." A promotion piece for the place went on to read, " 'Where Every Prospect Pleases,' The Mountain Panorama, Trout Streams, The River, The Forest Primeval, The Ideal All-the-Year 'Round Resort, Where Health is the Sure Result."

It quoted "the most reliable authorities" that "the most salubrious elevation above sea-level is from 1500 to 2500 feet. 'The Markleton,' either by accident or design is perched in the neighborhood of 1800 feet above sea-level."

The Markle pulp mill about 1881. The building with the tall smoke stack in the center of the engraving became part of the sanatorium. The track behind it led to a small coal mine. The building with the cupola at the end of the bridge was the railroad station that was built by the Markles. The building with the three gables at the extreme right is the only structure belonging to the sanatorium or pulp mill that still exists. From the *History of Westmorland.* Albert, 1882.

The "salubrious" altitude, coupled with the pure mountain water issuing forth from Icicle Spring, was supposed to cure what ailed the well-heeled Victorian gentleperson.

The place was a Victorian pile that assaulted the eye with its turrets, gables, long porches and sweeping staircases that led down to a network of boardwalks. It had a grand view of the Casselman River, the B&O Railroad (it must have been a wonderful place to watch trains) and the slopes of Negro Mountain.

The Barnett family of Mt. Pleasant, PA, built the sanatorium and it quickly became a popular resort, having frequent train service from Baltimore, Washington, and Pittsburgh. Four trains a day each way stopped there in 1916.

President Warren G. Harding is said to have had trysts here with "his lady friend" and visited often. Presumably, this was when Harding was still a Senator. He became President in 1921 after World War I when the Markleton was beginning its decline. The federal government took over the place during the war to serve as a hospital for soldiers who were wounded and who had tuberculosis. It was run by the U.S. Public Health Service and was expanded with new barracks and two Red Cross buildings.

After the war, the great resort hotels began to go out of fashion as the public rode their automobiles to new watering holes. The Markleton suffered even worse than most because of the stigma of tuberculosis that had become attached to it.

The old sanatorium was torn down in 1938 and its building materials were saved and used in homes all over Fayette and Somerset Counties.

Logging

After McCune and Lytle bought the Markle properties on the trail side of the river, they built a sawmill at the mouth of Isers Run where it joins Town Line Run (see map at the beginning of the chapter). One can assume there were still trees left that hadn't been blown to smithereens. H. C. Huston, who owned the adjoining operation in Pinkerton bought out McCune and Lytle in 1899. Huston died in 1902 and the whole shebang was sold once again, this time to the Enterprise Lumber Company which expanded it.

When the Western Maryland Railway was built in 1910-12, Enterprise abandoned the bridge over the Casselman at Markleton and shipped its lumber out on the new railroad. Enterprise closed the mill in 1917 and it was scrapped.

Mining

While the sanatorium was entertaining the great and near great, across the river men were mining coal. There were three mines in the Markleton area: M. A. Snyder and Sons operated the Snyder Mine; it had 10 employees and worked two coal seams. The Berger-Aiken Coal Co. of Pittsburgh had the Markleton Mine, a drift mine that had 25 employees and worked the 38-inch Upper Kittanning Seam. The Casselman River Smokeless Coal Co. (later the Darby Coal Co.) Mine No. 1, a drift mine, had 40 employees and also worked the Upper Kittanning Seam.

From the trail, you can see the remains of these mines and the railroad grades that served them.

CHAPTER 19: CASSELMAN

The Rockwood coaling station was strategically located about halfway between Cumberland and Connellsville to provide fuel and water to hungry steam locomotives which used huge amounts of both. When this picture was taken in 1955, steam engines had been gone from the Western Maryland for about a year and these facilities were no longer needed by the more efficient diesels. Courtesy Western Maryland Railway Historical Society.

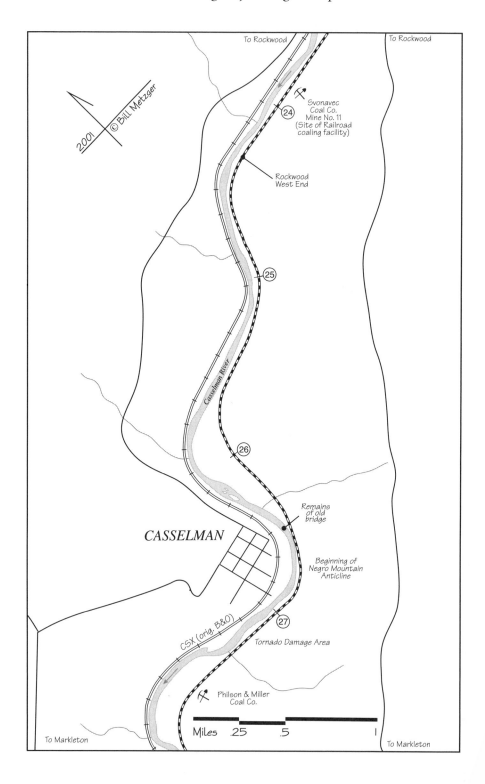

Mile 27.1 Tornado Damage

On two successive nights, June 6 and 7, 1998, a series of tornados touched down in Westmoreland and Somerset Counties causing considerable damage. About half of the town of Salisbury, PA was destroyed. One of the twisters knocked down the trees you see here.

This was said to be a freak occurrence, but on June 18, 1910 a similar storm raised havoc in the valley, knocking down trees, tearing off roofs and causing flooding.

Mile 26.8 Casselman

When the leaves are on the trees, the only way you know Casselman is there is when you hear the trains blowing for the crossing in town. Otherwise, you'll pass the town without having any clue you're even near it.

Many years ago there was a covered bridge that crossed the river here. It washed out and a suspension footbridge replaced it, but that's long since been removed.

There are no services and no access to the trail from Casselman.

You can see the remains of a mine here, the Millerton Coal Company's Millerton Mine. It had 53 miners in 1908.

Mile 24

When you come to a place where the trail right of way widens out, you've arrived at what the railroad called Rockwood West End, the beginning of double track. The railroad had a coaling facility and water tanks for the steam locomotives here. They were deactivated and removed in 1955.

The scars on the hill side of the trail was the Svonavec Mine. It was one of the last mines served by the Western Maryland. The decorative water spout was put there by the Sanner family, owners of the Rockwood Trail House. It uses water from a spring in the hill.

There were two brick yards in this area along the river side but they both closed about 1920.

A closer look at the Rockwood water tanks in 1955. They already had their spouts removed and were empty. They'd soon be torn down. Courtesy Western Maryland Railway Historical Society.

CHAPTER 20: ROCKWOOD

Part of a panoramic photo of Rockwood about 1920 looking across the Casselman River toward the Western Maryland. The bridge in the foreground belongs to the Quemahoning Branch and is one of the few structures in this picture that still stand. The B&O station, which also still stands, is partially obscured to the right of the bridge. Pennelec's power station is the building across the river. It was destroyed by fire in 1934. Courtesy Rockwood Historical Society.

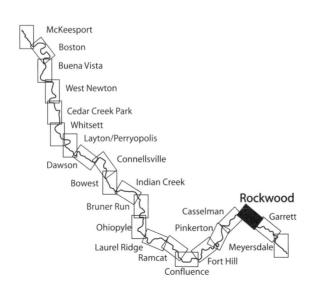

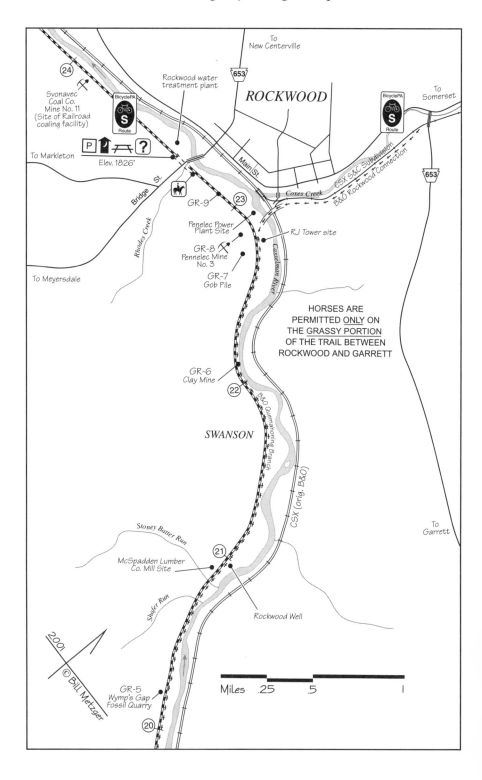

To
New Centerville

653

ROCKWOOD

To
Somerset

24

Svonavec
Coal Co.
Mine No. 11
(Site of Railroad
coaling facility)

Rockwood water
treatment plant

BicyclePA
S
Route

BicyclePA
S
Route

653

To Markleton

Elev. 1826'

Main St.

CSX S&C Subdivision

B&O Rockwood Connection

GR-9

23

Coxes Creek

Bridge St.

Rhodes Creek

Penelec Power
Plant Site

RJ Tower site

GR-8
Pennelec Mine
No. 3

Casselman River

To Meyersdale

GR-7
Gob Pile

HORSES ARE
PERMITTED <u>ONLY</u> ON
THE <u>GRASSY PORTION</u>
OF THE TRAIL BETWEEN
ROCKWOOD AND GARRETT

GR-6
Clay Mine

22

B&O Quemahoning Branch

SWANSON

CSX (orig. B&O)

Stoney Batter Run

To
Garrett

21

McSpadden Lumber
Co. Mill Site

Shafer Run

Rockwood Well

2001
© Bill Metzger

GR-5
Wymp's Gap
Fossil Quarry

MiLes   .25   .5   1

20

Mile 23.6

The Rockwood sewage treatment plant is along the river. It's operated by the Borough of Rockwood and processes about 80,000 gallons a day.

Rockwood station was situated just in front of the Rockwood Trail House. It was dismantled in the 1970s and rebuilt in the Mill Run area as a restaurant which has since closed.

Mile 23.5 Rockwood

As is the case with Confluence and Garrett, most of Rockwood is built on the other side of the river. The reason, quite simply, is that these towns all grew around the B&O and it got there first. The towns of the lower Casselman River valley all developed after the coming of the B&O in 1871. Before that, with the exception of the Turkeyfoot, nobody much had a need to travel through the rugged country. The through roads were to the north and south and most of the Casselman valley in the middle wasn't broad or fertile, so most settlers and travelers went elsewhere.

The Western Maryland Rockwood station in 1955. It was moved after the railroad was abandoned. The building behind it became the Rockwood Trail House. Courtesy Western Maryland Railway Historical Society.

Rockwood was originally named for John Shoaf, an early settler and farmer who came to the area in 1816. A wooden bridge was built across the river here and it—and the town—became known as Shoaf's Bridge. A later owner, Philip Wolfersberger, laid out a town on the property in 1857 and called it Mineral Point, wisely refraining from naming it after himself. But hardly anyone bought property in the new town and still called it Shoaf's Bridge. The official name was Mineral Point when the railroad came through and things started jumping.

> "There being already a Mineral Point post office in the state, the town could not take that name. After prolonged discussion, it was decided to name the town after about the only thing then in sight—rocks and woods—hence the name, Rockwood. The woods have about disappeared. The rocks still remain." History of Bedford and Somerset Counties Pennsylvania, Blackburn, Welfley & Koontz, 1906.

The woods around the town have grown considerably since 1906.

Industries, including a tannery, a lumber mill, three brick yards and a brewery, sprang up, and the B&O built its Somerset and Cambria Branch up to Johnstown. Rockwood became the commercial hub of the county; there were several hotels and businesses of every description. If you were going to Somerset by train, chances are you would have to lay over and spend at least one night at Rockwood.

It's no coincidence that the square in town was built where the street to the railroad station crossed Main Street.

There was an opera house in town and traveling theater companies would arrive by train and put on performances for the locals. At one time many of the towns along the trail had opera houses of some sort, but what sets Rockwood apart is that its opera house has been restored. It's now the Rockwood Mill Shoppes and Opera House on Main Street and worth a visit.

For what it's worth, the B&O station still stands. There is a strong movement afoot to make Rockwood a regular stop for Amtrak's Capitol Limited. It already stops here to change crews. By the time you read this, you may be able to ride the train to Rockwood and bike back downhill to McKeesport. Check with Amtrak.

There are two main industries in town: the Rockwood Casualty Insurance Company and the Rockwood Manufacturing Co. The town offers a variety of services including B&Bs, stores and restaurants.

This is where BicyclePA Route S leaves the trail and takes off north to Somerset and points east (see page 45).

Mile 23.1 Geology Classroom

As soon as you come up on the trail from Rockwood, there's a marker post that you haven't seen before. This is the first of a series that were placed on the trail by geologist Jim Shaulis and Tom Jones, a teacher in the Rockwood School District, to aid in using the trail as a geology classroom.

The top letter on the post, in this case "A," refers to a teacher's workshop guide Shaulis and Jones are preparing. The "GR" means Garrett to Rockwood and 9 is the reference number.

When you enter the trail here, you've entered the Negro Mountain anticline.

GR-9

If you look down at the bottom of the cliff at the bank side of the trail, right along the ditch, you'll see the Lower Kittanning Coal Seam. It's about 28" thick. Right on top of it is a formation of Lower Worthington Sandstone. What probably happened here was a sizeable flood washed over a peat bog, deposited a lot of sand and compressed the peat, which, over the course of about 300 million years, became coal. The rule of thumb is that 25 feet of peat will compress into about 2 feet of coal. You'll also see a healthy thicket of rhododendron growing here. Rhododendron likes acidic soil and both the coal and the sandstone are acidic.

Mile 22.9 GR-8

This is the mine entry for No. 3 mine, which fed the company's Rockwood power station. It's about ten feet above the trail. There's Abandoned Mine Drainage (AMD) flowing out at a pH of 2.5, about that of lemon juice.

Electricity came to Rockwood in 1896 with a small hydroelectric plant that was powered by a dam across the river here. In 1917, Pennsylvania Electric Co. (Pennelec) built a larger coal-fired power plant along the river below where the substation now sits. The remarkable thing about this particular power station is the mine that fed it. Pennelec Mine No. 3 worked a 28" coal seam. Think about this. A desk top is about 28" high. Now consider spending your entire day doing hard physical work in the dark and damp in a space no higher than the area under a desk, then try to tell yourself how tough you have it now. However bad you think you have it, the miners who worked in Pennelec No. 3 had it worse. This, by the way, is the same Lower Kittanning Coal Seam that you saw at GR-9.

By comparison, the guys who worked the 8-foot-thick Pittsburgh Seam on the other side of the mountain had it made. Ironically, says Shaulis, the hydro plant was destroyed by flood and the coal-fired plant was destroyed by fire. It burned in 1934.

The foundations of the plant, several company houses, the tipple, and suspension bridge that crossed the river to town are hidden down in the trees between the trail and the river.

Quemahoning Branch—RJ Cabin

Between Rockwood and Garrett the trail right of way is quite wide and there's a unique reason for this. In 1915, the B&O needed another track and didn't have enough room to lay one on its side of the river, so it bought some land along the Western Maryland and built the Quemahoning branch. The branch crossed back across the river here and connected with the B&O's Somerset and Cambria branch, which at that time was originating huge amounts of coal from a myriad of Somerset County mines and steel from the mills at Johnstown. The bridge still stands. It's just out of sight toward the river.

In actuality, both the Quemahoning Branch and the WM main line were operated as one railroad between Garrett and Rockwood, one track for each direction. In 1957, the B&O sold the Quemahoning back to the WM, but the WM still used the bridge into Rockwood.

There was a telegraph office here called RJ Cabin that controlled train movements on both the branch and the main line.

Pennelec Substation

Technically, the only functioning thing still remaining of the Rockwood power plant is the substation on the hillside. Pennelec is a subsidiary of GPU, General Public Utilities. When the leaves are off the trees, you can still see the track that leads into the substation. The rails that brought transformers in are still in place.

GR-7

This is the gob pile from the mine on the hillside. You can find plant fossils in the shale.

The gob pile you can see across the river on the power line marks the remains of the Pennwood Mine.

Mile 22.1 GR-6

The board fence on the river side marks the site of the clay mine for the abandoned brick works across the river. The grades to the mine are clearly visible. There was a tunnel under the railroad here which is now sealed up. There is also Pottsville Sandstone in the vicinity.

The Lower Kittanning Coal Seam slopes uphill along the trail. It's about 100' above the trail. This was all mined by Pennelec No. 3.

Mile 21 Rockwood Well

The green steel box is one of the wells for the borough of Rockwood. There are four wells, the deepest being 450 feet. The borough pays a lease on the wells which helps maintain the trail. The antenna is attached to radio equipment that controls the submerged pumps. The McSpadden Lumber Co. had a small logging operation along Stony Batter Run about 1911 that included a railroad.

Mile 20.1 GR-5

This is the Wymp's Gap Fossil Quarry. Stop here and poke around for a bit. Pick up just about any rock and examine it closely and you're sure to find fossils. Don't worry about picking up something and taking it with you—it's okay. It's been especially dug out for instruction. You'll notice there's already a hole where there's a lot of rock missing—it's all been hauled out by fossil-finding kids in their backpacks.

When fossils get in short supply, the Rockwood Maintenance Department comes up with a backhoe and digs out some more. The fossils are from the Mississippian Era and are between 323 and 360 million years old. The quarry is named for the gap in Fayette County where they were first identified.

"This quarry makes this a Class 1 geological trail," says Shaulis. "It's got everything you need to teach the area's geology."

You'll also notice how the rhododendron climbs up the mountainside following the Pottsville and Upper Mauch Chunk Sandstone.

Mile 19.5

There's a small stream here where the waterfall, when the stream's running, runs over Mauch Chunk Sandstone.

CHAPTER 21: GARRETT

A valuation photo of the Garrett station taken in 1917. Courtesy Western Maryland Railway Historical Society.

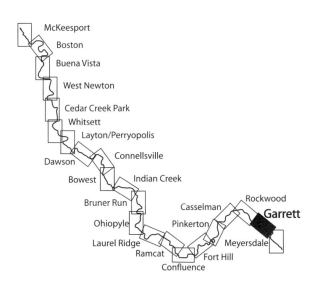

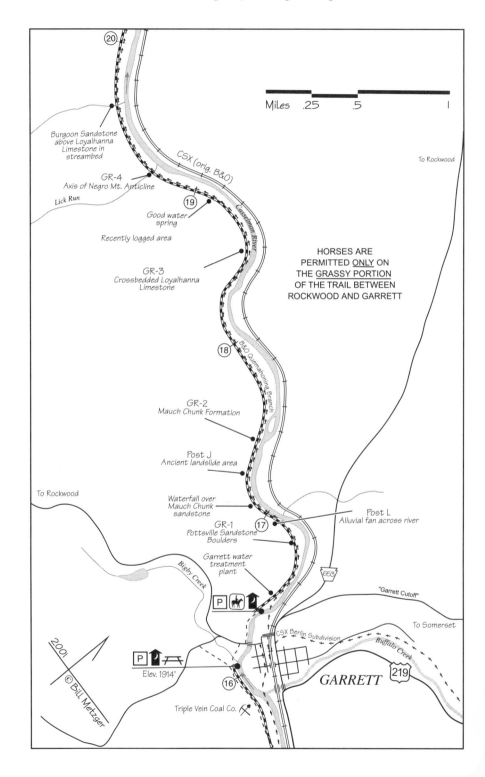

20

Burgoon Sandstone
above Loyalhanna
Limestone in
streambed

CSX (orig. B&O)

To Rockwood

GR-4
Axis of Negro Mt. Anticline

Lick Run

19

Good water
spring

Recently logged area

Cassleman River

GR-3
Crossbedded Loyalhanna
Limestone

HORSES ARE
PERMITTED <u>ONLY</u> ON
THE <u>GRASSY</u> PORTION
OF THE TRAIL BETWEEN
ROCKWOOD AND GARRETT

18

B&O Quemahoning Branch

GR-2
Mauch Chunk Formation

Post J
Ancient landslide area

To Rockwood

Waterfall over
Mauch Chunk
sandstone

Post L
Alluvial fan across river

GR-1
Pottsville Sandstone
Boulders

17

Garrett water
treatment
plant

653

"Garrett Cutoff"

P

CSX Berlin Subdivision

To Somerset

Bigby Creek

Buffalo Creek

2001
© Bill Metzger

P

Elev. 1914'

16

GARRETT

219

Triple Vein Coal Co.

Miles .25   .5   I

Mile 19.2 GR-4

The little stream here is Lick Run which marks the axis of the Negro Mountain anticline. The rocks here aren't inclined, but are perfectly flat. The stream flows down through a fracture in the rock.

GR-3

This is a place that only a geologist could love. It's called "festooned cross bedding" and was caused by either (a) sand dunes that were later submerged or (b) submarine dunes off a coast. They're red due to oxidation of the Mauch Chunk Sandstone mixing in with the sand. There are some shell fragments embedded in this stone.

The stone was cut in 1911 by the railroad and has slightly worn to where you can feel the relief in the face of the rock. Ninety years of exposure has weathered the rock about 0.1 inch. From that, you can calculate how long other rocks from this formation have been exposed. The answer is several thousand years. Or, to put it technically, a long time.

The white rock above this formation is Deer Valley Limestone, named for the YMCA camp near Mt. Davis.

Now you'll notice that the rocks are dipping to the east. You're on the other side of the anticline going forward in time.

The fractured rock you see along the trail was fractured when it was blasted by the railroad.

Mile 19

You can see recent evidence of clear-cut logging along the mountainside here. Large stumps are grown up with thick stands of small trees. Just east of Mile 19 there's a spring with potable water running out of the hill. You'll see the white plastic pipe in the hillside.

Mile 17.5 GR-2

You're looking at Mauch Chunk Sandstone here. You'll notice that the rhododendron doesn't grow outside the sandstone, but there's one tiny rhododendron growing out of a piece of fossilized wood.

Mauch Chunk (pronounced Maw-Chunk) Sandstone is named for the town of Mauch Chunk, Pennsylvania, that changed its name to Jim Thorpe in the early 1950s when the Olympic great died. Geologists, not caring much about the Olympics, stuck with the original name for the rock.

Mile 17.3 Post J

This post was added after the GR posts were all put in. It marks the site of a huge landslide that roared down the hill sometime around 10,000 years ago. The climate was arctic tundra back then. There was no vegetation to hold things together and warming was taking place. According to retired geomorphologist Bill Sevon, the rhododendron shouldn't be here, but is because of all the sandstone that slid downhill. Given the age of the slide it's conceivable that men could have witnessed it. When you stop seeing rhododendron, you're out of the slide area. You'll also see a drainage ditch that the railroad dug to keep the slide from sliding any farther.

Mile 17

You'll see a lot of conifers (evergreens) growing through here because they also like acid soil.

Post L

Refers to the Piney Run alluvial fan (delta) across the river that you can't see when the leaves are on the trees unless you climb down the bank which there's not much point in doing since it's not that big of a deal anyway.

Mile 16.9 GR-1

These are Pottsville boulders up close and personal that came down the mountainside in the post-glacial period when the soil was still like Jell-o and there wasn't much vegetation. Shaulis says "they're probably not moving at all now," so worry not.

Wind Farm

Without a doubt the most otherworldly experience on the whole trail is riding into Garrett and looking up and encountering the first windmill. It's completely out of context—you've been riding the trail for miles looking up and seeing nothing but trees and mountains and sky—and all of a sudden you feel like you're being attacked by giant aliens from The Planet of the Killer Windmills.

Do not be alarmed. They come in peace. You're looking at the Green Mountain Wind Farm, officially opened in May, 2000. National Wind Power Ltd., of England is the developer, owner and operator. They sell the power to Green Mountain.com of Vermont. There are eight windmills in this particular farm and two other farms nearby have opened.

Stats: Each turbine puts out 1.3 Megawatts and the whole farm has a combined output of 10.4 MW, enough to supply power to 2,500 average homes. Each tower is 200 feet high and each blade is 95 feet long. They rotate at either 12.7 or 19 revolutions per minute and start to generate electricity when the wind speed is 8 mph or higher. They'll automatically shut down when the wind exceeds 56 mph. The cool thing is that they're built on a former strip mine. You can see the mine's old dragline shovel from Salisbury Viaduct.

Mile 16.5

The building at the gate behind the chain link fence is the Garrett Water Works. Keep out.

Mile 16.4

You'll leave the trail here and go down a dirt road. If you look back downstream when you get close to the river you can see the piers from the abandoned B&O Quemahoning Branch where it went back across the river. When you get to the stop sign, you're in Garrett. Turn right and quick left if you want to continue up the trail. The left takes you into town.

The road originally crossed the railroad on a wooden bridge, but it was removed and filled in when the railroad was abandoned.

Mile 16.2 Garrett, Population 515

Named for John Garrett (1820-1884), president of the B&O from 1858 until his death. He was responsible for completing the Pittsburgh and Connellsville from Connellsville to Cumberland and for the expansion of the B&O to Chicago, St. Louis, and Cincinnati. Garrett led the railroad during the Civil War when it took a battering because of its location as a de facto boundary between the North and the South. His son Robert succeeded him in the railroad's presidency.

The town's situated at the mouth of Buffalo Creek. Just like the other towns in the Casselman Valley, it was laid out in 1871 when the railroad was built. It was a junction for the B&O's Berlin Branch and a coal mining town at one time. It was also the east end of the B&O's Quemahoning Branch and the terminal of the trolley line from Meyersdale. Garrett was home to blacksmiths, an ice house, a meat market, a bakery, a physician, several hotels, an opera house, clothing stores, a grocery store, a jewelry store, barber shops, and even a music studio and an art gallery. Today, there's a bank and a convenience store and gas station here. Should you feel like a bit of road biking, there's a covered bridge across Buffalo Creek about two miles north on Route 219. The road is busy but has good paving and a nice shoulder.

Mile 15.9 Enterprise Coal Co. Ponfeigh No. 7 and 8

This mine employed 55 in the 1930s and worked a 42-inch coal seam. There is a small AMD seep coming out of this mine.

CHAPTER 22: MEYERSDALE AND BEYOND

A short coal train crosses Salisbury Viaduct in 1952. The X-bracing on the piers makes this a true trestle. Courtesy Western Maryland Railway Historical Society, photo by William Price.

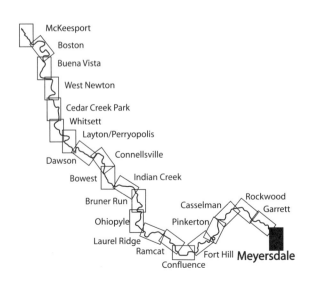

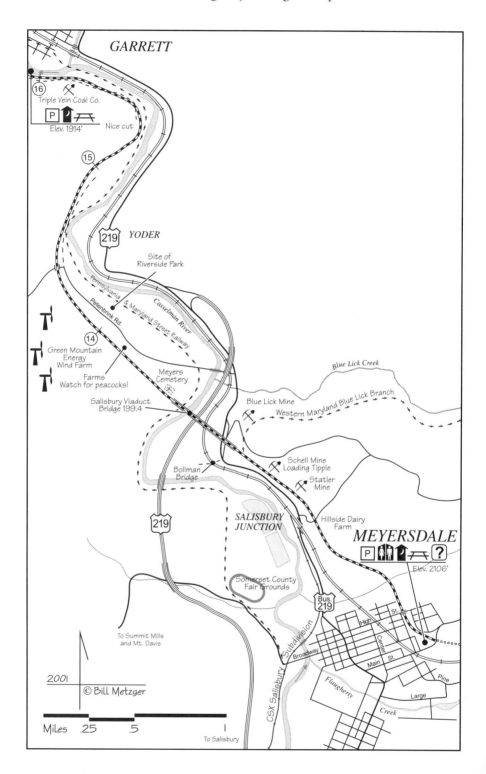

GARRETT

16
Triple Vein Coal Co.

P 🚻 📍 🪑
Elev. 1914'   Nice cut

15

219   *YODER*

Site of
Riverside Park

Pennsylvania & Maryland Street Railway

Casselman River

Petenbrink Rd.

14
Green Mountain
Energy
Wind Farm

Farms
Watch for peacocks!

Meyers
Cemetery

Salisbury Viaduct
Bridge 199.4

Blue Lick Creek

Blue Lick Mine

Western Maryland Blue Lick Branch

Schell Mine
Loading Tipple

Statler
Mine

Bollman
Bridge

*SALISBURY
JUNCTION*

Hillside Dairy
Farm

MEYERSDALE

P 🏠🏠 📍 🪑 ❓
Elev. 2106'

219

Somerset County
Fair Grounds

Bus.
219

High   St.

Center

Broadway

Main   St.

CSX Salisbury Subdivision

To Summit Mills
and Mt. Davis

2001

© Bill Metzger

Miles   .25   .5   1

Flaugherty

Creek

Pine

Large

To Salisbury

Mile 15.4

This a nice cut. Nothing special about it—I just like it.

Mile 14.5

The trail goes out on the township road for a bit here.

Mile 14

If you look toward the river across the road from the blue trailer, you can see the site of Riverside Park, which was built by the Pennsylvania and Maryland Street Railway (see page 187).

There are no mileposts from here to Meyersdale.

Like many trolley lines of the day, the Pennsylvania and Maryland Street Railway had its own amusement park, Riverside Park between Garrett and Meyersdale. Courtesy Meyersdale Public Library.

Farming

You've passed a field here and there, but between here and Meyersdale is the only section along the trail where you get close to any working farms. Farming is the biggest business in Somerset County, accounting for about twice the revenue of mining, but they keep strip mining farms anyway. Go figure. Keep a look out for the peacocks along here. That's right, peacocks.

Meyers Cemetery

The small cemetery near the south end of the Viaduct is the final resting place of the Meyers family, who originally farmed near here. Most of the graves date to the 19th century, including two sisters, Clara and Susan, who were killed in a house fire on June 4, 1891.

Salisbury Viaduct

Before you cross the viaduct, sit at the bench or picnic table and read about the bridge you're about to cross and all the things that it crosses. In order from south to north, you'll cross an abandoned trolley line, the Route 219 Bypass, the Casselman River, the CSX (old B&O) main line, the Casselman River (this is the last time you'll cross it on the trail), old Route 219 and a county road. Off to the east is a very historic bridge that also needs to be discussed.

A line of freshly-poured concrete piers marches across the Casselman River valley in preparation for Salisbury Viaduct. The track in the foreground belongs to the Pennsylvania and Maryland Street Railway. The Bollman Bridge can be just barely seen in the upper right corner of the picture. It was already in place when this picture was taken in 1911.
Courtesy Western Maryland Railway Historical Society.

Bridge No. 199.4 Salisbury Viaduct, Deck Plate Girder Trestle, 1908' Long, 101' High

Since this is the most spectacular surface structure on the trail, this is a good place to talk about how the railroad was built.

As you may have guessed, the B&O was somewhat less than thrilled about this upstart Western Maryland being built beside it (we talked about the B&O back in Chapter 1 and the WM in Chapter 10). The B&O made a great show of sending their surveyors out while the Western Maryland was being built and announced plans for a new two-mile-long super tunnel to eliminate their woefully inadequate Sand Patch Tunnel. They promised the citizens of Meyersdale all sorts of things, including a new railroad yard that would bring jobs and prosperity to the area. But the WM kept right on a-building. They did (very briefly) consider digging a tunnel under Meyersdale to keep the local citizenry mollified, but in the end, the folks settled for the biggest station on the WM between Cumberland and Connellsville. In 1911 the WM and B&O buried the hatchet after construction was well along on the new line, clearing the legal way for the new WM line. The super tunnel and yard never did get built by the B&O, but a new Sand Patch tunnel was completed in 1913.

The viaduct was built across the valley to maintain a favorable grade. Keeping to the south side of the valley would have meant extensive—and expensive—bridging and earthwork.

Ultimately the Western Maryland's Connellsville Extension would take two years and $10-$12 million to complete (see Route 219 on page 186). The Carter Construction Co. of Pittsburgh was the general contractor and oversaw the whole job. Construction began in earnest June, 1910. At one time 3,800 men and 34 steam shovels were at work and the neighboring B&O was choked with carloads of machinery and construction material.

McClintic-Marshall of Pittsburgh (later bought by Bethlehem Steel) was the construction company on the Salisbury Viaduct. Work progressed nicely until July 10, 1911 when an electric crane lifting a girder up to the deck of Salisbury Viaduct failed and fell about 100 feet to the valley floor taking 7 men with it, six of whom died: five instantly, one hours later. A month later another man was killed when he slipped and fell off the deck. Despite these accidents and another near miss, the viaduct opened on January 18, 1912 when the first train ran over it to the joy of hundreds of spectators.

The beautiful concrete deck on which you ride was completed in the spring of 1999 as a project of Somerset County. For the record, the bridge, according to the Western Maryland Historical Railway Historical Society, "consists of 37 alternating 39-foot and 60-foot girders, except at the railroad and river crossings where it consisted of 40 foot and 90 foot girders, placed on steel towers resting on concrete pedestals." Some of the pedestals are 40 feet deep. Like the rest of the Western Maryland bridges, Salisbury was built for two tracks.

"Viaduct" is just a fancy word for long bridge. Salisbury Viaduct actually qualifies as a trestle. Now it's time to talk about trestles. See the steel work under the viaduct? It's cross-braced—that's the X-shaped work and each one of those is called a "bent." Any bridge that uses bents in its structure is called a trestle.

It was named for the town of Salisbury even though the town is eight miles to the south. There might have been a worse name—Blue Lick Creek is right handy.

A Study In Contrasts

The Baltimore and Ohio's Pittsburgh and Connellsville and the Western Maryland Connellsville Extension are a study in contrasts. The P&C was built between 1854 and 1871 and the WM's Connellsville Extension took only 2 years: 1910-12. The P&C used hand labor, black powder and wood, stone and iron for construction materials.

The WM had the advantages of better engineering techniques coupled with steam shovels, compressed air drills, electricity, dynamite, concrete and steel. The engineers also built a railroad that's virtually flood proof. The B&O up Wills Creek has washed out several times. In some ways the B&O had the better route: it stayed on the right banks of the Casselman and Yough and never had to cross them. The WM crossed the rivers 9 times, but it only had to dig two tunnels; the B&O dug five and, worse, it had to re-dig Sand Patch Tunnel, its crossing of the Allegheny Front, after the first one proved to be something of a hellhole. In fact, much of the B&O had to be rebuilt. Little of the WM ever was. The WM had the shorter railroad between Cumberland and Connellsville and the gentlest grades.

But better railroad or not, the Western Maryland always had less traffic than the B&O and it only ran from Baltimore to Connellsville. It was competing with a railroad that had tracks to not only Baltimore, but Philadelphia, Washington, Buffalo, Chicago, St. Louis, and Cincinnati. And that, in the end, was what killed it.

Route 219, The Meyersdale Bypass

Think of this as a small part of a larger project. Some day, according to a local politician, this will be "the shortest route between Toronto and Atlanta." Right now, it's not exactly what you'd call heavily traveled; if you see 5 cars in 15 minutes you'll be doing good. But somebody decided that Meyersdale needed to be bypassed. And so it was.

The five and a half mile road cost $53 million and was finished in 21 months. The 87-mile Western Maryland Connellsville Extension cost $10-$12 million and was finished in about the same time.

The good news here is that were it not for the trail, PennDOT would have torn down the viaduct without thinking twice when they built the new road. When the original Route 219 was built, it was the first "hard road" in the area and was dubbed the "Transylvania Trail."

Archaeological Sites

This part of the Casselman River valley was once home to several Monongahela Native American villages and rock shelters. Two villages were located on the site of the Somerset County Fairgrounds, right where the racetrack is located now, and two rock shelters were about where new Route 219 branches off from the old road.

Blue Lick Mine And Branch

The Blue Lick Mine and Branch were named for Blue Lick Creek (it rhymes here). Yes, "blue lick" sounds silly, but what it refers to is a salt deposit along the creek where wildlife would come and lick. There are literally dozens of places in Pennsylvania with the word "lick" in them and each refers to a salt lick.

The Blue Lick Mine was a strip mine, as are most of the mines operating in Somerset County today. Aside from the fact that strip mining is a cheap way to pull coal out of the ground, there's really nothing good to say about it. Historically, strip mining was developed with the invention of the steam shovel and dynamite, which made it easy to remove large amounts of earth. A hole would be drilled, a dynamite charge would be placed in it, there would be a fine explosion that would loosen the rock above the coal seam (called overburden) and the steam shovel would scoop up the rock and set it aside. And before regulation of strip mining, that's where it would stay. The coal would be picked up by smaller shovels and trucks and the stripping operation would move on.

Vast sections of north central Pennsylvania in both the hard and soft coal regions look like moonscapes or war zones because of unregulated strip mining.

A drive on any main road in Somerset County today will pass a strip mining operation. Now the strippers use huge diesel-electric draglines that scoop up the rock three and four cubic yards at a time. And regulation makes them put the overburden back where they found it, sort of.

Once stripped, the water table in an area is usually ruined and the land when "reclaimed" looks like somewhere in western Nebraska. But it's a cheap way to mine coal. Our only consolation is that it's worse in West Virginia. The Blue Lick

Branch was built in 1928 to serve the Ponfeigh Mines. The word Ponfeigh was a registered trademark of the Merrill Coal Co. and was a word supposedly meaning "good" by the company's founder. It's anybody's guess how it's pronounced.

The branch was the last to be worked on this section of the Western Maryland; a train came up from Cumberland to serve the mines on the branch after the rest of the WM was shut down.

Bollman Truss Bridge

When you get to the east end of the bridge, look eastward and you'll see a small truss bridge crossing the railroad. This little jewel is all kinds of historic.

It was originally a railroad bridge on the B&O that carried the line over Wills Creek. In fact, it's the last of the original B&O iron bridges, and was moved here about 1910 to carry a farm road over the tracks. It was built by Wendell Bollman.

Bollman Truss Bridge.

Wendell Bollman (1814-1884) was a self-taught engineer who went to work for the B&O as a carpenter at a time when everyone was still learning the art and science of railroad building. He began designing bridges in the early 1850s and patented the first all-iron truss bridge design in 1852. Bollman's design wasn't used much by any other railroad than the B&O but it had a great influence with other designers at a time when iron was becoming the material of choice for building bridges.

Bollman became master of the road (chief of maintenance) of the B&O just before the Civil War. The railroad had the dubious distinction of running along the border between North and South and the Confederates had quite the time merrily blowing up the line and stealing entire trains as opportunities presented themselves. Bollman was the guy who got to patch the railroad up.

After the war, he left the B&O and started his own bridge construction company. The bridge here, which carries an 1871 construction date, is built by Bollman's company but isn't one of his designs; it's a Warren truss that uses both cast iron and wrought iron. There's some wonderful cast iron scrollwork over the portals.

Should you be interested, there is a Bollman-design bridge still in existence across the Patuxtant River in Savage, Maryland, near Baltimore, that's been nicely restored.

Pennsylvania and Maryland Street Railway

Running under the south end of the viaduct is the grade of the Pennsylvania and Maryland Street Railway, a trolley line that ran from Salisbury, PA to Garrett, a total of 12 miles. The line was started in 1906 with the grandiose plan of connecting Frostburg, Maryland with Johnstown, PA. Both towns already sported trolley net-

A group of local lads pose for the camera with a Pennsylvania and Maryland Street Railway trolley car at Riverside Park. Courtesy Meyersdale Public Library.

works; the Salisbury-Meyersdale-Garrett section was the only part of the scheme that was built. The first trolley arrived in Meyersdale at 4:30 a.m., Oct. 31, 1907. At first, the B&O railroad wouldn't allow the trolley line to cross its tracks, so passengers had to walk across the railroad from one car to the next—hardly rapid transit. The B&O finally relented and let the streetcar line build a crossing. It still took an hour for the cars to get from Salisbury to Garrett; service was every two hours.

Riverside Park, a small amusement park consisting of two pavilions, a fountain, a merry-go-round and some rowboats, was built to boost ridership—a scheme typical of the time—but that didn't help much, bearing in mind that the population of Garrett was 859 in 1920 and Meyersdale was 3,716. The park was popular, but you couldn't exactly call it Six Flags Over Garrett. Passengers could also choose between a train each way on the Western Maryland and two trains each way on the B&O, so the trolley line had plenty of competition. Still more typically, the line suffered from competition by automobiles and was abandoned from Meyersdale to Garrett in 1924 and from Salisbury to Meyersdale in 1927. The old P&M carbarn still stands in the town of Boynton between Meyersdale and Salisbury on Route 219.

Salisbury Junction

There were two mines on the section of the trail between the viaduct and Meyersdale. You can see a cleared spot up on the hill where the Schell Mine had a loading tipple and a grade going back in the weeds where the Statler Mine was located. The Statler Mine was a drift mine with 20 employees in 1918 and was owned by Emmanuel Statler.

There was a wooden overhead bridge here that was a private farm road. It was removed when the trail was built. The Hillside Farm raises Jersey cows which are brown and give milk that's higher in butterfat than the ordinary black and white Holsteins. The farm is private property and is guarded by a flock of watch geese.

For all its marvelous engineering, the Western Maryland skimped on building bridges over the railroad; they were all wood, not that there were all that many of them. In fact, between Cumberland and Connellsville there were seven highway overpasses all told and four of them were within a mile of Meyersdale. All but one have been removed.

Meyersdale Station

You know you're in Meyersdale when you come to the beautifully restored Western Maryland railroad station. The local historical society has done a fine job of bringing this once-derelict building back to life and today they run a visitors center here on the weekends. It includes full restrooms for those of you who are sick of trailside chemical toilets. It's also their headquarters.

In return for a right of way through town, the Western Maryland Railway promised the citizens of Meyersdale the biggest station on the line between Cumberland

Meyersdale station in 1955. "Speeders," or motorized hand cars, are parked next to the building, although difficult to spot in this photo. They were used by track and signal maintenance people. Courtesy Western Maryland Railway Historical Society.

and Connellsville and that's just what they got. The town fathers passed a resolution in 1911 allowing the railroad to come through and the station building was completed March 12, 1912.

The caboose next to the station was brought to the site after the Western Maryland was abandoned. The chances are excellent that it never ran on the WM, but it was available for purchase. It was built in 1969 for the Chesapeake and Ohio Railroad and is called a "wide vision" caboose because the cupola overhangs the carbody. No matter how quaint they were, and no matter how much fun it was to wave to the men riding in it, cabooses were expensive and dangerous to operate. They've been replaced by radio telemetry devices at the end of trains.

The concrete thingie by the caboose is a telephone booth that was commonly used by the B&O. Superman would have had a ball in this one.

Meyersdale, Population 2,453

Meyersdale's claim to fame is the Maple Festival, held the last weekend of March and the first weekend of April. Somerset County is a hotbed of maple sugaring if for no other reason than its altitude gives it a climate sort of like Vermont.

Maple sugaring is an important cottage industry in the county. There isn't any evidence of sugaring along the trail, but a drive or bike ride along the back roads reveals telltale scars on trees and "Maple Sugar for Sale" signs in front of houses.

Sugaring is done in February and early March when the sap is running. The sap is collected in buckets and boiled down to make maple syrup, which is expensive, or maple sugar, which is real expensive, reason being that it takes 43 gallons of sap to make a gallon of syrup. At the Maple Festival there's enough of both to make your pancreas scream in agony, all sorts of entertainment, and a parade complete with Maple Queen and Princesses. That's in the spring. In the summer, Meyersdale is home to the Somerset County Fair which happens the last week of August with all the requisite things one does at a county fair. Meyersdale was originally Meyers' Mills. It was settled by some farmers and millers, mostly German, in the late 1700s, got its current name and post office in the 1830s, and was a fair sized town when the Baltimore & Ohio came through. The town blossomed with the coming of the railroad and enjoyed a growth spurt that lasted 30 or so years. The boom was fueled by coal and lumber and included brickyards, lumber mills, and factories that made things out of wood. Like many of the other towns along the railroad, there were 5 hotels here to serve the drummer trade (see Sutersville Chapter 3).

In 1874, Meyers Mills and Dale City merged. Hence the name.

One of the gems of the era, the old Second National Bank building, is being restored by Somerset Trust Company. Meyersdale has a daily newspaper, a friendly library, and all the usual services.

South of Meyersdale, in the area of Summit Mills and St. Paul, is a fair-sized Amish community that's been there since at least 1772. There's some nice road riding in the area; just don't be obnoxious and try to take pictures of the locals. They really don't like it.

Also south of town is Mt. Davis, at 3,213 feet the highest point in Pennsylvania. If you're expecting a craggy peak with an awe-inspiring sense of altitude where Julie Andrews runs around singing "the 'heels' are alive," this ain't it. You know you're on top when the road you've been climbing starts going down, but it's something less than impressive.

On to Cumberland!

Meyersdale is currently the end of the Great Allegheny Passage. You've come 100 miles, climbed 1,354 feet and seen some gorgeous country. You've met our first President when he was just a lad and when he was a prosperous landowner; thieves that stole with guns and thieves that stole with pens; loggers, miners, farmers, millers, and railroaders. You've crossed ancient Indian paths and a superhighway that crosses the country. You've passed ghost towns and mansions; breweries and distilleries; mines, mills, and dams; railroad yards and coke ovens, waterfalls, and the tufa. You've seen a goodly portion of the fourteen ten thousandths of the Mississippi watershed. And there's more to come. The Great Allegheny Passage still isn't finished from McKeesport to Pittsburgh or from Meyersdale to Cumberland. You have yet to cross the Eastern Continental Divide, the Allegheny Front, and the Mason-Dixon Line.

And then there are the physical obstacles between here and Cumberland: namely Keystone Viaduct, a 1,000-foot-long monster; the 3,924-foot Big Savage Tunnel and relocating the Western Maryland Scenic Railway to accommodate the trail. But, given the track record of the Allegheny Trail Alliance so far, it won't be long until you'll be able to ride over and through each one of them.

We have it on good authority that the whole trail, including the Big Savage Tunnel, will be finished to Cumberland by the fall of 2005.

Likewise, the trail between McKeesport and Pittsburgh has its own set of obstacles, but they, too will be overcome.

On to Pittsburgh!

On to Cumberland!

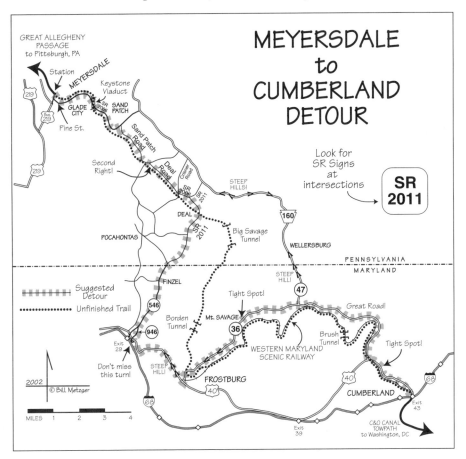

MEYERSDALE TO CUMBERLAND

For the next year or so, the trail between Meyersdale and at least the state line will be under construction. So you'll have to detour. You can either hire an outfitter from the website www.atatrail.org to ferry you between the two towns or you can do the detour yourself. It's not a bad ride, especially if you're going eastbound and makes a nice break from trail riding.

EASTBOUND

When you leave the Western Maryland station, turn right on Main Street and make a left on Pine Street just after you cross the railroad tracks going down hill. This becomes Glade City Road, State Route (SR) 2006. This is a lightly-traveled two-lane blacktop road. You'll gradually climb up through Glade City bearing in mind that any town in Pennsylvania with "City" in its name isn't.

You'll cross the railroad tracks again and pass under Keystone Viaduct. Keystone is slated to be rebuilt for trail use. Turn right on Sand Patch Road, SR 2006 and cross over the railroad again. This is Sand Patch, fabled among the railroad community as a great place to watch trains cross the Allegheny Mountains.

Stay on Sand Patch Road, a nice country blacktop road, and continue about a mile and a half. Turn right at the SECOND intersection, SR 2006, Deal Road.

In about 2 miles you'll come to two more intersections. Again, turn right at the SECOND, SR 2011, McKenzie Road. You'll cross over the filled-in crossing of the trail at Deal. This was the highest altitude on the old Western Maryland Railroad.

Stay on SR 2011 for about three miles and you'll cross into Maryland. Now you're on MD 546. The road gets wider and the pavement gets better. Stay on 546 for three more miles and make the left on MD 946. This takes you to US 40.

US 40 is a two lane blacktop road with wonderful shoulders. It also drops like a rock. You'll be in Frostburg in no time. Watch out for MD 36 on the left. MD 36 also drops pretty good. Be careful going through the town of Mt. Savage—the road becomes quite narrow here.

At Barrelville, MD 35 becomes bike paradise. This is some of the best bike riding you're ever going to experience: pretty scenery, wide shoulders, great paving—and it's down hill.

Turn left on US 40 at the red light. Now you're in the Narrows. Careful here. This is a narrow road with narrow shoulders. When US 40 starts over the bridge, stay straight on Mechanic Street. It'll take you directly to the C&O Canal Towpath Visitor's Center.

Westbound

Again, there are outfitters who will take you from Cumberland to Meyersdale by prior arrangement that you can find on the website or you have another fun option. The Western Maryland Scenic Railway offers train rides up to Frostburg. By prior arrangement you can put your bike on the train and ride about half the way up the mountain. From Frostburg you have about a two-mile climb up to the top. The train leaves Cumberland at 11:30 in the morning.

If you're gutsy and going to bike it, turn left on Mechanic Street in Cumberland at the Visitors Center. Mechanic Street is one way east, and Center Street is one way west. Take it. Center Street merges back into Mechanic Street which then joins US 40.

Take US 40 through the Narrows, be careful through here, and turn right at the red light at MD 36. This is a fine road with great shoulders. Stay on 36 through Barrelville and Mt. Savage, being careful in on the narrow street through town. Now you start to climb.

At the "T" intersection at the top of MD 36, turn right on US 40. You're still climbing through town and out the other side. Stay on US 40 to MD 946 which goes off to the left and loops over 40. This is your connection with MD 546. Don't miss it.

You're pretty much done climbing now. MD 546 rolls for about 3 miles into Pennsylvania where it becomes State Route (SR) 2011. This road will take you over the trail near Deal, the highest point on the old Western Maryland. At the "T" intersection, turn left on SR 2006, Deal Road. At the next "T" intersection, turn left on Sand Patch Road, still SR 2006. Cross the bridge over the railroad tracks at Sand Patch, and climb up to the stop sign where you'll make a left on Glade City Road, still SR 2006.

Cruise on down hill under Keystone Viaduct and be very careful crossing the railroad tracks—cross at a 90 degree angle. Keep cruising down through Glade City and into Meyersdale. Turn right on Main Street. The trail will be on the other side of the railroad tracks and a block up the hill on the left.

RESOURCES

TRAIL AND RELATED GROUPS
You can access all of these groups from www.atatrail.org or see the Allegheny Trail Alliance contact information below.

- Allegheny Highlands Trail in Pennsylvania, Somerset County Chamber of Commerce
  601 North Center Avenue, Somerset PA 15501
  814-445-6431 www.shol.com/smrst/somrst.htm

- Allegheny Highlands Trail of Maryland
  PO Box 28, Cumberland, MD 21501-0028
  www.ahtmtrail.org

- Allegheny Trail Alliance
  419 College Avenue, Greensburg, PA 15601
  724-853-BIKE www.atatrail.org

- C&O Canal Towpath, C&O Canal NHP Headquarters
  1850 Dual Highway, Suite 100, Hagerstown, MD 21740
  301-739-4200 www.nps.gov/choh

- Friends of the Riverfront/Three Rivers Heritage Trail
  412-488-0212 www.friendsoftheriverfront.org

- Montour Trail Council
  PO Box 11866, Pittsburgh, PA, 15228
  412-831-2030 www.montourtrail.org

- Somerset County Rails to Trails Association
  PO Box 413, Somerset, PA 15501
  814-445-6431

- Steel Valley Trail, Rivers of Steel National Heritage Area
  PO Box 318, Homestead, PA 15120
  412-464-4020 www.steelvalleytrail.org

- Youghiogheny River Trail, North, Regional Trail Corporation
  111 West Main Street, West Newton, PA 15089
  724-872-5586 www.youghrivertrail.org

- Youghiogheny River Trail, South
  See Ohiopyle Visitors Center below.

TOURISM GROUPS

- Laurel Highlands Visitors Bureau
  120 East Main Street, Ligonier, PA 15658
  724-238-5661 www.laurelhighlands.org

- Laurel Ridge State Park
  RD 3, Rockwood, PA 15557
  724-455-3744 www.dcnr.state.pa.us/stateparks/parks/l-rid.htm

- Ohiopyle Visitors Center, Ohiopyle State Park
  PO Box 105, Ohiopyle, PA 15470
  724-329-8591 www.dcnr.state.pa.us/stateparks/parks/ohio.htm

- Pennsylvania Visitors Guide
  1-800-VISITPA www.experiencepa.com

HISTORICAL SOCIETIES, LIBRARIES, & MUSEUMS

- Coal and Coke Heritage Center, Penn State University Fayette Campus
  PO Box 519, Uniontown, PA 15401
  724-430-4158 www.coalandcoke.org

- Connellsville Area Historical Society, Carnegie Free Library
  Connellsville, PA 15425
  724-628-5636 www.fay-west.com/connellsville/historic/

- Elizabeth Township Historical Society
  5811 Smithfield St Boston, PA 15135-1136
  412-754-2030 www.15122.com/eths/about.htm

- Fayette County Historical Society
  PO Box 193, Uniontown, PA 15401
  724-439-4422

- Historical and Genealogical Society of Somerset County
  10649 Somerset Pike, Somerset, PA 15501
  814-445-6077

- Historical Society of Western Pennsylvania and the Senator John Heinz
  Regional History Center
  1212 Smallman Street, Pittsburgh, PA 15222
  412-454-6000 www.pghhistory.org

- Mary S. Biesecker Public Library
  230 S. Rosina Ave Somerset, PA 15501-1937
  814-445-4011 www.somersetcounty.com/maryslibrary

- McKeesport Heritage Center
  1832 Arboretum Drive McKeesport, PA 15132
  412-678-1832 www.15122.com/MckHeritage/info.htm

- Meyersdale Public Library
  210 Center St Meyersdale, PA 15552-1323
  814-634-0512 www.meyersdalelibrary.org

- Pennsylvania Trolley Museum
  1 Museum Road Washington, PA 15301-6133
  1-877-PA-TROLLEY www.pa-trolley.org

- Perryopolis Historical Society
  Perryopolis PA 15473-0303
  724-736-8080

- Railroad Museum of Pennsylvania
  PO Box 15, Strasburg, PA 17579
  717-687-8628 www.rrmuseumpa.org

- Rockwood Historical and Genealogical Society
  PO Box 95, Main Street Rockwood, PA 15557
  814-926-1800

- Rockwood Public Library
  358 Market St Rockwood, PA 15557
  814-926-2540

- Somerset Historical Center
  RD 2, Box 238, Somerset, PA 15501
  814-445-6077 www.somersetcounty.com/historicalcenter

- Steel Industry Heritage Corporation, Rivers of Steel National Heritage Area
  PO Box 318, Homestead, PA 15120
  412-464-4020 www.riversofsteel.org

- Western Maryland Railway Historical Society
  41 N. Main St. Union Bridge, MD 21791-9100
  410-775-0150 http://trainweb.com/mvmra/wmrhs (note—don't use "www" prefix)

- Westmoreland County Historical Society
  951 Old Salem Road, Greensburg, PA 15601
  724-836-1800 www.wchspa.com

- West Overton Museums
  Overholt Drive, Scottdale, PA 15683
  724-887-7910 www.fay-west.com/westoverton

HISTORICAL SITES

- Fallingwater
  PO Box R, Mill Run, PA 15464
  724-329-8501 www.wpconline.org/fallingwaterhome.htm

- Fort Necessity National Battlefield
  One Washington Parkway, Farmington, PA 15437
  724-329-5512 www.nps.gov/fone/home.htm

- Fort Pitt Museum
  Point State Park, Pittsburgh, PA 15222
  412-281-9284 www.fortpittmuseum.com

- General Braddock's Grave site
  See Fort Necessity National Battlefield—the grave site is located about a mile west of the Fort.

- Kentuck Knob
  PO Box 305, Chalk Hill, PA 15421-0305
  724-329-1901 www.kentuckknob.com

OTHER ATTRACTIONS in the general area

- Hidden Valley Four Seasons Resort
  1 Craighead Drive, Hidden Valley, PA 15502
  800-458-0175 www.hiddenvalleyresort.com

- Linden Hall
  RD 1, Dawson, PA 15428
  724-529-7543 www.lindenhallpa.com

- Nemacolin Woodlands Resort & Spa
  1001 LaFayette Drive, Farmington, PA
  800-422-2736 www.nemacolin.com

- Seven Springs Mountain Resort
  777 Waterwheel Drive, Champion, PA 15622
  800-452-2223 www.7springs.com

GETTING THERE

Car:

The Great Allegheny Passage is accessible at a number of points along its length (see the Introduction for map).

Air

Pittsburgh International Airport (PIA): Several major airlines serve Pittsburgh, and PIA is a regional hub for USAirways. Access to the trail is currently by car only; the nearest trail head is in McKeesport (see Introduction for map).

Train—Amtrak Capitol Limited

Once a day, in each direction, Amtrak's Capitol Limited runs between Washington, DC and Chicago through the Yough Valley and along our trail. It's a pretty fancy train with double deck Superliners, a dining car, and sleeping accommodations. It stops in Connellsville. That's the good news. The bad news is there isn't any baggage service in Connellsville, let alone any Amtrak personnel, so you can't take your bike on the train to Connellsville, drop off and go for a ride on the trail. That would make too much sense. Same story for Cumberland. The stations in both Cumberland and Connellsville are shelters fondly known as "Amshacks" that are only open an hour before scheduled train time and aren't manned by ticket agents.

By the time you read this, the trail may also stop at Rockwood, but be warned: this train is habitually late, especially eastbound.

Baggage service is available in Pittsburgh for both the Capitol and the Chicago—New York trains that stop there. For more information, call Amtrak at 800-USA-RAIL.

FURTHER READING

GEOLOGY
In Suspect Terrain. John McPhee, 1983 (also part of *Annals of the Former World*, 1998).

FRENCH AND INDIAN WAR
Montcalm and Wolfe. Francis Parkman, 1999.

LOGGING
"Stemwinders" in the Laurel Highlands, *Book No. 13 in the Logging Railroad Era of Lumbering in Pennsylvania Series.* Benjamin F.G. Kline, 1973.

THE RAILROADS
Pittsburgh and Lake Erie RR. Harold McLean, 1980.
The Western Maryland Railway - Fireballs and Black Diamonds. Cook and Zimmerman, 1981.

THE YOUGHIOGHENY RIVER
Youghiogheny, Appalachian River. Tim Palmer, 1984.

COAL AND COKE
Wealth, Waste and Alienation. Kenneth Warren, 2001.
Cloud by Day. Muriel Early Sheppard, 1991.

HENRY CLAY FRICK
Henry Clay Frick - An Intimate Portrait. Martha Frick Symington, 1998.
Henry Clay Frick: The Gospel of Greed. Samuel Schreiner, 1995.

OTHER INTERESTING WEBSITES

• Virtual Museum of Coal Mining in Western Pennsylvania
   A great site to explore the coal mines of Westmoreland County
   http://theoldminer.virtualave.net (note—don't use "www" prefix)

• Climax Locomotives
   www.trainweb.org/climaxloco/index.html

Courtesy Meyersdale Public Library.

I N D E X

Page nmbers in italic indicate illustrations.

199

ORDER ADDITIONAL COPIES OF

THE GREAT ALLEGHENY PASSAGE COMPANION

Guide to History & Heritage along the Trail

by BILL METZGER

(ISBN 0-9711835-2-X)

from THE LOCAL HISTORY COMPANY

Publishers of History and Heritage

www.TheLocalHistoryCompany.com

sales@TheLocalHistoryCompany.com

ORDER FORM—PLEASE PRINT CLEARLY

NAME _____

COMPANY (if applicable) _____

ADDRESS _____

CITY _____ STATE _____ ZIP _____

PHONE _____ PLEASE include your phone number so we can contact you in case there is a problem with your order.

Please allow 2-4 weeks for delivery. Prices are subject to change without notice. All book sales are final. US shipments only (contact us for information on international orders). Payable by check, money order, or Discover/Visa/MC in US funds (no cash orders accepted).

PLEASE SEND _____ copies at $19.95 each .... Subtotal: $_____

Sales Tax: PA residents (outside Allegheny County) add 6% per copy

      Allegheny County, PA residents add 7% per copy $_____

Add $5 shipping/packaging for the first copy and $1 each additional copy $_____

               TOTAL AMOUNT DUE: $_____

PAYMENT BY CHECK/MONEY ORDER:

____ Enclosed is my check/money order made payable to *The Local History Company* for the total amount due above.

PAYMENT BY DISCOVER, VISA, OR MASTERCARD:

Bill my ___ Discover ___ Visa ___ MasterCard   Account # _____

(Address above must be the same as on file with your credit card company)

Expires _____   Name as it appears on your card _____

         Signature _____

Mail or Fax your order to: The Local History Company

(Fax 412-362-8192)   112 NORTH Woodland Road

               Pittsburgh, PA 15232

          Or—Call 412-362-2294 with your order.

QUANTITY ORDERS INVITED

This and other books from The Local History Company are available at special quantity discounts for bulk purchases or sales promotions, premiums, fund raising, or educational use by corporations, institutions, and other organizations. Special imprints, messages, and excerpts can also be produced to meet your specific needs.

For details, please write or telephone:

Special Sales, The Local History Company

112 NORTH Woodland Road, Pittsburgh, PA 15232-2849, 412-362-2294.

Please specify how you intend to use the books (promotion, resale, fund raising, etc.)